ISBN 978-1-333-18479-7
PIBN 10527566

Forgotten Books is a registered trademark of FB &c Ltd.
Copyright © 2017 FB &c Ltd.
FB &c Ltd, Dalton House, 60 Windsor Avenue, London, SW19 2RR.
Company number 08720141. Registered in England and Wales.

For support please visit www.forgottenbooks.com

English
Français
Deutsche
Italiano
Español
Português

www.forgottenbooks.com

Mythology Photography **Fiction**
Fishing Christianity **Art** Cooking
Essays Buddhism Freemasonry
Medicine **Biology** Music **Ancient
Egypt** Evolution Carpentry Physics
Dance Geology **Mathematics** Fitness
Shakespeare **Folklore** Yoga Marketing
Confidence Immortality Biographies
Poetry **Psychology** Witchcraft
Electronics Chemistry History **Law**
Accounting **Philosophy** Anthropology
Alchemy Drama Quantum Mechanics
Atheism Sexual Health **Ancient History**
Entrepreneurship Languages Sport
Paleontology Needlework Islam
Metaphysics Investment Archaeology
Parenting Statistics Criminology
Motivational

PREFACE.

The portion of this outline which is devoted to criminal law, was printed a year ago; that relating to procedure is now added, and the whole is intended to furnish to students a brief synopsis of the law upon those subjects, as a basis for study in connection with a course of lectures. Lectures alone constitute a very unsatisfactory method of imparting elementary instruction in law. Illustrations and explanations may be readily retained, but the classification and main principles need to be more accurately and firmly fixed in the mind than is possible from merely hearing them stated. The assistance of notes for this purpose is very unreliable. The student not yet familiar with the subject finds it difficult to gather out just those things of primary importance, and the labor of noting them distracts the mind so that he is not able to follow the line of thought of the lecture. This outline, then, is intended to enable the student to acquire by collateral study a fuller, more accurate and systematic knowledge than he could get from oral lectures and hasty notes. And in order that he may carry on collateral reading upon each subject, references are given to leading text-books and pertinent cases.

The references to cases are more numerous than would otherwise be necessary, in order that students in a class, having access to but one library, may all find something bearing upon each subject; and the reading of these cases, with the making of brief notes on the blank pages, stating the principle decided, or the application of the principle to facts, in each case read, is especially urged upon the student, not merely that he may acquire correct knowledge, but also that he may learn the use of the tools of his trade. The cases cited are to be looked upon, not strictly as authorities in support of the text, but as proper to be read in connection with it.

By the use of this printed synopsis in connection with lectures and collateral reading, or even with such collateral reading alone, it is believed the student may acquire a better general knowledge of the subject than by the study of those large treatises which are now the standard text-books. Indeed, it would be inexpedient, if not wholly impracticable, to give, either in a class or in private instruction, sufficient time to this branch of law, to go through the four or five large volumes which Bishop and Wharton each devote to the law and procedure. As to smaller works, none of them cover procedure, and in treating of the law they devote too much attention to a multitude of offences which are either no longer of practical importance, or which are purely statutory, and too little to the general doctrines. There is a need here, as in other branches of the law, for a book designed for the student, rather than the practitioner. The author has not presumed to attempt to supply such a book, but has resorted to an expedient, by no means original with him, to bridge over the difficulty.

The matter here given is intended to be equally applicable in every state, and to furnish that general knowledge of the common law of crimes and criminal procedure which is essential to a correct understanding of those subjects, even in states where the whole ground of criminal law and procedure is covered by statute. It is believed that it will be found expedient to study it in connection with the statutes of the particular state in which the student lives.

Law Department,
  State University of Iowa,
    October, 1883.

TABLE OF CONTENTS.

CRIMINAL LAW.

PART I.—PRINCIPLES.

General Nature and Sources 1
Construction of Penal Statutes 14
The Criminal Intent 19
    Ignorance or Mistake 28
    Necessity and Compulsion 30
    Coverture 38
Want of Mental Capacity 39
    Infancy 39
    Insanity 40
    Intoxication 46
    Corporations 48
Principal and Accessory 49
Classification of Crimes 55

PART II.—SPECIFIC CRIMES.

Introductory 56
Offences Against Government 57
    Treason 57
Offences Against the Person 60
    Homicide 60
    Mayhem 80
    Robbery 81
    Rape 83
    Assault and Battery 84
    Felonious Assaults 88

Offences against the Habitation 88
    Arson 90
    Burglary 91
Offences against Property 94
    Larceny 94
    Embezzlement . . . . 10£
    False Pretences 102
    Malicious Mischief 103
    Forgery 104
    Counterfeiting 105
Offences against Justice 105
    Perjury 105

CRIMINAL PROCEDURE.

General Nature and History 107
The Machinery 111
    In States 112
    In the United States 117
Jurisdiction 120
Prevention of Offences 131
Proceedings in the Punishment of Past Offences . 133
Arrest and Preliminary Examination . . 133
    Information and Warrant 134
    The Arrest 136
    Fugitives from Justice 143
    Preliminary Examination 149
    Bail 151
Method of Accusation 155
Pleading 164
    The Accusation 165
        Formal Parts . . 169
        Matters of Description . . . 172
    Defendant's Pleadings 186
The Trial 188
The Execution . . . .

ABBREVIATIONS.

[The usual abbreviations for names of states are used, and are omitted from this list. All reference by pages is to marginal paging, if any.]

Abbott's U. S. Prac.,	Abbott's U. S. Practice, (2d Ed.)
Alb. L. Jour.,	Albany Law Journal.
Allen,	Allen's Reports, (Mass.)
Am. Law Rev.,	American Law Review.
Am. Rep.,	American Reports.
Austin's Jurisp.,	Austin's Jurisprudence, [Am. Ed., 1875.]
Binn.,	Binney's Reports, (Penn.)
Bish. Cr. L.,	Bishop's Criminal Law, (6th Ed.)
Bish. Cr. Pr.,	Bishop's Criminal Procedure, (3d Ed.)
Bish. Stat. Cr.,	Bishop's Statutory Crimes.
Blackf.,	Blackford's Reports, (Ind.)
Bl. Com.,	Blackstone's Commentaries.
Bliss, Code Pl.,	Bliss on Code Pleading.
Bos. & P.,	Bosanquet & Puller's Reports, (Eng.)
Broom's Leg. Max.,	Broom's Legal Maxims.
Burr,,	Burrow's Reports, (Eng.)
Bush,	Bush's Reports, (Ky.)
Campb.,	Campbell's Nisi Prius Reports, (Eng.)
Cent. L. Jour.,	Central Law Journal.
Cl. & Fin.,	Clark & Finnelly's Reports, (Eng.)
Comst.,	Comstock's Reports, (N. Y.)
Cooley's Const. L.,	Cooley's Constitutional Law.
Cooley, Const. Lim.,	Cooley's Constitutional Limitations.
Cow.,	Cowen's Reports, (N. Y.)
Cranch,	Cranch's Reports, (U. S. Sup. Ct.)
Cr. L. Mag.,	Criminal Law Magazine.
Cro. Car.,	Croke's Reports, *tempore* Charles I., (Eng.)
Cro. Eliz.,	Croke's Reports, *tempore* Elizabeth, (Eng.)
Cro. Jac.,	Croke's Reports, *tempore* James I., (Eng.)
Cush.,	Cushing's Reports, (Mass.)
Dall.,	Dallas' Reports, (Penn.)
Dean's Med. Jur.,	Dean's Medical Jurisprudence.
Denio,	Denio's Reports, (N. Y.)
Dill.,	Dillons' Reports, (U. S. Cir. Ct.)
East, P. C.,	East's Pleas of the Crown, or Crown Law.
E. C. L.,	English Common Law Reports.
Eng. L. & E.,	English Law and Equity Reports.
Eng. Rep.,	English Reports, Moak's Notes.
Exch.,	Exchequer Reports, (Eng.)
Fed. Rep.,	Federal Reporter.
Foster,	Foster's Report and Crown Law.
Grant's Ca.,	Grant's Cases, (Penn.)
Gray,	Gray's Reports, (Mass.)
G. Greene,	Greene's Reports, (Iowa.)
Green, Cr. L. Rep.,	Green's Criminal Law Reports.
Greenl. Ev.,	Greenleaf on Evidence.
H. & N.,	Hurlstone & Norman's Reports, (Eng.)
Hale, P. C.,	Hale's Pleas of the Crown.

Harris, Cr. L.,	Harris' Criminal Law, (Am. Ed.)
Hawk. P. C.,	Hawkin's Pleas of the Crown.
Heisk.,	Heiskell's Reports, (Tenn.)
Hill,	Hill's Reports, (N. Y.)
Hobart,	Hobart's Report, (Eng.)
Hor. & T. Ca.,	Horrigan & Thompson's Ca. on Self-Defense.
How.,	Howard's Reports, (U. S. Sup. Ct.
Ibid.,	Ibidem (same as last preceeding.)
Johns.,	Johnson's Reports, (N. Y.)
Kent, Com.,	Kent's Commentaries.
L. R. C. C.,	Law Reports, Crown Cases Reserved, (Eng.)
L. R. P. C.,	Law Reports, Privy Council, (Eng.)
L. R. Q. B.,	Law Reports, Queen's Bench, (Eng.)
La. Ann.,	Louisiana Annual Reports.
Lea,	Lea's Reports, (Tenn.)
Lead. Cr. Cas.,	Bennett & Heard's Lead. Crim. Cas., (2d Ed.)
M. & S.,	Maule & Selwin's Reports, (Eng.)
M. & W.,	Meeson & Wellsby's Reports, (Eng.)
May, Cr. L.,	May's Criminal Law.
McCrary,	McCrary's Reports, (U. S. Cir. Ct.)
Met.,	Metcalf's Reports, (Mass.)
Mod.,	Leach's Modern Reports, (Eng.)
N. W. Rep.,	Northwestern Reporter.
Ohio St.,	Ohio State Reports.
Penn. St.,	Pennsylvania State Reports.
Pet.,	Peters' Reports, (U. S. Sup. Ct.)
Pick.,	Pickering's Reports, (Mass.)
R. S. of U. S.,	Revised Statutes of United States.
Rawle,	Rawle's Reports, (Penn.)
Reeves' Hist. Eng. L.,	Reeves' History of Eng. Law, (Am Ed. 1880)
Rep.,	The Reporter.
Root,	Root's Reports, (Conn.)
Russ. Cr.,	Russell on Crimes.
S. C.,	Same Case.
S. & R.,	Sergeant and Rawle's Reports, (Penn.)
Salk.,	Salkeld's Reports, (Eng.)
Sedg. Constr. Stat.,	Sedgwick on Construction of Statutes.
Sergeant's Const. L.,	Sergeant's Constitutional Law.
Stephen, Hist. Cr. L.,	Stephen's History of Crim. Law of England.
Story, Const.	Story on the Constitution.
Story, Eq. Jur.,	Story's Equity Jurisprudence.
Stra.,	Strange's Reports, (Eng.)
Stubbs, Const. Hist.,	Stubbs' Constitutional History of England.
Term R.,	Term Reports, (Durnford & East, Eng.)
Tex. Ct. App.,	Texas Court of Appeals' Reports.
U. S.,	United States (Sup. Ct.) Reports.
U. S. C. C.,	United States Circuit Court.
U. S. S. C.,	United States Supreme Court.
Ventris,	Ventris' Reports, (Eng.)
Wall.,	Wallace's Reports, (U. S. Sup. Ct.)
Watts & S.,	Watts & Sergeant's Reports, (Penn)
Wend.,	Wendell's Reports, (N. Y.)
Whart. Am. C. L.,	Wharton's American Crim. Law, (6th Ed,)
Whart. Cr. Ev.,	Wharton's Criminal Evidence.
Whart. Cr. Pl. & Pr.,	Wharton's Criminal Pleading and Practice.
Wheat.,	Wheaton's Reports, (U. S. Sup. Ct.)
Wheat. Int. Law,	Wheaton's International Law, (8th Ed.)
Yeates,	Yeates' Reports, (Penn.)

CRIMINAL LAW.

PART I. PRINCIPLES.

GENERAL NATURE AND SOURCES.

A Subdivision of Municipal Law. —Municipal law (or internal positive law) is usually divided into public law and private law. Criminal law is a branch of the public law, that is, the law which relates to rights and duties subsisting between state and subject   In other words, the state regards certain acts as violations of the duty owed by the subject to it. The acts may, in themselves, be primarily injurious to private individuals, or the public in general, or the state as such, but they are also regarded as breaches of public duty.   Holland, Jurisp., Chap. 9, Div. II.

Rights and Duties.—The general province of law is to protect the individual in the enjoyment of what it recognizes as rights, and to enforce the observance by him of what it designates as duties. Although the great body of the law seems to be taken up in defining rights and duties, yet it must be apparent that this is only to determine what shall be protected as rights and what shall be enforced as duties. The ultimate object of the law is to protect and enforce, rather than to define. Right and duty are in this sense correlative, every right recognized as belonging to an individual giving rise to a duty on the part of others to refrain from infringing upon it, and every duty imposed implying a right on the part of some one, or many, to have that duty performed. It is sometimes more convenient to speak of the right, as when it is specific and every one, in' general, is under the common duty of not infringing upon it while on the other hand, the attention turns more naturally to the duty, when it is something which each person, or specific persons, are required to observe as to all others. Austin, Jurisp., Lecture XII; Holland, Jurisp., Chap. 7.

How Protected or Enforced.—There are two principal methods in which the law protects rights and enforces duties. The one is a civil proceeding, in which a right is protected by giving to the person entitled to enjoy it, a judgment against the person violating or about to violate it, and a duty is enforced by giving a judgment against the person omitting or about to omit to perform it, in favor of any person injured or about to be injured by its omission. The judgments in such cases may be various in form, but they affect primarily only the persons directly implicated in the proceeding, that is the person suffering the injury and the person causing it; and their main purpose is to prevent the violation of the particular right, or the omission of the particular duty, as the case may be, or to compensate the person directly injured by such violation or omission. But a very important secondary result from such judgment is, that they operate, also, to a considerable extent, as a punishments upon the person guilty of such violation of right or omission of duty, and they thus serve, in a general way, to protect all other persons in the enjoyment of similar rights, and to enforce upon all others the observance of similar duties. Austin, Jurisp., Lecture XXVII.

Another Method.—But there may be classes of rights and duties which cannot be adequately protected and enforced by judgments in civil proceedings. For example, murder would not be considered as adequately punished by rendering a judgment against the offender in favor of the relatives of the deceased for the pecuniary damage suffered by them in his death, for, aside from the fact that such a loss cannot be compensated in money, the offender might be so rich that such a penalty would be but a light punishment; or, as would more frequently happen, he might be so poor that a judgment against him would be of no value. So in case or theft, it would be no adequate punishment

to render a judgment against the thief for the value of the property stolen, for if he escaped detection his theft would be a gain, while if detected he could only be compelled to restore what he had stolen, and he would thus stand a chance of profit without a corresponding danger of loss. Again, there is a large class of acts which are violations of duty toward what is called the public, which are not so directly injurious to any one individual that he could recover any judgment in a civil action; and there is another class of acts injurious to the government, such as, for example, treason, etc., which could hardly be considered as producing any pecuniary injury to even the government, though a direct breach of duty toward it.

Damages as a Punishment.—In some such cases a greater penalty than a mere judgment as compensation for the injury done, is provided by giving to the person injured a judgment for a greater amount than sufficient to cover his injury, not because he is entitled to it, but because the transgressor ought to be more severely punished. Such amount included in the judgment, in addition to the real damages suffered by the injured party, is called punitive damages. But it is apparent that this expedient would not obviate the difficulty in many cases.

Criminal Punishments.—The law therefore employs another and quite different method of protecting rights and enforcing duties. It provides direct punishments for some violations of right and breaches of duty, which punishments are inflicted in pursuance of a judgment in a criminal proceeding. The object of the civil proceeding is primarily to protect or recompense the person injured by the violation of a right or breach of a duty, and punishment of the wrong-doer is only a secondary result. In the criminal proceeding the law regards, primarily, the person committing the injury, and punishment is the direct object. Very generally it may be said that in the one case the law considers, primarily, rights, while in the other it looks, primarily, at duties.

Distinction between Civil and Criminal Proceedings.—
The difference in the nature of the two proceedings, renders
them quite dissimilar in some of their main features. In the
civil proceeding the person injured must take the initiative in
procuring the redress which the law grants, and if he for any
reason chooses to remain silent, the wrong-doer goes unpunished.
In the criminal proceeding, no redress is, in general, granted the
injured party; hence there must be some other agency to set in
motion the machinery which the law provides in such cases; and
therefore the government, acting as the representative of the
public and for its interests, undertakes to see to the taking of the
proper steps to secure the punishment of the offender, and it
becomes, in such case, an active party to the proceeding, a litigant
in the case.

Object of Punishment.—The object of the criminal proceeding being punishment of the wrong-doer, it is not essential
that it be pecuniary in any sense. It may be that he be deprived
of life, or of liberty, or undergo physical suffering; but while the
direct object of the criminal proceeding is to punish the wrong-
doer for the specific wrong committed, yet the object of the law
in providing such a proceeding, and of the government in acting
as a litigant therein, is, not to secure specific punishment for
wrongs already done, for that in itself could be of but little
advantage to any one, as no benefit therefrom results to the
injured party, but to prevent the recurrence of such acts, either
by that particular offender or by others; and in determining the
course of criminal procedure, and the punishments to be inflicted,
that is the object to be kept in view.

Crimes.—Those breaches of duty or violations of right
which the law deems it proper and expedient to discourage by
causing a punishment to be inflicted upon any one who is, in a
proper proceeding, found guilty thereof, are called crimes. What
specific acts, injurious to individuals or the state, shall be deemed,
either by reason of their grave nature, or the difficulty of otherwise preventing them, such that it is expedient to discourage

their commission by punishing them as crimes, will depend upon the varying notions and conditions of each nation or age. Austin, Jurisp., Lecture XVII.

Classification: Form.—The foregoing untechnical suggestions as to the nature and bounds of criminal law are intended to illustrate rather than to define. Law is not a natural science, and it is doubtful if any system of classification and definition of its several branches, which would be generally recognized as natural, could be formed. It must also be borne in mind, that anything here suggested as to the reasonableness, or desirability, or necessity of the existence of a branch of the law corresponding to criminal law, is not intended as a statement of the reason why it exists in that form. Its form is to be accounted for, not by abstract speculation on law as "the perfection of human reason," but by tracing its growth and development from the rude form in which it is found to have existed in the earliest times of which we have any knowledge through the various vicissitudes and surroundings of the peoples from which we are descended.

Genesis of our Criminal Law.—The best information attainable as to the earliest times, seems to indicate that the punishment of crimes was then left to those directly interested, the injured person himself and his kinsmen ; in other words, to private vengeance. The existence among the ancient Hebrews and among the early Anglo-Saxons of rights of sanctuary apparently point to a time when such was the case, or rather to a time when, in the earliest mitigation of complete barbarism, it began to seem desirable to have some slight relief from the severity of the unlimited rule of private vengeance. See account of Cities of Refuge in Old Testament, Numbers, xxxv. As to sanctuary among the Anglo-Saxons, see 1 Reeves' Hist. Eng. Law (Am. Ed., 1880), 198. The earliest codes of the Germanic tribes indicate a further progress in amelioration. By them an elaborate system of money compensation was provided, to be accepted by the injured person or his relatives in lieu of the private vengeance, to which it seems to be assumed they would otherwise be entitled. The price of each man's life, according to his rank, etc., was duly fixed ; also the price of each of his important members, as a tooth, finger, etc. The amount thus fixed was to be recovered by the injured party from the wrong-doer, by an action corresponding in general characteristics to a civil action. The idea that the governing power should take cognizance of every case of violence to life or property, and punish it, in behalf of the public, for the better security of the public, does not seem to have been then entertained, but the legislative power did seem to assume jurisdiction to punish some flagrant offenses which more especially threatened the security of the government. Such punishment, however, was not meted out in accordance with any definite system of criminal law, but arbitrarily, at the will of the legislative body, after the offense was committed. It does not seem clear just when or how the doctrine arose that a crime was an offense against the ruling power, as representative of the people and the source of all justice, and that it should be punished by a proceeding in the name of the ruling power against the wrong-doer ; but when criminal law took definite form it had crystalized around that idea, which has ever since remained the most marked feature of the system. The leading authority on these points seems to be the brief but pregnant chapter of Maine's Ancient Law (Chapter x). See also, Holmes' Common Law, Lecture 2; 1 Reeves' Hist. Eng. Law (Am. Ed., 188.), 188–202, and especially, Finlason's notes; 1 Stephen's Hist. Cr. L., 57, 244; Holland, Jurisp., Chap. 17, Div. III.

Definitions.—A crime is: "An act committed or omitted in violation of a public law, either forbidding or commanding it." 4 Bl. Com., 5.

"An act of disobedience to a law, forbidden under pain of punishment." But punishment in this definition must be limited to such penalties as are inflicted by the law-making power specifically as punishments, and not such as are authorized directly by

way of compensation to the injured party, but operate indirectly as punishments. 1 Stephen's Hist. Cr. L., Chap. 1.

"Criminal law, as a branch of the juridicial law of the country, treats of those wrongs which the government notices as injurious to the public, and punishes, in what is called a criminal proceeding, in its own name." 1 Bish. Cr. Law (7th Ed.), Sec. 32; see also, *Rex v. Wheatly*, 2 Burr., 1125; S. C., 1 Lead. Cr. Ca., 1.

Distinction between Tort and Crime.—Considering only those rights and duties which the law recognizes as existing independently of any contract obligation—for in discussing criminal law, contract obligations are seldom to be considered—torts may be said to be those wrongs recognized by the law as affecting private individuals, and for which it gives the injured person private redress by judgment in a civil action. The distinguishing feature of a crime, therefore, as differing from a tort, is that it is regarded as a wrong to the public, or the state, rather than to any particular individual, and is therefore punished in a proceeding by the government as the representative of the public. Cooley on Torts, 81; 4 Bl. Com., 5, and note in Cooley's Ed. "An offense which is pursued at the discretion of the injured party or his representative, is a civil injury. An offense which is pursued by the sovereign or by the subordinate of the sovereign, is a crime." Austin, Jurisp., Lecture XVII.

What acts shall be made Criminal.—The public may be said to have a general interest in seeing that every infraction of a private right shall be punished, for the infringement of any right enjoyed by one individual renders the enjoyment of similar rights by others less perfect and secure. As to some wrongs, the mere liability to a judgment for damages at the suit of the party injured may well be considered as sufficient to deter from their commission. As to others, the act may so little affect the public, that it may not be worth while to punish it as a crime. It is for the sovereign power to determine what acts shall be punishable as crimes, and in so determining it is to be guided, not only by considerations of morality, but by those of expediency. But when the sovereign power has determined what shall be punished as a crime, the courts have nothing to do with the morality or expediency of such determination, but have only to enforce the law as it is laid down. It is to be constantly borne in mind, that while the precepts of morality should be regarded in making laws, the respective provinces of law and morality are entirely distinct, and that only those acts are punishable as crimes which are made criminal by the law of the land; and it is for the sovereign power to determine how far the public good requires it to go in punishing as crimes those acts which are wrongful as infringing upon the rights and privileges of others. The mere sinfulness of an act is not a ground for punishing it as criminal; it is only when it affects others injuriously that the government can properly interpose to punish it. 1 Bish., Cr. L. (7th Ed.), Chap. 14; Stephen Cr. Dig., Introd.

Malum in se: Malum Prohibitum.—A distinction is sometimes made between *malum in se*, an act which is in its nature wrongful, and *malum prohibitum*, an act which is not essentially wrongful, but is so only because prohibited by law 1. Bl. Com., 54, 57. Such a distinction is no longer regarded with favor, and every act prohibited by law, or to the doing of which a penalty is attached by way of punishment, is, in the eye of the law, looked upon as illegal and wrongful in every sense. There is no legal test by which to determine what acts are, in their nature, morally wrongful, and what are merely wrongful because prohibited. An act not expressly prohibited, but to the doing of which a penalty in the nature of a criminal punishment is affixed, is a crime and illegal. The payment of the penalty does not render the act legal and right. *Pike v. King,* 16 Iowa, 49; *Watrous v. Blair,* 32 Iowa, 58; Cooley's note (12) to 1 Bl. Com., 58.

A Wrong may be both a Tort and a Crime.—It is evident from the foregoing discussion that the same act which, when

looked at as a private injury committed by one person upon
another, would be a tort, might, when viewed as an injury to the
public, be considered also as a crime. If a person should
maliciously burn his neighbor's house, he would thereby
commit a wrong for which the neighbor might recover a judgment, in a civil action, for the damages suffered; but he
would also do a wrong which the law, for the general protection of the public, has seen fit to designate as a crime, and for
which it provides a punishment, entirely different from the mere
liability to a judgment in a civil action, which punishment is
imposed for the purpose of deterring others from committing a
like offense.

Tort not merged in Crime.—The purpose of the action for
the tort and that of the criminal prosecution being thus distinct,
there is no reason, in principle, why both might not proceed,
each irrespective of the other, and it is strictly true, both at
common law and under code procedure, that judgment in one
action will not bar the other. The tort is not merged in the
crime. But there was a rule at common law, in England, that
the injured party could not maintain the action in tort for his
private damages until he had procured the prosecution to final
judgment of a criminal action against the defendant for the
criminal offense, and then he might maintain his civil action, irrespective of what the judgment in the criminal prosecution might
be. This rule is said to have obtained for the reason that there
were, in England, no public prosecutors, and a criminal prosecution could only be set on foot and maintained by a private prosecutor, and the rule was necessary to secure the enforcement of
the criminal law by private prosecutions. But as conviction, in
case of a felony, worked a forfeiture of all defendant's goods to
the crown, and all considerable offenses were felonies, the civil
remedy, in case a conviction was procured, was of little value, and
the criminal prosecution in fact defeated the civil remedy. This
English common law rule, however, was never adopted in this
country, even where the common law as to crimes was recog-

2

nized, and is expressly abrogated by statute in some of the states. 4 Bl. Com., 6, and note in Cooley's Ed.; 1 Bish. Cr. Law (7th Ed.), Chap. 16 ; *Gimson v. Woodfall,* 2 Car. & P., 41; *White v. Spettigue,* 13 M. & W., 603; *Boston, etc., R. Co. v. Dana,* 1 Gray, 83; *Pettingill v. Rideout,* 6 N. H., 454.

How the Criminal Law is Prescribed.—As the criminal law consists essentially of prohibitions and penalties, it comes more strictly than any other branch of the law within the general definition of law given by Blackstone : "A rule of civil conduct prescribed by the supreme power in a state, commanding what is right and prohibiting what is wrong." (1 Bl. Com., 44.) But it is true of criminal law, as it is of other branches of the law, that its commands and prohibitions are not necessarily laid down by legislative enactment.

Criminal Law is both written and unwritten.—Criminal law, then, is both written and unwritten, although the proportion of written to unwritten is very much larger than in many other branches. By the common law many wrongs were punishable as crimes, and their respective punishments determined without statutory enactment in relation thereto. Thus larceny, burglary, arson, etc., were punishable at common law, the definition and punishment thereof not being, so far as is known, originally fixed by statute, but in each case there are statutes extending the definition to cover cases not included under the common law definition, and also changing the punishment.

Codification.—As the criminal character of an act is not dependent upon the nature of the act itself, or the belief entertained by the person who does it as to its inherent wrongfulness, but is determined entirely by the prohibition of the law, it is manifest that the law of crimes and punishments should be plain, unambiguous and easily ascertained, in order that, on the one hand, a man shall not be liable to punishment for an act done without reasonable means of knowing that it was prohibited, and on the other, that one, having intentionally done a criminal act,

may not enlist sympathy in his own behalf by a false claim that
he had not knowledge of the law. Therefore, the arguments for
codification have been more cogent and reasonable in regard to
criminal law than to any other branch, unless it be procedure.
As to codification, see Cooley on Torts, 11–19, quoting Ben-
tham's Works, Vol. IX., page 8; articles in 20 Am. Law Rev., 1,
315. In many, perhaps in a majority of the states, there are,
therefore, criminal codes, defining what acts are punishable by
law as crimes, and prescribing the punishments therefor.

Common Law Crimes.—In the states where there are no
such criminal codes, common law crimes, that is, crimes which
are recognized and punishable by the common law without
express statutory provision, are still recognized. Massachusetts,
Pennsylvania and Illinois are examples of such states. Thus acts
which openly outrage decency, or disturb the peace and public
order, or are injurious to public morals, or are a breach of official duty, if done corruptly, are included in common law crimes
and are subject to indictment, although such precise acts have
never before been defined or punished as crimes at common law.
So, exciting, encouraging and aiding one to commit a misdemeanor, is a misdemeanor. *Com. v. Harrington*, 3 Pick.,
26; *Brockway v. People*, 2 Hill, 558; *Smith v. People*, 25 Ills.,
17.

Common Law Crimes in States Having Criminal Codes.
—In some states which have adopted criminal codes, it is held
that such codes do not entirely abrogate the common law, so
far as it prescribes what shall be crimes, but simply supplant it,
so far as the statutory provisions extend, and that any act punishable as a crime by the common law, but not coming within the
provisions of the code, may be still punished as a common law
crime. *State v. Pulle*, 12 Minn., 164; 1 Bish. Cr. Law (7th Ed.),
Chap. 3; and see *State v. Danforth*, 3 Conn., 112.

Common Law Crimes not Recognized.—But in Ohio and
Iowa, and perhaps in other states having criminal codes, common law crimes are not recognized. As is said in an Ohio case:

"We have no common law offenses. No act or omission, however hurtful or immoral in its tendencies, is punishable as a
crime in Ohio, unless such act or omission is expressly
enjoined or prohibited by the statute laws of the State."
Smith v. The State, 12 Ohio St., 466 ; and see *Key v. Vattier*,
1 Ohio, 132, 144; *Allen v. The State*, 10 Ohio St., 287, 301.
The rule in Iowa is the same; the reason given being (1),
that the constitution (Art. v., Sec. 6,) confers jurisdiction in
criminal cases upon the district court, "in such a manner
as shall be prescribed by law," and (2), the statutory offenses
cover nearly the whole ground of common law crimes, and it
must be inferred that those omitted were intended to be excluded.
Estes v. Carter, 10 Iowa, 400. (The reasoning in this case is
criticised in *State v. Pulle, supra.*) In other states it is enacted
that only such offenses as are made punishable by statute are to
be punished as crimes. The doctrine in Iowa and Ohio seems
the more reasonable one, and more in harmony with the principle
that no one should be punished for an act as a crime which the
law has not distinctly declared to be such. See note J, in Ham-
mond's Ed. of Lieber's Hermeneutics, page 293.

In Federal Courts.—The judicial power of the United
States government being only such as is given it under the constitution, and the general power to punish crimes not being
granted by that instrument, it is doubtful whether the United
States government could confer upon its courts general criminal
jurisdiction. At any rate it has not attempted to do so. The
legislative authority of the Union must first make an act a crime,
affix a punishment to it, and declare the court that shall have
jurisdiction of the offense, before that act can be punished as a
crime in a federal court. Nor is the exercise of criminal jurisdiction in common law cases within the implied powers of such
courts. They have no jurisdiction not given by written law.
U. S. v. Hudson, 7 Cranch, 32; *U. S. v. Coolidge*, 1 Wheat.,
415 ; 1 Bish. Cr. Law (7th Ed.), Chap. 10; 1 Whart. Am. Cr. Law,
Sec. 163, *et seqq.;* 1 Kent's Com., 331; *U. S. v. Walsh*,
5 Dillon, 58.

The Common Law a Part of Criminal Jurisprudence.— The common law is, however, still recognized as a part of criminal jurisprudence, even in those states where common law crimes are not recognized. Thus the statutes prohibiting offenses in many cases do not define them, but leave their definitions as at common law. *Smith v. State*, 12 Ohio St., 466; *Estes v. Carter*, 10 Iowa, 400; *State v. Twogood*, 7 Iowa, 252; *Ex parte Bollman*, 4 Cranch, 75; *U. S. v. De Quilfeld*, 2 Cr. L. Mag., 211.

Legislative Power to Define Crimes and Prescribe Punishments.— The power to say what acts shall be regarded as crimes and what punishments shall be inflicted therefor, is inherent in the legislatures of the states as a part of their general legislative powers, and is unlimited except as restricted by constitutional provisions usually contained in the bill of rights of each state constitution ; as for example, the provisions guaranteeing religious freedom, liberty of speech and the press, etc., etc. So long as the legislature does not transgress these express limitations of its power, it may exercise its own discretion in determining what acts shall be punished as crimes, and the courts cannot interfere with that discretion or pass upon the propriety of the legislation.

Same as to United States Government.— The government of the United States possesses, however, only limited or delegated powers, and has power to define and punish crimes only so far as that power is conferred by the constitution, either in express terms or by implication.

Express Power.— The constitution gives congress power to provide for the punishment, (a) of certain classes of crimes, as counterfeiting the securities and current coin of the United States, piracies and felonies committed on the high seas, offenses against the law of nations, etc.; (b) of all crimes within certain territory under its exclusive jurisdiction, as the District of Columbia, places ceded to the United States for the erection of forts, arsenals, etc., etc. U. S. Const., Art. I., Sec. 8; *U. S. v. Clark*, 31 Fed. R., 710, 10 Cr. L. Mag., 59.

Implied Power.—In granting to congress general powers, the constitution, by implication, gives it the power to prohibit and punish the commission of acts which would interfere with, or hinder the exercise by the government of the powers conferred. Thus congress has defined and provided for the punishment of a large number of offenses, as to which it is given no express power to legislate, as for instance, offenses against the existence of the government, against the revenue laws, etc. Also under the power to regulate commerce with the Indian tribes, congress provides for the punishment of crimes committed within the Indian country, by whites against Indians, or Indians against whites. *U. S. v. Barnhart*, 22 Fed. R., 285; *Ex parte Crow Dog*, 109 U. S., 556. The admiralty jurisdiction given to the federal courts includes power to punish crimes. U. S. Const. Art. III., Sec. 2.

Ex Post Facto Laws.—There is this limitation imposed by the Federal Constitution upon the power of congress and state legislatures to define offenses, and provide punishments therefor, that no *ex post facto* law shall be passed (U. S. Const. Art. I., Secs. 9 and 10), and the same limitation upon the power of the state legislature is usually found in state constitutions. An *ex post facto* law is one which makes acts, innocent when done, criminal, or if criminal when done, aggravates the crime, increases the punishment, or reduces the measure of proof. The term applies only to criminal laws. Retrospective or retroactive laws are not in conflict with the constitution of the United States, and the power of the legislature to pass them has been uniformly recognized, unless they interfere with vested rights. *State v. Squires*, 26 Iowa, 340; see also, *Calder v. Bull*, 3 Dall., 386; Cooley's Const. Law, 285; *People v. Campbell*, 3 Cr. L. Mag., 29; *Kring v. Mo.*, 107 U. S., 221; *Hopt v. Utah*, 110 U. S., 574. The act must be contrary to the law at the time committed, and the law must be in force at the time of judgment. *Com. v. Marshall*, 11 Pick., 350, 22 Am. Dec., 377.

CONSTRUCTION OF PENAL STATUTES.

Important.—The criminal law being very largely statutory, even in states where there is no systematic criminal code, it is important to notice a few of the rules governing the interpretation and construction of such statutes.

Strict Construction.—The most important rule of construction applied to penal statutes, is that they are to be strictly construed, and this rule arises from the policy of the criminal law which presumes innocence; that is, the accused is not to be punished until, not only the act charged is proven, but it clearly appears that such act is one forbidden by the law. Any ambiguity on that question, as well as any doubt on the other, is to be resolved in favor of accused. Bish. Stat. Crimes, Sec. 192–201; 1 Bl. Com., 88, and notes 18 and 19 in Cooley's Edition; Sedgwick on Constr., 279; Potter's Dwarris on Stat., 245; *U. S. v. Wiltberger*, 5 Wheat., 76, 95; *State v. Lovell*, 23 Iowa, 304. But this rule of strict construction must not be carried to the extent of nullifying the statute. *U. S. v. Wiltberger, supra; Am. Fur Co. v. U. S.*, 2 Pet., 358, 366; *U. S. v. Morris*, 14 Pet., 464; *Nash v. State*, 2 G. Greene, 286, 296; *Com. v. Martin*, 17 Mass., 359; *Com. v. Loring*, 8 Pick., 370; Sedgwick on Constr., 279–288. In general, as to construction of penal statutes, see article in 2 Cr. L. Mag., 1.

Only applicable as against Accused.—This rule of strict construction applies only to so much of the statute as defines the offense and prescribes the punishment, and not to portions relating to collateral matters; and it is applicable only as against the accused. The reason of the rule requires a liberal construction of everything favorable to the accused. Bish. Stat. Crimes, Sec. 196, 197.

Purpose of the Statute to be considered.—The general policy or purpose of the statute, and the mischief which it was intended to remedy, are to be considered in construing it.

General Language.—General language should be limited in application to cases within the policy or purpose of the statute, or, as it is sometimes expressed, the mischief to be remedied. *Commonwealth v. Slack,* 19 Pick., 304; *Brown v. Thompson,* 14 Bush, 538, 29 Am. R., 416.

Casus Omissus.—But, on the other hand, the fact that a case is within the mischief to be remedied, will not warrant the application of the statute to it, unless the case is within its letter or language, even though it be apparent that the omission was an oversight. A statute is not to be stretched beyond its language, to cover a *casus omissus.* This is the rule as to all statutes, and of course, is to be even more strictly applied to those of a criminal nature. Bish. on Stat. Crimes, Sec. 193; Broom's Leg. Max., [47], [85]; *Jones v. Smart,* 1 Term R., 52; *Lane v. Bennett,* 1 M. & W., 73; *Pitman v. Flint,* 10 Pick., 504, 506.

Letter and Mischief.—In order, therefore, that a case may be considered as covered by a statute, it must come within both the letter and the mischief of the act.

Legislative Intent.—It is but putting the rule, requiring the purpose of the statute to be considered, in another form, to say that the legislative intent is to be ascertained and followed. This is the primary object of all rules of construction or interpretation. When that is made plain by the signs or indications which the law regards as authoritative, there is no further room for such rules to operate. "Where the language is clear and explicit, and susceptible of but one meaning, and there is nothing incongruous in the act, a court is bound to suppose the legislature intended what the language imports." 1 Bl. Com., 59, and Cooley's note.

How the Intent is to be ascertained.—Where there is some apparent ambiguity in the statute itself, or where a doubt arises as to its meaning when it is sought to apply it to particular facts, then it is proper, in seeking the legislative intent: (1) to compare the different parts of the statute with each other; and, (2) to consider certain matters outside the language of the statute.

I. **The whole Statute considered together.**—In getting at the meaning of any part of the statute, the whole of it is to be considered together, and such construction is to be put upon it that each part may have some meaning, and all may be consistent. 1 Bl. Com., 88; Bish. Stat. Crimes, Secs. 81, 82; Sedgw. Constr. of Stat., 199; *Dist. Twp. v. City of Dubuque*, 7 Iowa, 262, 275; *Leversee v. Reynolds*, 13 Iowa, 310; *U. S. v. Fisher*, 2 Cranch, 358, 399; *Opinion of the Justices*, 22 Pick., 571, 573; *Attorney General v. Detroit &c. Plank Road*, 2 Mich., 138; *San Francisco v. Hazen*, 5 Cal., 169; *Gates v. Salmon*, 35 Cal., 576, 586.

Title and Preamble.—The title and preamble of an act are not strictly parts of it. Indeed the latter is now commonly omitted from acts of a general nature. Nevertheless they may, in case doubt arises from a consideration of the statute without reference to them, be considered as throwing light upon the legislative intent. They are not to be allowed, however, to control the plain provisions of the body of the act. Bish. Stat. Crimes, Secs. 42–51; Sedgw. Constr. of Stat., 38–44; 1 Kent's Com., 460; *U. S. v. Fisher*, 2 Cranch, 358, 386; *Com. v. Slifer*, 53 Penn. St., 71; *Hadden v. The Collector*, 5 Wall., 107; *Rex v. Athos*, 8 Mod., 136, 144; *Wilson v. Spaulding*, 19 Fed. R., 304.

Particular Words followed by General.—Where particular words are followed by general ones, the general ones are restricted in meaning to objects of the like kind with those specified in particular. Bish. Stat. Crimes, Secs. 245, 246; Sedgw. Constr. of Stat., 360 and note.

II. **Matters outside the Statute.**—In construing a doubtful statute the court may also look at certain matters outside the language of the statute itself. The statute is to be looked at in the light of the law, both statutory and common, existing at the time of its enactment. Bish. Stat. Crimes, Secs. 86–90.

Statutes in pari materia.—A statute is to be read in connection with previous statutes relating to the same subject matter (*in pari materia*). Sedg *n*. Constr. of Stat., 209; *Rex v. Loxdale*, 1 Burr., 445, 447; *Converse v. U. S.*, 21 How., 463; *State v. Shaw*, 28 Iowa, 67, 78.

Particular Provision.—As between a general and a particular provision, in different statutes covering the same subject, the particular provision will govern. *Brown v. County Comrs.*, 21 Penn. St., 37, 43; Sedgw. Constr. of Stat., 98, note.

Common Law.—The rules and reason of the existing common law are to be observed, and may modify the statute. Thus criminal statutes usually declare that "any person" or "every person" doing the prohibited act, shall be punished as provided; and the expressions, "any person" and "every person," are broad enough, as ordinarily used, to include a child five years old; yet it is a principle of the common law relating to crimes, that a child under seven years of age is not subject to criminal responsibility, and so all such statutes would be construed as applying only to such persons as under the rules of the common law are held to criminal responsibility. *Coy v. Coy*, 15 Minn., 119; *Osgood v. Breed*, 12 Mass., 525; *Wilber v. Crane*, 13 Pick., 284; *Norris v. State*, 25 Ohio St., 217; 18 Am. R., 291; *Cutter v. State*, 36 N. J. L., 125; *U. S. v. DeQuilfeld*, 2 Cr. L. Mag., 211.

Mischief to be Remedied.—It was a favorite doctrine with some early English judges that they might, in construing a statute, look at the mischief intended to be remedied. *Rex v. Hodnett*, 1 Term R., 96, 100; 1 Bl. Com., 87. But now it is pretty clearly settled that the judge cannot undertake to say what motives led the legislature to the passage of the act except as the motive can be gathered from the act itself and the law previously existing. Sedgw. Constr. of Stat., 2 2–209.

Exceptions and Provisos.—Where a statute contains a clause in the nature of a proviso, under which a defendant seeks protection from the general language of the act, he must insist upon it as a defense and prove that his case is within the proviso; but if the statute contains an exception, the prosecution

must negative the exception and prove that defendant's case is not within it. Sedgw. Constr. of Stat., 50, 93; Potter's Dwarris on Stat., 119; *Spieres v. Parker*, 1 Term R., 141; *State v. Stapp*, 29 Iowa, 551; *U. S. v. Cook*, 17 Wall., 168; *King v. Turner*, 5 Maule & S., 206.

Repeal of Statutes.—A statute may, of course, be repealed by a subsequent statute expressly so declaring. It may, also, be repealed by implication by the passage of a subsequent act inconsistent with it, for evidently the last expression of the legislative will must govern. But an implied repeal is not favored and is not to be presumed. If possible the later enactment is to be construed as in harmony, and not in conflict, with prior ones. Bish. Stat. Crimes, Secs. 149–163; Sedgw. Constr. of Stat., 97–106.

Consequences of Repeal.—The criminality of an act is to be determined by the law in force at the time it is committed. Any law making an act criminal which was not so when done, would be *ex post facto* and unconstitutional. See *ante*, p. 14. The punishment is determined by the law in force at time of sentence. Therefore it follows that if an act be not a crime when committed, but is afterward made a crime, it cannot be punished, while if it be a crime when committed and the law by virtue of which it is a crime and is punishable is repealed before sentence, it still cannot be punished. However, if an act is repealed and re-enacted in the same language except that the punishment is reduced, a crime committed within the language of the act before the change may still be punished. *State v. Wish*, 15 Neb., 448.

If the repeal does not take place until after sentence, it does not prevent the full execution of the sentence. The proceedings must be in accordance with the law in force at the time of the trial, and a change of the method of proceedure after commission of the offense and before trial, cannot be objected to by defendant, unless it is such as to bear harder on the criminal than before. See generally, Bish. Stat. Crimes, Secs. 175–187; 1

Hale's Pleas of the Crown, 291; *Yeaton v. U. S.*, 5 Cranch, 281; *The Irresistible*, 7 Wheat., 551; *Com. v. Kimball*, 21 Pick., 373; *Com. v. McDonough*, 13 Allen, 581; *Calkins v. State*, 14 Ohio St., 222; *Hartung v. People*, 22 N. Y., 95; *State v. Ingersoll*, 17 Wis., 631..

By special provision in the repealing act, or by a general statutory provision, the repealed statute may be kept in force as to crimes already committed. *State v. Showers*, 34 Kan., 269.

THE CRIMINAL INTENT.

Essential to Constitute Crime.—The object of punishment being, not to recompense either the state or the injured party for the wrong done, but to deter from a repetition of the crime, it is evident that it would be useless, as well as morally iniquitous, to punish one who, though in fact committing the forbidden act, does so without any fault being imputable to him, that is without any wrongful intent. Therefore it is a common saying in the books that an evil intent must be shown, in addition to the forbidden act, to render the act punishable as a crime. 1 Bish. Cr. L. (7th Ed.), Chap. 18; Broom's Leg. Max. [301]; *Rex v. Harris*, 7 Car. & P., 428; *Reg. v. Allday*, 8 Car. & P., 136; *Coward v. Baddeley*, 4 H. & N., 478, 481; *Cutter v. State*, 86 N. J., 125, 2 Green's Cr. L. R., 589; *Gordon v. State*, 23 Am. R., 575; *State v. Sheeley*, 15 Iowa, 404; *State v. McKean*, 36 Iowa, 343; article, 7 Cr. L. Mag., 273; *Queen v. Tolson*, 26 Q. B. D., 168, 12 Cr. L. Mag., 96, 40 Alb. L. J., 250.

Not Always Essential in Civil Actions.—The distinction between criminal and civil liability is made very apparent in considering the extent to which such liability is affected by the intent. While absence of wrongful intent so complete as to show freedom from fault is usually sufficient to relieve from criminal punishment, it will not relieve from liability to recompense a party injured by the wrongful act. Thus in an old case it was held that a soldier, who, while engaged with his company by way of practice in a skirmish, or sham fight, injured a comrade

by the accidental discharge of his gun, was liable, in a civil action, for damages, though he would not have been liable to criminal prosecution. *Weaver v. Ward*, Hobart, 134. So, also, a sheriff is civilly liable for the acts of his deputy, but not criminally, as for instance for allowing a prisoner to escape. *Rex v. Fell*, 1 Salk., 272; *State v. Berkshire*, 2 Ind., 207; *Campbell v. Phelps*, 17 Mass., 244; *Miller v. Lockwood*, 17 Penn. St., 248, 252.

How Ascertained.—The true intent with which an act is done may be difficult, often impossible, to ascertain. But when the law has forbidden or commanded certain acts under penalty of punishment, it is the duty of every person to know and obey, irrespective of his convictions as to the propriety or morality of the act forbidden or commanded, and the law presumes that an act of disobedience arises from a wrongful intent and it will not allow the accused to say that he had no such intent unless he can show the fact by proving circumstances which the law recognizes as proper to be shown for that purpose. In other words it is not everything which in general acceptation or in morals might be considered as showing that the intent was not bad which the law will consider in that light, but a person seeking to escape criminal liability for his acts must prove some fact, such as mistake, accident, insanity, or the like, which the law recognizes as sufficient to show absence of criminal intent.

Motive and Intent Distinguished.—The law looks at the intent, rather than the motive. The man who should set fire to his neighbor's barley to prevent it being manufactured into intoxicating liquor might be said, possibly, to be actuated by a good motive, but the specific intent of that act would be to destroy his neighbor's property, and that intent the law brands as evil, and it refuses to inquire further into the motive. The intent is the immediate purpose with which the act is done, while the motive is the desire in the mind to attain some ultimate object, which may be the very thing done, or may be, and often is, some entirely different object to which the thing done is looked upon as merely a means. May Cr. L., Sec. 6; Broom's Com., 866–872.

Malice.—As the term is used in criminal law, malice means essentially the same thing as wrongful intent, but it is generally employed in speaking of homicide and will be again referred to in that connection.

Intent inferred from the Act.—It is a common doctrine in the books that a man is presumed to intend the natural consequences of his acts. An unlawful act being shown to have been committed by the accused, the rule as formerly stated was that the law conclusively presumes an evil intent, while as others now insist this is a presumption of fact to be drawn by the jury unless rebutted by the accused. *Rex v. Woodfall,* 5 Burr., 2661, 2667; 1 Greenl., Ev., Sec. 18; 3 id, Sec. 13; *U. S. v. Taintor* (U. S. C. C.), 2 Green's Cr. L. R, 241, and note; *R. v. Moore,* 3 B. & Ad., 184, 188; *The Ambrose Light,* 25 Fed. R., 408, 426. Whichever rule be correct the principle is unquestioned that where an act is done which is in itself unlawful, the intent with which it was done need not be proved, but will be presumed from proof of the act itself, unless the accused can show some fact which the law regards as sufficient to rebut such presumption. It is not necessary that the act be done with intent to violate the law; if the person intended to do the thing he did do, and that was in violation of law, it is sufficient to constitute a crime. *U. S. v. Baldridge,* 11 Fed. R., 552. Ignorance of law or fact as affecting the question of intent will be considered further on.

Good Motives.—If the act is one forbidden, it is immaterial what the motive under which it is done. The law does not allow the doing of something unlawful that good may follow. *Reg. v. Hincklin,* L. R., 3 Q. B., 360; 1 Bish. Cr. L. (7th Ed.), Chap. 22.

Religious Belief.—As against the presumption of criminal intent arising from the doing of an act made a crime by law, it is no excuse to show that the act was one commanded by the religious belief of the party accused. So *held,* as to polygamy, *Reynolds v. U. S.,* 98 U. S., 145. See also, *Guiteau's Case,* 10

Fed. R., 161, 175; *Com. v. Has*, 122 Mass., 40; *Specht v. Com.*, 8 Penn. St., 312.

Where Specific Wrongful Intent is Essential.—But there are acts, not criminal in themselves, which may be criminal or not according to the intent with which they are done. For instance, to have in possession a counterfeit bank note would be perfectly innocent in itself, but to have it *with intent to defraud* is criminal. So too, in many cases an act which is in itself criminal · is made criminal in a higher degree when done with intent to commit a different offense. Thus to make an assault upon another is criminal, but to make an assault with intent to commit murder is made a higher crime though the act really committed be no more than a mere assault. In such cases a specific wrongful intent must be alleged and proven as a fact and will not be presumed from the possession of the counterfeit bills in one case or the mere assault in the other. 3 Greenl. Ev., Sec. 15; *Com. v. Hersey*, 2 Allen, 173, 180; *State v. Bell*, 29 Iowa, 316.

Proof of Specific Intent.—The testimony of the defendant as to his intent in doing the act may be received where he is a witness. *People v. Baker*, 96 N. Y., 340; Art. 22 Cent. L. J., 271; *Delano v. Goodwin*, 48 N. H., 203; *Bolen v. State*, 26 Ohio St., 371. Direct proof of the intent is not required, but the intent may be inferred from the act. *State v. Teeter*, 69 Iowa, 717; *State v. McBryde*, 1 S. E. R., 925, 9 Cr. L. Mag., 508; *Patterson v. State*, 11 S. E. R., 620; *State v. Meche*, 7 So. R., 573.

Intent alone not Punishable.—The law does not undertake to punish criminal intentions not carried out in acts. Though the intent may render an act, when done, more or less criminal, until some act is done no criminality attaches. 1 Bish. Cr. L., (7th Ed.), Chap. 11; *Dudgale v. Regina*, 16 Eng. L. & Eq., 380; Broom's Com., 875. The case of conspiracy is only an apparent, not a real exception to this rule. *U. S. v. Walsh*, 5 Dillon, 58.

Intent and Act must Concur.—Thus it appears that to constitute a crime there must be both a wrongful act and a wrongful intent. They must also concur; that is, the wrongful intent must have existed at the time the wrong act was done. A subsequent wrongful intent will not be sufficient. *People v. Anderson*, 14 Johns., 294; *People v. Cogdell*, 1 Hill, 94; *State v. Dean*, 49 Iowa, 73; *State v. Wood*, 46 Iowa, 116; *Gates v. Lounsbury*, 20 Johns., 426; *Tuberville v. Savage*, 1 Mod., 3.

Act producing Unintended Result.—It is not necessary that the thing actually done be the thing intended. If a man shooting at one person with intent to murder should hit and kill another the act would still be murder. 4 Bl. Com., 201; 1 Bish. Cr. L. (7th Ed.), Chap. 21; Broom's Leg. Max. [318]; *State v. Gilman*, 69 Maine, 163, 31 Am. R., 257; *Dunaway v. People*, 110 Ills., 333, 4 Am. Cr. R., 60.

Intent of One, Acts of Another.—Criminal intent, carried out through the wrongful acts of another, may be punishable. For instance, one may be guilty of a crime in procuring an agent to do an act, and it would be immaterial as affecting the question of the criminal intent of the procurer whether the agent joined therein or was innocent, But upon that point would turn the question of liability as principal or accessory, to be discussed hereafter. *State v. Dowell*, 11 S. E. R., 525.

In cases of Agency.—Where the agent does the wrongful act by express authority from his principal, or the servant by direct command from his master, there is no question as to the criminal liability of the principal or master. But where it is sought to hold the principal or master thus liable for acts done in the course of his employment without express authority or command, the question is more difficult. In prosecutions for libel in the sale of libelous publications, the owner of the establishment has been held criminally responsible for sales made by a clerk in his general employ without direct proof that he knew of the character of the publication or expressly authorized its sale. *Rex v. Almon*, 5 Burr., 2686; S. C. 1 Lead. Cr. Ca., 145 and note; *Com. v. Morgan*, 107 Mass., 199. And the same principle has been followed in cases of illegal sales of intoxicating liquors

by clerks (*Carrol v. State*, 7 Cr. L. Mag., 77); though it is said proof of the sale by the clerk is only *prima facie* proof of the master's complicity. *Com. v. Nichols*, 10 Met., 259; *Com. v. Park*, 1 Gray, 553; *People v. Park*, 49 Mich., 333; and the master may show that he in no way knew or was responsible for the illegal sale, or forbade it. *Burns v. State*, 19 Conn., 398. But the general rule is that one is not liable, criminally, for acts of his servants or agents unless committed by his command or with his assent. *Sloan v. State*, 8 Ind., 312; 1 Bish. Cr. L. (7th Ed.), Sec. 889.

In case of Husband and Wife.—It will appear further on that the wife acting in the presence of her husband is presumed to act under his compulsion so as to relieve her from criminal liability, but it does not follow, on the other hand, that all such acts are to be presumed, as against the husband, to be his acts. The question becomes one of agency : did the husband authorize or procure the wife to do the act. However, it is said the husband has the right to regulate and control his own household, and if the wife carries on an illegal business therein (such as unlicensed sale of intoxicating liquors), he becomes a participator and may be punished. *Com. v. Barr*, 115 Mass., 146; S. C., 2 Green's Cr. L. R., 285, and notes.

In case of Combination.—Where two or more persons unite to commit a criminal offense each is punishable for all that is done in pursuance of the common intent and in furtherance of the common object, even though the result was not intended. *Rex v. Murphy*, 6 Car. and P., 103; *Brennan v. People*, 15 Ill., 511; *Spies v. People*, 9 Cr. L. Mag., 829, 12 N. E. R., 865; *McRae v. State*, 5 Am. Cr. R., 622; *Jennings v. Com.*, 16 S. W. R., 348. But one of the parties is not responsible for what another does beyond the object intended, or even in the prosecution of the common object, if not germane to such object, but for a collateral purpose. *State v. Lucas*, 55 Iowa, 321; *Watts v. State*, 5 W. Va., 532; 2 Green's Cr. L. R., 676. And see further discussion under the subject of principal and accessory.

4

Carelessness and Negligence supplying Intent.—A general wrongful intent may be evinced in willfully disregarding the rights or welfare of mankind as well as in intentionally violating the rights of one particular person. Thus it is that carelessness or negligence may supply a criminal intent. Death caused by shooting into a crowd, or throwing timbers from the roof of a house into the street without warning to passers, will constitute criminal homicide. The carelessness or negligence may be in connection with either a legal or an illegal act, or may consist in a mere omission, but in such case the omission must be of some duty. It is said that contributory negligence on the part of the person injured will not relieve the act from criminality, though it would relieve from liability to damages in a civil action. 1 Bl. Com., 192; 1 Bish. Cr. L. (7th Ed.), Secs. 313–322; 1 Lead. Cr. Ca., notes, 51, 62, 68, etc.

Negligence Considered.—The commands of the law are of a twofold character. On the one hand they may *forbid* the doing of certain things; on the other hand they may *require* the doing of certain things. One who does what the law forbids is guilty of a wrong founded in malice; one who omits to do what the law commands is guilty of a wrong founded in neglect. A neglect may be as willful and wicked as a wrongful act. But in the nature of things, as government aims to protect each person in as large a freedom as he can enjoy consistently with the like privilege in others, and does not undertake to regulate or compel action within that limit of freedom, it has much more occasion to forbid than to require action, and crimes committed by wrongful doing are much more numerous that those by wrongful failing to do. The requirement, a failure to perform which will be negligence, may be either that a person perform some positive duty, or that in doing something which he has a right to do he shall not omit such other action as shall be necessary to prevent what he proposes to do from proving injurious to others. The positive duty of one person to do something for another, irrespective of any previous action done, or obligation

incurred, by the first, only arises out of the relations of men as members of a body politic. The government may require, as a duty toward it, that a person cognizant of a crime shall disclose it, or that an officer properly appointed shall perform his functions. But as to private affairs there is, in general, no breach of duty in failing to act except in so far as an obligation to act has been assumed. If one person has in some way assumed an obligation to support another, he may be guilty of a breach of duty in failing to render such support. If he has put another in danger it may be his duty to protect the other from such danger. If he has the control of property he may be guilty of a breach of duty in not protecting others from injuries resulting from the condition or management of such property.

Illustrations.—In support of the statements of the last paragraph no further authority need be offered than a few pertinent illustrations. A person carelessly handling a dangerous instrument is guilty of manslaughter if death inadvertently results. *State v. Hardie*, 47 Iowa, 647; S. C., 29 Am. R., 496; *Robertson v. State* (Tenn.), 31 Am. R., 602. A person pretending to act as a physician and causing the death of his patient by gross want of attention is guilty of manslaughter. *Rex v. Spiller*, 5 Car. & P., 333. The owner of a river failing properly to scour it, may be indictable for a nuisance in thereby causing the overflow of another's land. *Rex v. Wharton*, 12 Mod., 510. If a person knowingly or carelessly employs an incompetent servant to perform an act and the servant by reason of his incompetence causes an injury in doing the act, the master may be criminally liable. *Rex v. Dixon*, 3 M. & S., 11, 14; *Rex v. Medley*, 6 Car. & P., 292. Mere failure to furnish support to another is not criminal unless there is a legal duty to furnish such support. *Rex v. Smith*, 2 Car & P., 447.

Intent Measures desert of Punishment.—As already seen, liability to punishment does not arise until some act is done; but when a wrongful act is committed, the punishment which shall be meted out to the perpetrator is often made to depend upon the degree of criminality in the intent. Thus an act innocent in itself may become criminal by reason of the intent with which it is done, or an act criminal in itself may thus become a higher offense, or it may become a higher degree of the same offense; and finally, after conviction, the judge, in determining the degree of punishment within the discretionary limits allowed him, will take into account the intent, as appearing from the facts of the case, and make the sentence light or heavy accordingly. 1 Bish. Cr. L. (7th Ed.), Sec. 334.

IGNORANCE OR MISTAKE.

Ignorance or Mistake of Law.—It is a fundamental ˉprinciple of both civil and criminal law that ignorance of the law excuses no one. (*Ignorantia legis neminem excusat.*)   Broom's Leg. Max., [249];   4 Bl. Com., 27, and   Cooley's note ; 1 Bish. Cr. L. (7th Ed.), Chap. 19 ; *Com. v. Bagley,* 7 Pick., 279 ; *State v. Goodenow,* 65 Maine, 30 ; 1 Story Eq. Jur., Sec. 110; 3 Greenl. Ev., Sec. 20. The difficulty or impossibility of knowing the law, as in the case of a statute passed to take effect immediately in all parts of the country, or in. the case of a foreigner just landed, does not prevent the operation of the rule. *Matter of Barronet,* 1 El. & B., 1; *The Ann,* 1 Gallis., 62; *Ship Cotton Planter,* 1 Paine, 23; Bish. Cr. L. (7th Ed.), Sec. 296. Though the doctrine, as thus applied, seems harsh, it is seldom oppressive, for acts are not often made wrongful by law which are not generally considered wrong in morals. The entire rule is based upon evident considerations of public policy.

Mistake or Ignorance of Fact.—It is an equally well recog-. nized principle, both in civil and criminal jurisprudence, that a mistake of fact or ignorance of a fact, may relieve a person from the consequences of acts which would otherwise render him civilly or criminally liable.   4 Bl. Com. and Broom's Leg. Max., *supra ;* 1 Bish. Cr. L. (7th Ed.), Secs. 301–310; 1 Story Eq. Jur., Sec. 140. Thus a person will be justified in acting as would be proper under circumstances as they appear to him, although, owing to a mistake or delusion as to the real facts, his act is such that it

would be criminal if he was aware of the real facts. *Com. v. Rogers*, 7 Met., 500 ; *Com. v. Powers*, 7 Met., 596 ; *Yates v. People*, 32 N. Y., 509 ; *Queen v. Tolson*, 23 Q. B. D., 168 ; 40 Alb. L. J., 250.

Party required to know the Facts.—It seems to be still an open question whether in all cases ignorance of an essential fact may be shown as an excuse, or whether a party may not be required *at his peril* to know the facts with regard to which he acts and be held accountable for any mistake as though it were intentional. The weight of authority seems to be in favor of the proposition that where by statute the doing of an act in a particular manner or under particular circumstances is prohibited, the person who undertakes to do such act must see to it that he does not do it in the manner or under the circumstances forbidden. May's Cr. L., Sec. 5, and article by same author in 12 Am. Law Rev., 469 ; 3 Greenl. Ev., Sec. 21 ; *Com. v. Elwell*, 2 Met., 190 ; *Com. v. Mash*, 7 Met., 472; *Com. v. Raymond*, 97 Mass., 567 ; *Com. v. Farren*, 9 Allen, 489 ; *Barnes v. State*, 19 Conn., 398 ; *State v. Hartfiel*, 24 Wis., 60 ; *McCutchern v. People*, 69 Ill., 601 ; *Jamison v. Burton*, 43 Iowa, 282 ; *Redmond v. State*, (Ark.) 38 Am. Rep., 24; *Dudley v. Sautbine*, 49 Iowa, 650; *State v. Heck*, 23 Minn., 549; *Beckham v. Nacke*, 56 Mo., 546 ; *State v. Newton*, 44 Iowa, 45 ; *Halsted v. State*, 41 N. J., 552, 32 Am. R., 247 ; *Reg. v. Prince*, L. R., 1 C. C., 150, 13 Moak's Eng. R., 385; *Com. v. Uhrig*, 138 Mass., 492. *Contra*, 1 Bish., Cr. L. (7th Ed.), Sec. 304 ; Bish. Stat. Cr., Secs. 1021, 1022 ; *Stern v. State* (Ga.), 21 Am. R., 266 ; *Farrell v. State*, 32 Ohio St., 456 ; S. C., 30 Am. R., 614, and note, 617 ; *Birney v. State*, 8 Ohio, 230, 237 ; *State v. Kalb*, 14 Ind , 403 ; *Williams v. State*, 48 Ind., 306 ; *Faulks v. People*, 39 Mich., 200 ; S. C., 33 Am. R., 374 ; *People v. Parks*, 49 Mich., 333 ; *Hunter v. State*, 6 Cr. L. Mag., 544, and note ; S. C., 5 Am. Cr. R., 336 ; *Hamline v. State*, 101 Ind., 241 ; 6 Cr. L. Mag., 544, 5 Am. Cr. R., 336.

Mixed Mistake of Law and Fact.—Where the mistake is one of fact, but arising from a mistake of law as to a collateral matter, as for instance a mistake as to the ownership of property resulting from a mistake of law as to the effect of a conveyance, the mistake is considered one of fact and not of law. *Rex v. Hall*, 3 Car. & P., 409; *Reg. v. Reed*, Car. & M., 306; and see note to *U. S. v. Anthony*, 2 Green's Cr. L. R. 215; *People v. Long*, 50 Mich., 249.

NECESSITY AND COMPULSION.

Showing Lack of Intent.—If a criminal act is done under compulsion or overruling necessity, it is evident there is lack of criminal intent, and therefore the act is not to be punished as a crime. If a strong person should seize the hand of a weaker one and by mere superiority of strength compel the latter unwillingly to hold a lighted torch to a building until it should take fire, the weaker person would be as innocent as the torch itself of any crime, and the stronger person as guilty as though the torch had been in his own hand. (Broom's Leg. Max., 17, 18). So if the duty which the law imposes is not the passive one of desisting from a wrongful act, but the active one of doing something, the absolute impossibility of doing the thing required would be a complete excuse. But the usual cases of compulsion or necessity cited in the books are those where such compulsion or necessity arises from fear. Thus in time of rebellion a citizen falling into the hands of the enemy might, to save his life, join and act with them so far as absolutely necessary for his safety, until he should have opportunity to escape. 1 East P. C., 294; 1 Bish. Cr. L. (7th Ed.), Sec. 348. Or the officer of a bank who should find himself in the power of robbers with good cause to believe that if he did not obey their commands his life would be sacrificed would be excusable for opening the bank's vaults and permitting its money to be taken. But in such cases there is evidently not entire absence of intent but a choosing between two evils, and the question is whether the danger threatened is such as to justify the doing of the act done. 4 Bl. Com., 27–32; 1 Bish. Cr. L. (7th Ed.), Chap. 23; Broom's Leg. Max., [11].

Taking Life.—One person has not the right to take the life of another who is guilty of no wrong, for the purpose of saving

his own life. *Queen v. Dudley*, 14 Q. B. D., 273, 6 Cr. L. Mag., 361, 5 Am. Cr. R., 559, and see 19 Am. L. Rev., 118 ; *U. S. v. Holmes*, Hor. & T. Ca., 757 ; 1 Hale, P. C., 51 ; 4 Bl. Com., 186 ; 1 Bish. Cr. L. (6th Ed.), Sec. 845 ; *State v. Dowell*, 11 S. E. R., 525.

Injury to Another.—Necessity may excuse the doing of an insignificant injury to another to avoid a much greater injury to one's self. But, in general, if the injury threatened is only to be averted by a corresponding injury to another, the necessity will not excuse.

Defense of Person or Property.—It is the right of a person about to be injured by an unlawful assault upon his person or trespass upon his property to resist such threatened injury, and in thus resisting he will be considered as acting under compulsion or necessity, and therefore excusable. But the resistance must have regard to the threatened offense. *State v. Kennedy*, 20 Iowa, 569.

It is to be noticed that in cases of defense the question is not between two innocent persons, but between one person who is in the right and another who is in the wrong. The law takes away from the individual, to a great extent, the right of private redress, both in civil and criminal injuries, and supplies him with legal remedies to take its place, but it does not, to any great extent, because it cannot, furnish him direct protection against sudden injuries to his person or the property in his possession, and it leaves him therefore a correspondingly greater right of self-protection. He may, as against one interfering with his possession of property or his personal liberty and security, resist force with force so far as is necessary for his protection. He is not required to yield and look to legal remedies for redress of an injury which may be irremediable. Of course, when it is borne in mind that the excuse for what is done rests on the ground of necessity, it will be apparent that he must go no further than necessity requires in the use of force, and that whatever is done be done for protection and not for injury.

Extent of the Right.—The law puts no limit to this right except that it shall not extend to the taking of life. However insignificant the damage to property, or however trifling the bodily restraint or injury threatened, the right of necessary resistance exists, up to this point; but in this protection the defender is not to resort to any means reasonably calculated to endanger life, or he will be criminally liable for the consequences. This is as far as the right of resistance for the mere selfish end of protection of property can be clearly traced on legal grounds. 1 Bish. Cr. L. (7th Ed.), Sec. 860–863; *State v. Moore*, 31 Conn., 479, Hor. & T. Ca., 891, and note, 900; *State v. Gilman*, 69 Maine, 163, 31 Am. R., 257; *Filkins v. People*, 69 N. Y., 101, 25 Am. R., 143; *State v. Benham*, 23 Iowa, 154, Hor. & T. Ca., 115; *State v. Kennedy*, 20 Iowa, 569, Hor. & T. Ca., 106; *State v. Thompson*, 9 Iowa, 188, Hor. & T. Ca., 92.

Defense of the Habitation.—The law looks upon the habitation as distinguishable, in some respects, from other property, and allows it to be defended further than other property, even to the extent of taking life when necessary. A man's house is said to be his castle and is held peculiarly sacred, as will appear by the fact that acts of breaking and entering, or burning, when committed as to the habitation, were at common law felonies, while like offenses as to buildings not inhabited or closely connected with the habitation were misdemeanors. See also, "duty to retreat," *infra*, p. 35. In general, the right to protect the habitation from violence is the same as that to protect the person. 1 Bish. Cr. L. (7th Ed.), Sec. 858; *Pond v. People*, 8 Mich., 150, Hor. & T. Ca., 814. But it seems the threatened danger to the habitation must be such as would amount to a breach of the peace, and it is doubted whether the right to defend the habitation goes further than the right to defend other property unless the assault be with intent to take life or inflict great bodily harm. *State v. Patterson*, 45 Vt., 308, 12 Am. R., 200, 211, and note; *Carroll v. State*, (Ala.), Hor. & T. Ca., 804.

Duty to Prevent Felony.—But it seems that, irrespective of this right to protect person and property, the law imposes as a positive duty the resistance to and prevention of the commission of a felony. No such duty is imposed in case of misdemeanor. It will hereafter become apparent that this distinction between a felony and a misdemeanor is not a merely arbitrary or fanciful one, but is well recognized and sufficiently marked to serve as the dividing line between those offenses which it is a duty to prevent and those which may be resisted or disregarded as private inclination may dictate. 4 Bl. Com., 180, 183; 1 Bish. Cr. L. (7th Ed.), Secs. 842–859; Foster, 273; 1 Russ. Cr., 660; 1 Hawk. P. C., Chap. 28, Sec. 21; *Pond v. People,* 8 Mich., 150, 173, Hor. & T. Ca., 814, 820; *State v. Burke,* 30 Iowa, 331, Hor. & T. Ca., 126; and it seems immaterial whether the felony is one at common law or is only made so by statute. *State v. Smith,* 32 Maine, 369; *Pond v. People, supra.*

Great Bodily Injury.—Although an assault with intent to commit great bodily injury and even the inflicting of great bodily injury (not amounting to maiming or disfiguring) are not, either by common law or, in general, by statute, made felonies, yet it is said that resistance to such assault may be carried to the extent of taking life just as in the case of felonious assaults. *State v. Burke,* 30 Iowa, 331, Hor. & T. Ca., 126; 1 Bish. Cr. L. (7th Ed.), Sec. 865.

Riot.—It is also said to be justifiable to proceed to the extreme measure of force necessary to suppress a riot. *Pond v. People,* 8 Mich., 150, Hor. & T. Ca., 814, and note, 737; 1 Hawk. P. C., Chap. 28, Sec. 14. But, as to this and the preceding case, although not strictly felonies in themselves they are acts likely to lead to felonies and endanger life, and are rather apparent than real exceptions to the rule limiting this extreme defense to a resistance of felonies. They are acts which would become felonies if death should result. 1 Bish. Cr. L. (7th Ed.), Sec. 867.

Extent of Duty to Resist.—This duty of preventing a felony (that is, the necessity which the law imposes) has no limit. It extends even to taking the life of the person committing the felony. But here again it is to be borne in mind that the whole doctrine rests on necessity, and the means adopted are only to be those which the necessity of the particular case demands. If the duty to prevent can be performed otherwise than by personal violence endangering life, such a remedy should not be resorted to, and thus it is that in cases of felonies not attempted by sudden and forcible measures, violence in resistance is not usually justified. *State v. Thompson,* 9 Iowa, 188, Hor. & T. Ca., 92; *Oliver v. State,* 17 Ala., 587, Hor. & T. Ca., 725, and ibid. notes, 30, 236.

Justification and Excuse Distinguished.—As resistance to prevent the commission of a felony is a duty imposed by law, it is a justification for anything necessarily done in the line of that duty, but protection of person and property from non-felonious assaults or injuries, being looked upon not as a duty imposed by law, but as the exercise of a right recognized for private ends merely, serves only as an excuse, not a justification It is optional with a party whether he avail himself of the right or not. He may waive it and look to legal remedies for redress, and if he insists on the right he must do so carefully, that he may not pass the limits which the law has fixed. That there is a difference between mere excuse and full justification will appear in connection with the subject of homicide. 1 Bish. Cr. L. (7th Ed.), Sec. 852; *U. S. v. Wiltberger,* 3 Wash. C. C., 515, Hor. & T. Ca., 34; *Pond v. State,* 8 Mich., 150, Hor. & T. Ca., 814; *Erwin v. State,* 29 Ohio St., 186, 23 Am. R., 733; *Com. v. Riley,* Hor. & T. Ca., 155.

Duty to Retreat.—There is much confusion in the cases relating to self-defense as to the duty of the person assailed to retreat so far as he can ("retreat to the wall" as the old books put it) before resisting in such a way as to imperil life. The true doctrine as to the necessity of retreat seems to be this: where the person assailed is acting merely in the protection of his person or property, and resisting an assault not felonious in

its nature, while he may repel force with force and return blow
for blow so long as he does not imperil life, yet as he is acting
in the view of the law from a selfish standpoint he is not particularly favored and must conduct his defense with caution. If the
combat reaches such a pitch that life is threatened, the assailed
must retreat if he can and avoid the danger, and it is only when
he has retreated so far as he can with safety, or when the
onslaught is so fierce that there would be danger in retreat, that
he will be excused in resorting to the extreme measure of self-
defense. But if he is engaged in repelling a felonious assault,
he is looked upon as doing a duty, and therefore favored in the
eye of the law, and is under no obligation to retreat, but may
stand his ground, using such means, even to the extent of
endangering or taking life, as may be necessary in resisting the
felony. 1 Bish. Cr. L. (7th. Ed.), Sec. 869–871; *State v. Thompson*, 9 Iowa, 188, Hor. & T. Ca., 92; *Philips v. Com.*, 2 Duv.,
328, Hor. & T. Ca., 383, 385; *Erwin v. State*, 29 Ohio St., 186,
23 Am. R., 733; *Runyan v. State*, 57 Ind., 80, 26 Am. R., 52;
State v. Donnelly, 69 Iowa, 705. But the duty to retreat does
not arise when the assailed is in his habitation, and here he may
stand his ground, repel force with force, and without yielding,
exercise the highest right of defense. *Pond v. People*, 8 Mich.,
150, Hor. & T. Ca., 814; *Carroll v. State*, 23 Ala., 28, Hor. &
T. Ca., 804; *State v. Middleham*, 62 Iowa, 150; *Lee v. State*,
(Ala.), 9 So. R., 407.

Right to Pursue.--Where the assault is felonious and the
assailed is justifiable in defending to the full limit, he not only
has the right to resist without retreating, but he may pursue the
assailant until he finds himself out of danger. But this right
to pursue does not exist in cases of mutual combat, or of non-
felonious assault. *Stoffer v. State*, 15 Ohio St., 47, Hor. & T. Ca.,
213, and note, 230; *Young v. Com.*, 8 Bush, 366, Hor. & T. Ca.,
400 (in note).

Party in the Wrong.—The necessity which is urged as showing the act to be in self-defense, must not be one growing out of

the party's own wrong.　Having taken the aggressive and brought on a combat, he cannot excuse himself for using extreme means even to save his life só long as that combat continues.　To be entitled to act in self-defense he must have withdrawn and declined further combat.　*Adams v. People*, 47 Ill., 376, Hor. & T. Ca., 208; *Stoffer v. State*, 15 Ohio St., 47, Hor. & T. Ca., 213; *State v. Rogers*, 18 Kan., 78, 26 Am. R., 754.

Apparent Necessity.—It is evident that in applying this doctrine of necessity as an excuse, the appearances, and not the actual facts, must guide in determining whether the necessity would justify or excuse.　If a person in a lonely place should see a stranger suddenly rush toward him drawing and pointing a pistol, .ne would doubtless be warranted in supposing that the intent was to rob or murder, and if he did actually believe so he might resist accordingly, without fault, although it should turn out that the stranger acted merely in sport and without criminal intent, and that the pistol was not loaded.　*Selfridge's Case*, Hor. & T. Ca., 1., 16 ; *Shorter v. People*, 2 Comst., 193, Hor. & T. Ca., 256 ; *Logue v. Com.*, 38 Penn. St., 265, Hor. & T. Ca., 269 ; *Campbell v. People*, 16 Ill., 17, Hor. & T. Ca., 282 ; *Pond v. People*, 8 Mich., 150, Hor. & T. Ca., 814; *Panton v. People*, 114 Ill., 505, 5 Am. Cr. R., 425, and note.

Reasonable Belief.—But the person seeking to justify or excuse his acts on the ground of apparent and not real danger, must show that he acted properly under the circumstances as they would appear to a *reasonable person* in his position.　The jury are to judge whether, as matter of fact, the appearances were such as to justify or excuse a reasonable person in so acting. The fact that the person assailed was naturally of a nervous or timid nature, will not excuse him from acting otherwise than a reasonable person would have been justified in acting.　*Shorter v. People*, 2 Comst., 193, Hor. & T. Ca., 256, and ibid, note 242; *State v. Thompson*, 9 Iowa, 188, 193; *Darling v. Williams*, 35 Ohio St., 58.

Actual Danger.—The reasonable belief must, however, be of actual and imminent danger, otherwise the case would not be one of necessity. *Evans v. State*, 44 Miss., 762, Hor. & T. Ca., 329, 336; *State v. Neely*, 20 Iowa, 108; *People v. Lombard*, 17 Cal., 317.

Threats and Character of Assailant—Previous threats of assailant against the person assailed, and also the character of assailant for violence and lawlessness, if known to the person assailed, may properly be shown as indicating the light in which he might reasonably look upon the acts actually done in determining their nature and intent. *People v. Scoggins*, 37 Cal., 676, Hor. & T. Ca., 596; *Monroe v. State*, 5 Ga., 85, Hor. & T. Ca., 422, 446, *et seq.*, and note; *State v. Nett*, 50 Wis., 524, 2 Cr. L. Mag., 78; *State v. Graham*, 61 Iowa, 608. But to justify one in acting upon fears arising from known threats or character, there must be *some overt act*, with which such threats or character can be connected so as to give rise to a reasonable belief of immediate danger. *Lander v. State*, 12 Tex., 462, Hor. & T. Ca., 366; *Bohannan v. Com.*, 8 Bush, 481, Hor. & T. Ca., 395, 403; *Evans v. State*, 44 Miss., 762, Hor. & T. Ca., 329, 336; *People v. Campbell*, 59 Cal., 243, 3 Cr. L. Mag., 29. Threats and violent character of which he has no knowledge cannot be shown as affecting the reasonable belief of assailed, but where the question is whether the assailant in fact made such an assault as would justify assailed in repelling it in a manner dangerous to life, such threats and character may be shown as indicating what the nature of the assault was. *Stokes v. People*, 53 N. Y., 164; *Campbell v. People*, 16 Ill., 17; *People v. Lombard*, 17 Cal., 317; *State v. Turpin*, 77 N. C., 473, 24 Am. R., 455; *Turpin v. State*, (Md.), 2 Cr. L. Mag., 532; *Wiggins v. People*, 93 U. S., 465; *State v. Spendlove*, 44 Kan., 1.

Defense of Person or Property of Another.—The doctrine runs through all the personal relations in life, whether of husband and wife, parent and child, master and servant, etc., etc., that the one may do for the other, by way of defense, whatever he may do for himself. So a guest in the habitation, or the neighbors, may defend it to the same extent as the owner might. As to prevention of felony, the duty rests upon every one in condition to resist it, as well as upon him against whose person or property it is directed. And it is even said, generally, that whatever a man may lawfully do for himself he may do for another. 1 Bish. Cr. L. (7th Ed.), Sec. 877: note, Hor. & T. Ca., 750; *Cooper's Case*, Cro. Car., 544; *Rex v. Bourne*, 5 Car. & P., 120; *Bush v. People*, 10 Colo., 566, 16 Pac. R., 290.

Compulsion of Authority.—As the ordinary relations existing among human beings by virtue of which one person may have authority over another, as for instance the relation of master and servant, parent and child, etc., contemplate a free moral agency on the part of the one under authority, no control by virtue of such relations exercised by the one in authority can be considered as compulsion justifying the commission of a crime at his command by the other. *Com. v. Hadley*, 11 Met., 66 ; *Hays v. State* 13 Mo , 246.

COVERTURE.

Coercion Presumed.—At common law the wife is considered so completely subject to the will of her husband that criminal acts done by her in his presence is presumed to be done under his coercion and not of her own will ; and for such act she is not held criminally responsible. If the act is done in the presence of the husband no command or compulsion other than that resulting from his presence need be shown. But for criminal acts done out of the presence of the husband the married woman is held liable as fully as a man, and a direct command from her husband would not excuse her. Some crimes, it is said, by reason of being either so malignant in their nature, or such that they are more likely to be committed by a woman, are excepted from the rule, e. g., treason, murder, keeping house of ill-fame, etc.; and in any case the presumption of compulsion from the presence of the husband is only *prima facie* and may be rebutted by proof that the wife is the real criminal. 4 Bl. Com., 28, and note; 1 Bish. Cr. L. (7th

Ed.), Secs. 356–366; *Com. v. Burk*, 11 Gray, 437; *Com. v. Butler*, 1 Allen, 4; *Com. v. Neal*, 10 Mass., 152, 6 Am. D., 105; *Com. v. Gannon*, 97 Mass., 547; *People v. Wright*, 38 Mich., 744, 31 Am. R., 331; *State v. Fitzgerald*, 49 Iowa, 260; *State v. Kelley*, 74 Iowa, 589, 38 N. W. R., 503; *Tabler v. State*, 34 Ohio St., 27,

WANT OF MENTAL CAPACITY.

As showing want of Intent.—Mental incapacity of greater or less degree, resulting from infancy, insanity, or intoxication, is recognized to some extent as showing want of criminal intent and therefore as relieving from criminal responsibility.

INFANCY.

How far Excuses.—Under seven years of age an infant is conclusively presumed incapable of entertaining a criminal intent. From seven to fourteen the presumption is that the infant is incapable of crime, but this presumption is not conclusive and may be overthrown by proof that a criminal intent existed, the question of his responsibility being for the jury. *Rex v. Owen*, 4 C. & P., 236; *York's Case*, Foster, 70; *Com. v. Mead*, 10 Allen, 398; *McClure v. Com.*, 5 Cr. L. Mag., 210, and note; *State v. Fowler*, 52 Iowa, 103, 106. Such proof, however, ought to be strong and clear beyond all doubt and contradiction. *Angelo v. People*, 96 Ill., 209, 36 Am. R., 132; *State v. Adams*, 76 Mo., 355. After fourteen the infant is held accountable. *People v. Kendall*, 25 Wend., 399. However, it is said that for omissions in relation to the management of property, etc., in regard to which he is not supposed to have full capacity until majority, he is not to be held criminally liable, as for instance, for failure to repair a bridge or highway. 4 Bl. Com., 22, and see *People v. Townsend*, 3 Hill, 479. See, generally, as to the criminal capacity of infants, 1 Bish. Cr. L. (7th Ed.), Secs. 367–373; 1 Russ. on Cr., 1; 1 Whart. Am. Cr. L., Sec. 48; 2 Stephen Hist. Cr. L., 97; Broom's Leg. Max. [311]; 1 Lead. Cr. Ca., 71; 4 Bl. Com., 22; Cooley on Torts, 97. The distinction between crimes and torts in regard to the importance of the intent is here very notice-able. An infant is, in general, liable to respond in damages for his torts irrespective of his age. Cooley on Torts, 103.

Showing Absence of Criminal Intent.—Idiocy and insanity, the former a congenital want of, or deficiency in the mental powers, and the latter a total or a partial loss of such powers previously possessed, are considered both in morals and in law as an excuse for acts otherwise wrongful. When the lack or loss of mind is quite complete, so that there can be said to be no reasoning mind, the law regards and has always regarded the person as free from criminal responsibility. It may provide for his restraint if his propensities are such as to make it danger-ous for him to be at large, but it confines him, not as a punish-ment, but merely as a protection to society. 4 Bl. Com., 24.

Partial Insanity.—But the difficulty which arises is that the deficiency in understanding, or mental powers, is not usually complete nor always permanent. It may be either partial in degree, or intermittent in duration. As to intermittent, or tem-porary insanity, the rule is unquestionable that for an act com-mitted during an insane period there is no criminal responsi-bility, while for an act committed during a sane period respon-sibility attaches. The difficulty which arises is to determine, as matter of fact, what was the mental condition at the time of the commission of the act.

Insane Delusions.—Partial insanity exists in many forms. One of the forms earliest and most clearly recognized by the law is that of insane delusions. It is claimed that there may exist in the mind delusions as to certain facts while as to other matters the mind is clear and rational; and there is no contro-versy about the doctrine that if there exist such insane delusions and the person acts as he would be justified in doing if the facts actually were as he believes them to be, he is not to be held criminally responsible. *McNaghten's Case*, 10 Cl. & Fin., 200; S. C. (in a note), 47 E. C. L., 130.

Knowledge of Right and Wrong.—Also it is said that in cases of partial insanity the test whether there is sufficient insanity to free the person from criminal responsibility is to be applied by inquiring whether he, at the time of doing the act, knew right from wrong, and that the act which he was committing was wrong. Here again there is no controversy that if the person does not know right from wrong, or does not have sufficient mind to understand the nature of the act as being right or wrong, he is free from responsibility. *Hart v. State*, 14 Neb., 572; *State v. Nixon*, 32 Kan., 205, 4 Pac. R., 159; *State v. Mowry*, 37 Kan., 369, 15 Pac. R., 282; *State v. Lewis*, 20 Nev., 333, 22 Pac. R., 241.

Debatable Ground.—The difficulty arises as to the converse of each of the two preceding propositions. If the person, though laboring under an insane delusion, acts in a manner which would be criminal even if the facts were as they are imagined to be, or if, with mind unbalanced, but still knowing right from wrong and knowing the act to be punishable as a wrong, he nevertheless does it, is he to be held fully responsible for his acts?

Medical View.—Those who study insanity from a medical standpoint and look upon it as a disease, usually insist that the theories of insane delusions and knowledge of right and wrong do not go far enough; that a man who labors under a delusion, not only is not responsible for the effects of that delusion, but has in every sense an *unsound mind*, that is, one which is impaired and likely to be unbalanced in all its operations; that one who knows the distinction between right and wrong and knows that a contemplated action is wrong, at least that it is an act prohibited by law, may yet be possessed of insane impulses which he cannot control; and that in either case he should not be held to the same degree of responsibility as one who is possessed of a wholly rational and sound mind. See Maudsley's Responsibility in Mental Disease, International Series; and criticism of his views, 2 Stephen, Hist. Cr. L., Chap. 19.

Difficulties.—But if we accept this theory where is the stopping place? No two persons have minds so equal in strength

6

that we have a right to expect just as much of one as the other. Those who investigate mental diseases and conditions insist that evil tendencies are transmitted from parent to child; and so it would seem unjust to impose upon one who, without any fault of his own, is born of depraved parents and reared among surroundings which tend to develop his worst tendencies, the same strict responsibility as upon one whose every inducement has been to virtue and obedience to law And the theory is often carried further and mental states and acts are attributed to precedent external causes to such an extent as to materially restrict the domain of freedom of the will and moral accountability. It would not be difficult to argue that every act amounting to a crime, at least an atrocious crime, *must* proceed from some tendencies for which the individual is not accountable, and that such tendencies are to be dealt with as a disease rather than a fault.

Susceptibility to Restraint as a Test.—It is evident that such considerations and discussions pertain to moral rather than legal accountability, and law does not make moral accountability the basis of criminal responsibility. The object of punishment is the protection of society by preventing a repetition of similar acts by the same person or others, and while it would outrage the public sense of justice and defeat the ends of the law if innocent men should be punished, yet where a person knows that an act is contrary to law and has sufficient mind to be restrained by a fear of punishment, it would seem that the law, in its protection of society, might well punish him for his transgressions, both to restrain him from further offense and as a warning to others of like class.

Irresistible Impulse.—It does appear, however, that there may exist irresistible impulses, originating in well defined disease of the mind, for which the unfortunate subject should not be held accountable. If the impulse is, by reason of mental disease, *irresistible*, then it ought, undoubtedly, to be allowed as a defense, but if it is the result of depraved propensities which

might have been checked by their possessor, or which fear of consequences would induce him to restrain, then the case would seem a proper one for punishment. *Spann v. State*, 47 Ga., 549, 1 Green's Cr. L. R., 391, and note; *People v. Hoin*, 62 Cal., 120.

Latest Doctrine.—The general result indicated by the tendency of modern authorities seems to be this: The "delusion" theory, by which the character of the act is made to depend upon whether it would be right or wrong if the delusion under which the perpetrator labored were true, and the "right and wrong" theory by which knowledge of the difference between right and wrong in the abstract, or of the moral character of the particular acts, is the test of responsibility, are both inadequate to meet all cases and constitute too narrow and harsh a rule. A person may, owing to disease of the brain, be in such condition that he is not responsible for his acts and is beyond restraint by fear of punishment, and in such case he should not be punished. But to justify the impulse being considered irresistible, it must appear that the person is otherwise insane. Wharton's note to *Guiteau's Case*, 10 Fed. R., 189; *State v. Jones*, 50 N. H., 369, 9 Am. R., 242; *Parsons v. State*, 81 Ala., 577, 9 Cr. L. Mag., 812, 2 So. R., 854; *State v. Felter*, 25 Iowa, 67; *Looney v. State*, 10 Tex. Ct. App., 520, 38 Am. R., 646; *Harris v. State*, 18 Tex. Ct. App., 287, 5 Am. Cr. R., 357; *Fain v. Com.*, 78 Ky., 183, 39 Am. R., 213; *Conway v. State*, 118 Ind., 482, 21 N. E. R., 285, 11 Cr. L., Mag., 640.

Emotional and Moral Insanity.—The doctrine of irresistible impulses must not be confounded with that of "moral," or "emotional" insanity, as being a state of disease of the moral nature, or the emotions, distinct from any impairment of the intellect. The law does not recognize any such disease as relieving from responsibility. See Wharton's Note, *supra;* May Cr. L., Secs. 18, 19; *Boswell v. State*, 63 Ala., 307, 35 Am. R., 20; *Guetig v. State*, 66 Ind., 94, 32 Am. R., 99.

Authorities.—On the general subject the following authorities, in addition to those already referred to, may be consulted.

1 Bish. Cr. L. (7th Ed.), Chap. 26; 1 Lead. Cr. Ca., 100; Articles,
7 Cr. L. Mag., 431, 567, and 10 *id.*, 641, 805.

Presumption.—Sanity is the usual and natural condition of
human beings and insanity is the exception. Therefore every
person is presumed sane until the contrary appears. While
criminal intent is an essential element in most crimes and it is
the duty of the prosecution to show that all the elements of the
crime exist before conviction, yet this presumption of sanity
renders it unnecessary to introduce any evidence tending to show
sanity or overthrow the possible excuse of insanity until some
evidence of insanity is introduced in the defense. See authorities
under next paragraph.

Burden of Proof.—The burden of proving defendant's guilt
rests upon the prosecution; every element necessary to make
out the crime must be shown, and as criminal intent is, in general, a necessary element, it must be proven. That there may be
criminal intent there must be a mind sufficiently sane to be
responsible, and therefore sanity must appear to warrant a conviction, and the burden of proving it is on the prosecution. But
the presumption of sanity referred to above is sufficient to make
out a *prima facie* case and to warrant the defendant being considered sane until he introduces some evidence to the contrary.
When such evidence is introduced the prosecution must overcome it and establish sanity as it must every other essential
element of the crime. This doctrine seems to be the most
reasonable and the one to which the authorities are tending.
Cooley's note to 4 Bl. Com., 24; 1 Greenl. Ev. Secs. 81 b., and
81 c.; 2 Bish. Cr. Pr., Secs. 669–673; May Cr. L., Sec. 20; *Com.
v. McKie*, 1 Gray, 61, and note thereto in 1 Lead. Cr. Ca., 299;
Com. v. Kimball, 24 Pick., 366; *People v. Garbutt*, 17 Mich., 9;
Brotherton v. People, 75 N. Y., 159; *State v. Crawford*, 11 Kan.,
32; S. C. 2 Green's Cr. L. R., 638; Article by Dr. Ordronaux,
1 Cr. L. Mag., 432, and notes, ibid., 465; *Cunningham v. State*,
56 Miss., 269, 31 Am. R., 360; *State v. Nixon*, 32 Neb., 205, 2
Am. Cr. R., 307; *Ballard v. State*, 19 Neb., 609.

Contrary View.—On this rule as to burden of proof the authorities are irreconcilably in conflict. Many of them hold that the defense of insanity is in the nature of an affirmative defense, or matter in confession and avoidance, as to which the burden is on defendant. But this is a misconception of the state of the issues. The prosecution, in fact, alleges the *crime*, not merely the commission of the act. The defendant by pleading "not guilty," denies all the essential elements of the charge. This denial throws upon the prosecution the burden of proving each of these essential elements, one of which is the criminal intent. Although the presumption of sanity relieves the prosecution from the necessity of introducing any evidence in the first instance to show sanity, such presumption simply serves to supply the requisite evidence to make out a *prima facie* case and does not shift the burden of proof. Cases supporting the view here criticised are very numerous; a few only can be cited. *State v. Lawrence*, 57 Maine, 574; *Boswell v. State*, 63 Ala., 307, 35 Am. R., 20, and *Webb v. State*, 9 Tex. Ct. App., 490 given at length in note to that case; *Parsons v. State*, 81 Ala., 577, 9 Cr. L. Mag., 812; *State v. Felter*, 32 Iowa, 50; *State v. Hoyt*, 46 Conn., 330; *Lynch v. Com.*, 77 Penn. St., 205, 213; *People v. McDonnell*, 47 Cal., 134, 2 Green's Cr. L. R., 441; *State v. Smith*, 53 Mo., 267, 2 Green's Cr. L. R., 597; *State v. Redemeier*, 71 Mo., 173, 1 Cr. L. Mag., 456 and note; *State v. Lewis*, 20 Nev. 333, 22 Pac. R., 241.

Sufficiency of Proof.—There is also great conflict among the authorities as to the amount of evidence of insanity necessary to entitle defendant to acquittal on that ground. A few cases have held that defendant relying upon insanity as a defense, must establish it beyond a reasonable doubt; others hold that the defense must be established by a preponderance of evidence or by satisfactory evidence, while still others only require defendant ,to introduce such evidence of insanity as to raise a reasonable doubt of guilt. The first of these three rules is not now recognized anywhere. The second is announced by many cases, probably a majority of all, among which are the cases cited to the last preceding paragraph. The last of the three rules finds support in *Chase v. People*, 40 Ill., 352, and *Guetig v. State*, 66 Ind., 94, 32 Am. R. 99. But if the rule as to the burden of proof, which is stated in the next to the last paragraph as the one best founded in reason, is correct, then there is no difficulty as to the amount of evidence required. The rule is universally recognized that all things as to which the prosecution has the burden of proof, must be proven beyond a reasonable doubt to warrant conviction, and if it be conceded that the burden of proof as to sanity rests on the prosecution, then it follows that if, on all the evidence, there is a reasonable doubt of defendant's sanity, the jury must acquit. See the authorities cited under the paragraph just referred to. These questions as to the burden and sufficiency of proof come more properly, however, under criminal procedure in connection with similar questions as to other defenses, and will be found there further discussed.

INTOXICATION.

Does not Excuse.—Voluntary drunkenness or intoxication is no defense in a prosecution for a crime, although it amounts for the time being, to temporary insanity. But *delirium tremens* is looked upon as a kind of insanity, resulting, it is true, from habitual intoxication, but different from mere intoxication, and may be sufficient to render its victim not criminally responsible. Also, an act done under the influence of involuntary intoxication, produced through the fraud of another, or through mistake, would not be imputed as a crime. 4 Bl. Com., 25, and Cooley's note (3); 1 Bish. Cr. L. (7th Ed.), Chap. 27; *U. S. v. Drew*, 1 Lead. Cr. Ca., 131, and note; May's Cr. L., Secs. 21–24; *Com. v. Hawkins*, 3 Gray, 463; *People v. Garbutt*, 17 Mich., 9, 19; *Rafferty v. People*, 66 Ill., 118; *McIntyre v. People*, 38 Ill., 514; *Maconnehey v. State*, 5 Ohio St., 77; *People v. Ferris*, 55 Cal., 588, 2 Cr. L. Mag., 19; *State v. Mowry*, 37 Kan., 369, 15 Pac. R., 282, 10 Cr. L. Mag., 23; *Garner v. State*, (Fla.), 9 So. R., 835.

As Showing Want of Specific Intent.—Where the criminality of an act is made to depend upon the specific intent with which it was done, or the state or condition of the person's mind with reference thereto, then the defendant will usually be allowed to prove intoxication for the purpose of showing that such specific intent, or necessary mental state, was not present. *Ford v. State*, 5 Cr. L. Mag., 32; *People v. Blake*, 65 Cal., 275. In such cases the act is considered as taking its complexion from the intent with which it was done, and intoxication may furnish an explanation for the doubtful act without attributing it to a specific intent to do some other wrong. Thus the crime of burglary consists of breaking and entering the dwelling house of another with intent to commit a felony, and defendant may be allowed to prove his intoxicated condition by way of defense, not to show that he did not intend to break and enter when he did so, but to rebut any evidence or presumption in favor of the prosecution that he broke down the door *for the purpose* or *with the intention* of doing some other wrongful act amounting to a felony. So, also, drunkenness may be proven to show the absence of the deliberation and premeditation necessary to make a homicide murder in the first degree, where the statute makes two degrees of murder. *Aszman v. State*, 123 Ind., 347, 24 N. E. R., 123. Again, in homicide, the question may be whether the killing was the result of sudden provocation which is shown to have existed, or of a deliberate intent, irrespective of such provocation; for the crime would be greater in the latter case than in the former. In deciding whether the provocation was sufficient to have caused the act, intoxication may be considered as showing the defendant to have been peculiarly susceptible to provocation, and thus rendering the probability that the provocation caused the act stronger than it would be in case of a sober person. But it will be seen that in none of these instances is intoxication admitted to show that accused did not intend the natural and ordinary consequences of the act which he did. 1 Bish. Cr. L. (7th Ed.), Secs. 408–416; 1 Lead. Cr. Ca., 137; May's Cr. L., Sec. 22; *Crosby v.*

People, (Ill.), 27 N. E. R., 49, 43 Alb. L. J., 387; *State v. Bell*, 29 Iowa, 316; *Jones v. Com.*, 75 Penn. St., 403; *People v. Langton*, 67 Cal., 427; *State v. Garvey*, 11 Minn., 154; *Roberts v. People*, 19 Mich., 401, 416; *Rogers v. State*, 33 Ind., 543; *People v. Belencia*, 21 Cal., 544; *Rex v. Carroll*, 7 Car. & P., 145; *Wood v. State*, 34 Ark., 341, 36 Am. R., 13; *State v. Cross*, 27 Mo., 332; *Pigman v. State*, 14 Ohio, 555; *People v. Harris*, 29 Cal., 678; *Hopt v. People*, 104 U. S., 631; *State v. Johnson*, 40 Conn., 136 and 41 ib., 584; *Shannahan v. Com.*, 8 Bush, 463, 1 Green's Cr. L. R., 373; *Cline v. State*, 43 Ohio St., 332.

CORPORATIONS.

May Commit Crime.—Corporations can only act through agents, and can only authorize agents to do for them such acts as are proper for the accomplishment of the objects for which they are created. A corporation organized and empowered to buy and sell cattle would have no power to authorize an agent to steal cattle, and if such agent should do so he would be considered as acting on his own responsibility, and punished accordingly, and the corporation would not be criminally responsible for his acts. But if a corporation should fail to do something which it had authority to do, and such failure was made criminal in an individual, it would be equally criminal in the corporation; that is, a corporation may be punished for a criminal non-feasance. Also, where a corporation has power to do an act, and causes it to be done in a manner which is criminal, it is criminally liable for such misfeasance. However, to render a corporation amenable to criminal law, there must be some method beyond the ordinary one for bringing the defendant within the jurisdiction of the court, and the punishment authorized must be such that it can be inflicted upon such an artificial or fictitious being. 1 Bish. Cr. L. (7th Ed.), Chap. 28; 1 Lead. Cr. Ca., 158, 166, and note, 174; May Cr. L., Sec. 15; 2 Morawetz Corp. (2d Ed.), Secs. 732, 733; *Com. v. Proprietors, etc.*, 2 Gray, 339; *Reg. v. Birmingham, etc., R'y*, 3 Q. B., 223; *Reg. v. Great North of England R'y*, 9 Q. B., 315; *People v. Albany*, 11 Wend., 539; *State v. Atchison*,

etc., R. Co., 3 Lea., 729, 31 Am. R., 663; *State v. B. & O. R. Co.*, 15 W. Va., 362, 36 Am. R., 803; *Stewart v. Waterloo Turn Verein*, 71 Iowa, 226; *contra, State v. Great Works, etc., Co.*, 20 Maine, 41; *State v. Pres't, etc., of O. & M. R. Co.*, 23 Ind., 362; *State v. Cincinnati Fertilizer Co.*, 24 Ohio St., 611; 1 Bl. Com., 476.

PRINCIPAL AND ACCESSORY.

Some Participation Necessary.—To render a person guilty of a crime, he must, to some extent, participate therein. Thus one who should stand by and see another murdered, would, if he had had no share in instigating the murder, and was not present to render assistance, be innocent of the crime of murder, though he might, by common law, be guilty of misprison of the felony in not preventing it, if he might have done so, or in afterward concealing it. *Hilmes v. Stroebel*, 59 Wis., 74; *State v. Farr*, 33 Iowa, 553; *People v. Ah Ping*, 27 Cal., 489; *People v. Woodward*, 45 Cal., 293; *Connaughty v. State*, 1 Wis., 159; article 20 Cent. L. Jour., 3. But a person present and assenting to the commission of a crime from which he alone is to derive benefit, may be presumed to have procured it to be done. *Com. v. Stevens*, 10 Mass., 181; Foster, 350.

The Principal.—The guilty perpetrator of the wrongful act is the principal. It is immaterial whether he do the act himself, or cause it to be done by an irresponsible or innocent agent, but if he acts merely as instigator to another responsible will, then he ceases to be a principal, as will be shown further on. In every crime there must be a principal, and if the act is done by an agent who is not responsible, as by reason of infancy, or ignorance of the object of the act, the person procuring the act to be done is responsible as principal. Thus it was held that one who, by fraudulently substituting one instrument for another, procured a party's signature to a deed which he had no intention of signing, was thereby guilty of forgery. *State v. Shurtliff*, 18 Maine, 368. And see, generally, *Adams v. The People*, 1 N. Y., 173; *Com. v. Hill*, 11 Mass., 136; 2 Stephen's Hist. Cr. L., 229.

Joint Principals.—Two or more persons may join to accomplish the same wrong and thereby become joint principals. Even though each should be engaged in only a part of the common enterprise and his acts, in themselves, not amount to a completed crime, yet if what he does is in pursuance of a common object which, when accomplished, constitutes a completed crime, each person engaged therein is guilty of the crime, as a principal thereto. 1 Bish. Cr. L. (7th Ed.), Secs. 628–642, 650; *Rex v. Cassey*, 7 Car. & P., 282. All who join in the plan at the time it is formed or afterward, and are present at the commission of the wrongful act in pursuance thereof, are guilty of the crime intended to be committed, though actually accomplished by one or a portion of the number, and each is also guilty of any crime committed in the execution of, or attempt to execute the common purpose, or naturally resulting therefrom. *Spies v. People*, 122 Ill., 1, 12 N. E. R., 865, and 17 N. E. R., 898, 9 Cr. L. Mag., 829; *Williams v. State*, 88 Ala., 80, 7 So. R., 106, 9 Cr. L., Mag., 480; *State v. Shelledy*, 8 Iowa, 477, 505; *Ruloff v. People*, 45 N.Y., 213; *Brennan v. People*, 15 Ill., 511; *Smith v. People*, 1 Col., 121, 138; *Reg. v. Wallis*, 1 Salk., 334; *State v. Underwood*, 57 Mo., 40; *Com. v. Fortune*, 105 Mass., 592; *Reg. v. Young*, 8 Car. & P., 644. But if one of the wrong-doers turns aside from, or goes beyond the common purpose to commit an act not contemplated and aside from that purpose, or proceeds after the accomplishment of the purpose to do something further, the others are not joint participators in that wrong. *Reg. v. Canton*, 12 Cox C. C., 624, 10 Moak's Eng. R., 506; *Rex v. Hawkins*, 3 Car & P., 392; *Lamb v. People*, 96 Ill., 73, 2 Cr. L. Mag., 472. The foregoing matters are also treated somewhat in connection with the doctrine of intent in the paragraph concerning the intent of one joined to the wrongful acts of another.

Presence Actual or Constructive.—To constitute one a principal in a joint crime he must be present at its execution, but this presence need not be immediate and actual. What is called constructive presence is sufficient. In other words he must par-

ticipate, or be prepared to participate, or render some assistance, in the actual accomplishment of the design. One of the wrong-doers who remains at a distance but within hearing, to be called if needed, is constructively present. Note to 4 Bl. Com., 33; *Breese v. State*, 12 Ohio St., 146; *Rex v. Skerritt*, 2 Car. & P., 427.

Principals in First and Second Degree.—By early common law a distinction was made between actual participants in the wrongful act and those who were actually or constructively present in pursuance of the common purpose, aiding and abetting, but took no active part, the former being called principals in the first degree, the latter principals in the second degree. The latter were also sometimes designated as accessories *at the fact*. The distinction is now obsolete and of no value whatever. All principals are equally guilty and proof of either of these degrees of participation will warrant conviction as principal. 1 Bish. Cr. L. (7th Ed.), Secs. 644–659; *Warder v. State*, 24 Ohio St., 143; *Doan v. State*, 26 Ind., 495; *Reg. v. Howell*, 9 Car. & P., 435; *People v. Bearss*, 10 Cal., 68; 2 Bish. Cr. Pr., Sec. 3; *State v. Davis*, 29 Mo., 391; May Cr. L. Sec. 30; 4 Bl. Com., 33, and note; Foster, 347.

Intermediate Responsible Agents.—There are various relations in life which give rise to an obligation on the part of one person to render obedience to the commands of another, but the obedience due to the law is higher than any such obligation. The wife is excused, as has been stated, for criminal acts done in the presence of the husband, but no other relation will excuse or justify the commission by a responsible being of a criminal act in obedience to a command. And as the law looks primarily at the person immediately causing the wrong, such person is deemed the principal unless he is the mere unwilling, irresponsible, or otherwise innocent tool of another. 4 Bl. Com., 37; *Com. v. Drew*, 3 Cush., 279; *Hays v. State*, 13 Mo., 246; May Cr. L. Sec. 34; *People v. Lyon*, 99 N. Y., 210; 6 Cr. L. Mag., 865.

Accessory Before the Fact.—But the person who has originated the plan, and at whose instance the crime has been committed, or who has given aid or encouragement toward its execution, though not present at its commission, is not held guiltless. He is, however, looked upon as further removed from the act than the actual perpetrator, and is designated as accessory before the fact, the only distinction between such and a principal in the second degree being that the former commands, aids, abets, or encourages, but is not present at the commission, while the latter is present, either actually or constructively, though not actually participating. 1 Bish. Cr. L. (7th Ed.), Secs. 660–689; 4 Bl. Com., 36; May Cr. L , Sec. 31.

Procurement Necessary.—To constitute one an accessory before the fact he must have exercised his will in some way toward the accomplishment of the object; mere knowledge of the intent, and concealment will not suffice. And this assent must continue until the commission of the act, for there is a time for repentance, and if it take place before the actual commission of the act, and the person originally instigated insist on proceeding on his own motion, the original instigator is relieved from liability. *Reg. v. Taylor*, L. R. 2 C. C. R., 147, 12 Moak's Eng. R., 636. But the procurement need not be direct, and if one should command another to get a third person, whether specified or not, to commit the crime, the original instigator would be an accessory, and it would be immaterial that the perpetrator did not know who the original instigator was. *Rex v. Cooper*, 5 Car & P., 535. The act committed must be, however, substantially the one instigated, or for the commission of which assistance was rendered, and not a totally different one, or one not implied in that contemplated. *State v. Lucas*, 55 Iowa, 321; 4 Bl. Com., 37; Foster, 369.

Aider and Abettor: Accomplice.—Aiders and abettors, or accomplices, may be either accessories before the fact or principals, according as they are present or absent at the commission. May Cr. L., Sec. 36; Foster, 130.

Accessory After the Fact.—One who harbors and conceals, comforts and assists, or otherwise aids the principal, knowing

that he has committed the crime, and after it is complete, is an accessory after the fact. Such comfort and assistance must be rendered for the purpose of hindering or preventing the apprehension, trial, or punishment of the principal. A wife may render such aid and comfort to her husband without incurring guilt, but no other relationship will excuse such complicity. Something more than mere knowledge of the commission of the offense and concealment of the fact, or acceptance of the benefits of the crime, or compounding with the criminal is necessary to constitute the relation of accessory after the fact. The offense of receiving stolen goods is akin to that of accessory after the fact to larceny, but it is not the same. 1 Bish. Cr. L. (7th Ed.), Secs. 690–708; 4 Bl. Com., 37; May Cr. L., Sec. 35.

Punishment of Accessories.—An accessory before the fact was, at common law, and is now, generally held equally guilty with the principal, and liable to the same punishment. He is guilty of the same crime as the principal, and they may be jointly indicted, the former being charged as accessory. The accessory after the fact was also at common law deemed guilty of the same crime as the principal, and might be indicted with him, but his punishment was lighter. In either case the relation to the crime as charged in an indictment must be proved as alleged. Proof that defendant was guilty as principal will not support the charge of being accessory, nor *vice versa*. 2 Bish. Cr. Pr., Sec. 11; *People v. Mather*, 4 Wend., 229, 256.

Principal must be Convicted.—As the guilt of the accessory, as viewed from the common law standpoint, depended on the relation which he sustained to the principal, it was held that the accessory was not liable to punishment until the principal had been tried and sentenced, and so he could only be put on trial, unless by his consent, jointly with, or after the conviction of his principal. If for any cause, such as the death of the principal, or his escape, or pardon, the prosecution against him failed to proceed as far as sentence, the accessory could not be punished; and even in a case where the statute authorized the trial of accessories to proceed irrespective of the previous trial and conviction of the principal, and after the trial of the accessory and the finding of a verdict of guilty, but before sentence, the principal was acquitted, it was held that the accessory was thereby released. *McCarty v. State*, 44 Ind., 214, 2 Green's Cr. L. R., 715, 15 Am. R., 232. The previous conviction of the principal is only *prima facie* evidence of his guilt on the trial of the accessory, and he may overcome it and exonerate himself by proving, notwithstanding, that the principal was in fact innocent. *Com. v. Knapp*, 10 Pick., 477. The accessory can not be convicted of a higher offense than his principal. Generally, as to the matters of this section, see 1 Bish. Cr. L. (7th Ed.), Secs. 666–669; 4 Bl. Com., 40.

Statutory Provisions.—The absurdity of the rules of the common law with reference to the trial of accessories has led to its modification by statute in, probably, every state. Many states entirely abrogate the distinction between principal and accessory before the fact, and make the latter in every sense a principal, to be indicted, tried and punished as such, without regard to the conviction or acquittal of any other participant in the crime. *State v. Stanley*, 48 Iowa, 221; *People v. Bearss*, 10 Cal., 68; *State v. Cassady*, 12 Kan., 550, 1 Am. Cr. R., 267. At common law benefit of clergy (as to which, see 1 Steph. Hist. Cr. L., 459–472; 1 Bish. Cr. L., 936–938) was allowed to accessories after the fact when it was denied to principals and accessories before the fact. In some states there is now no provision for their punishment, except for the distinct offenses of assisting a prisoner to escape, receiving or aiding to conceal stolen property and the like.

In what Crimes Accessories Recognized.—The foregoing discussion has gone on the assumption that the relation of principal and accessory might exist as to every crime, and that relation may, in fact, exist as to every crime unless something in the nature of the crime itself renders it impossible; but the relation is recognized under the names above given only in certain

classes of crimes. Thus it is said that in treason there are no accessories, but all are principals. But under the definition of treason in the U. S. Constitution, or the same definition in a state constitution, an accessory after the fact would clearly not be guilty of treason. Similarly, in cases of misdemeanor the distinction between principal and accessory before the fact is not preserved, and the latter is called and treated as a principal; but a person standing in the relation of accessory after the fact to a misdemeanor is disregarded. The result is that it is only as to felonies that we have either the two degrees of principals or any such term as that of accessory. 1 Bish. Cr. L. (7th Ed.), Secs. 681–689, 701–708; 4 Bl. Com , 36; May Cr. L., Sec. 32. But although petit larceny was a felony at common law, it was held there could be no accessories therein. *Evan's Case*, Foster, 73; *Ward v. People*, 3 Hill, 395.

CLASSIFICATION OF CRIMES.

At Common Law.—The common law divided crimes into treasons, felonies, and misdemeanors. The characteristics of treason will be briefly mentioned hereafter under that head. The distinction which it is important to notice is that between the latter two. The derivation of the term felony is given as *fee-lon*, importing (in relation to feudal tenure of lands) the forfeiture of the fee; and it was used to designate that class of crimes the conviction of which occasioned a forfeiture of lands, or goods, or both. To this consequence was also usually added capital punishment, so that the term came to mean those crimes punishable with death, and had attached to it an idea of enormity, although some crimes not felonies, as for instance, perjury, would be acknowledged to be more heinous than some felonies, such as petit larceny. Many acts were made felonies by statute which were not so at common law and an act making a crime punishable capitally was said to constitute it a felony without express words, and so, to declare a crime a felony was to thereby make it punishable with death. The term misdemeanor was used to signify all crimes not treasons or felonies. 4 Bl. Com., 94; 1 Bish. Cr.

L.(7th Ed.), Secs. 615–625; May Cr. L., Secs. 25–27; 2 Stephen Hist. Cr. L., 55.

In the United States.—Aside from statutory provision, the terms felony and misdemeanor have no fixed meaning in the United States. Felonies may be said, in such cases, to include all those crimes which were so at common law (unless otherwise declared by statute), and also all crimes expressly made felonies by statute. In some states the term is regarded as having no significance. *Ward v. People*, 3 Hill, 395; *Drennan v. People*, 10 Mich., 169; *Matthews v. State*, 4 Ohio St., 539, 542; *State v. Felch*, 58 N. H., 1; *U. S. v. Coppersmith*, 1 Cr. L. Mag., 741.

Meaning by Statute.—A common usage in this country is to speak of felonies as those crimes punishable capitally or by imprisonment in the penitentiary, and this is the meaning given the term in some states by statute; misdemeanors being at the same time defined as including all offenses not felonies. See Code of Iowa, Secs. 4103–4105; 1 Bish. Cr. L. (7th Ed.), Sec. 618; *State v. Smith*, 32 Maine, 369; *State v. Waller*, 43 Ark., 381, 5 Am. Cr. R., 631.

Use of the Distinction.—The distinction between felonies and misdemeanors being arbitrary would be valueless, except that, as most of the graver offenses are included in the one class and most of the lighter ones in the other, certain differences in the methods of procedure, etc., in the two classes of cases are recognized or expressly declared. Thus the presence of defendant in court in the trial of a felony is indispensable, while it is immaterial in case of a misdemeanor.

PART II.—SPECIFIC CRIMES.

INTRODUCTORY.

How Treated Here.—Having thus considered the most important general doctrines affecting all crimes, it is now necessary to notice the various particular crimes and the characteristics and peculiarities of each. As has already been said, the common

law as to crimes, even in states where common law crimes are not recognized, is regarded as the great storehouse in which to find definitions of terms and enunciations of principles necessarily existing and used in criminal jurisprudence, and in construing the criminal statutes the courts do not confine themselves to the language used, but look also at the law as it previously existed to determine what is the meaning of the enactment, thus attempting to ascertain what of the previous law was intended to be retained and what rejected. *Com. v. Webster*, 5 Cush., 303.

Common Law Meaning of Terms.—It is a recognized rule of interpretation that words in a statute which have acquired a legal meaning are to be understood in that sense, and not in the ordinary sense. Bish. Stat. Cr., Secs. 93, 97. Therefore it becomes necessary to discuss the general doctrines applied to particular common law crimes in order that the corresponding statutory crimes may be understood.

What Crimes Considered.—It will only be possible to consider the more important common law and statutory crimes. The fact that in states where common law crimes are recognized, some old common law crime might be discovered to exist which had not before been recognized by their courts or regulated by their statutes, would not make it worth while to discuss the whole field of such crimes as they existed in England. Neither would it be worth while to discuss statutory crimes specified in the statutes of particular states, unless they belong to some general class of offenses defined and regulated in a similar manner in many states and in regard to which they are judicial decisions throwing light on the whole class. For special statutory provisions the statutes of each state must, of course, be consulted.

OFFENSES AGAINST GOVERNMENT.

TREASON.

High and Petit.—By the early common law, treasons were of two kinds, high and petit, the former being an offense by a citizen against the sovereign, such as is now called treason, and the latter being a violation by an inferior of the allegiance due from him to his superior. The term petit treason included originally various offenses, but by statute (25 Edw., 3, which defined both petit and high treason,) it was confined to three: where a servant kills his master; where a wife kills her husband; where an ecclesiastical man, secular or religious, kills his prelate to whom he owes obedience. 1 Hawkins P. C., Chap. 32; 4 Bl. Com., 75. Petit treason was never recognized in this country and is now abolished in England, and those acts which would have constituted petit treason are now murder, the crime of murder having been considered, at common law, as being included in petit treason.

High Treason in United States.--The Constitution of the United States specifically defines what only shall constitute treason, following substantially the language of 25 Edw., 3 (U. S. Const., Art. 3, Sec. 3). A similar provision is contained in most State Constitutions. The object in putting the definition of this crime into the constitution, while all other crimes under the laws of the United States are left to be defined by Congress, seems to have been to prevent the prosecution for treason being made an engine of tyranny and oppression as it had been in England, by reason of the power exercised by the judges to punish acts which they held to be constructively treasonable. Story on the Const., Secs. 1796–1802; Cooley's Const. Law, 287; Sergeant's Const. Law, 379.

What Acts Constitute.—To constitute "levying war" within the definition, it is said there must be some overt act; that a conspiracy to levy war is not sufficient, nor is the mere enlistment of men, but there must be an actual assemblage of men for the treasonable purpose. But war having been commenced, all who perform any part, or are actually leagued in the general conspiracy, are guilty, however remote they may be from the scene of action. It is also said that an insurrection to prevent the execution of an act of Congress (e. g.), the excise law, would be treason. 2 Bish. Cr. L. (7th Ed.), Secs. 1214–1236; 3 Whart. Am. Cr. L. (6th Ed), Secs. 2719–2738; 3 Greenl. Ev,, Secs. 240–244; *Ex parte Bollman*, 4 Cranch, 75, 136; *U. S. v. Mitchell*, 2 Dall., 348; May Cr. L , Secs. 211–213; 4 Bl. Com., 74.

Allegiance.—To constitute treason the person committing the act must owe allegiance and fidelity to the government, either state or national, against which the act is committed. Such allegiance is due at all times and places from a citizen of the sovereignty, and from an alien resident so long as such residence continues. 2 Bish. Cr. L. (7th Ed.), Sec. 1235; 3 Greenl. Ev., Sec. 239; R. S. of U. S., Sec. 5331; *Resp. v. Chapman*, 1 Dall., 53; *Carlisle v. U. S.*, 16 Wall., 147.

Treason against a State.—The question has been much discussed whether there can be a levying of war against a state, or adherence to its enemies, which may be treason against the state as distinct from treason against the United States. On principle it seems doubtful, but the tendency of authorities has been from the first to recognize and punish treason against the state as an offense under state law, cognizable in the state courts. The parties engaged in Dorr's and Shay's rebellions were so tried and punished, as was also John Brown. It is to be noticed, however, that where the constitution of the state does not confine treason to levying war upon the state and adhering to its enemies, other acts might be made treason against the state and properly punished in the state courts as such. Therefore the fact that the United States Constitution (Art. 4, Sec. 2,) recognizes treason as among the offenses for which the surrender of a fugitive from justice may be demanded by the state from which he has fled, does not prove that levying war against a state is not treason against the United States and therefore punishable only in the federal courts. ·1 Bish. Cr. L. (7th Ed.), Secs. 177, 456; 3 Whart. Am. Cr. L. (6th Ed.), Secs. 2766–2774; 1 Kent's Com., 403, note; *People v. Lynch*, 11 Johns., 549.

Punishment.—By statutes of the U. S. (Rev. Stat., Sec. 5332,) treason is made punishable with death, or fine and imprisonment, and disqualifies for holding office.

Misprison of Treason.—Misprison, in general, is a term applied to the concealment of a crime, and was itself, as to treasons and felonies, an offense at common law. There was no such offense, however, in connection with a misdemeanor. Misprison of a felony is no longer an offense in many states, but is so as to some felonies under the laws of the United States. As to treason, it is an offense under the laws of the United States (U. S. Rev. Stat., Sec. 5333), and those of Iowa (Code, Sec. 3846), and is made to consist in having a knowledge of the crime of treason and concealing it and not revealing as soon as may be to the executive or a judge. It is punishable in either case by fine or imprisonment, which imprisonment by the state statute is to be in the penitentiary, so that the offense is felony, as it was originally at common law. 4 Bl. Com., 120 ; 1 Bish. Cr. L. (7th Ed.), Secs. 717–722.

Other Offenses against the Government.—The statutes of the United States (U. S. Rev. Stat., Secs. 5334–5338) provide for the punishment of other acts as offenses against the government, such as inciting or engaging in rebellion or insurrection, carrying on criminal correspondence with foreign governments, conspiring to overthrow or levy war against the government, recruiting armed forces against it, etc., etc.

OFFENSES AGAINST THE PERSON.

HOMICIDE.

Defined.—Homicide is, as the derivation of the name literally implies, the killing of a human being by a human being.

The Killing.—To kill a being is to cause its death. It is a matter of importance to determine how closely the death must be the result of the act of the person charged therewith to constitute a "killing" by him. If such act, as a cause, starts a chain of effects which finally result in death without the intervention of any other independent cause which alone would have produced that result, that act is said to amount to a killing. Where there is a concurrence of causes more or less instrumental in producing a result, it is often mere casuistry to say that one rather than another of them is *the* cause. Here the law gives some assistance by indicating what it will regard as the cause in certain

classes of cases. 2 Bish. Cr. L. (7th Ed.), Secs. 635–641; 1 Hawk. P. C., Chap. 31, Secs. 4–8; 4 Bl. Com., 196, 197.

Examples.—Familiar examples of acts which constitute a "killing" are wounding, striking, poisoning, strangling, drowning, etc., etc., and the intent with which an act is done is of no consequence in determining whether it is homicide, though it may affect its criminality. To accidentally shoot and kill an unseen person in shooting at game would be homicide.

Direct or Indirect Cause: Wound.—It is not necessary, in order to constitute homicide, that the act be the direct cause of the death, or that it be such a cause as necessarily produces death. If one being dangerously wounded, but in a manner not necessarily mortal, simply fails to attend to the wound, or is treated in an unskillful or careless manner, so that death results, the act is still looked upon as homicide, although by skillful treatment and care a cure would have been effected. 1 Hawk. P. C., Chap. 31, Sec. 10; 1 Hale P. C., 428; 3 Greenl. Ev., Sec. 139; *Com. v. Hackett*, 2 Allen, 136; *State v. Bantley*, 44 Conn., 537, 26 Am. R., 486; *State v. Morphy*, 33 Iowa, 270, 11 Am. R., 122, and note; *Denman v. State*, 15 Neb., 138. If the injury, however, whatever it be, is not in itself dangerous, but the person dies solely in consequence of the improper treatment, the death would not render the act producing the original injury homicide. For instance, if by some act or carelessness of another, a person was slightly, but not dangerously, poisoned, and in taking an antidote should, by his own carelessness or that of his physician, take a dose which in itself would cause death, the original poisoning would not be homicide, although it gave rise to the occasion for taking the dose which was fatal. 1 Hale P. C., 428; *Coffman v. Com.*, 10 Bush, 495, 1 Am. Cr. R., 293.

Hastening Death.—The most that can be said of any injury is that it hastens death, for the agencies tending to final dissolution are always at work. An injury that in any degree hastens death, provided the death result within a year and a day as hereafter specified, will amount to homicide, although the party was already mortally wounded or diseased. 2 Bish. Cr. L. (7th Ed.), Sec. 638; *Com. v. Fox*, 7 Gray, 585; *People v. Ah Fat*, 48 Cal., 61.

Negligence.—An *act* directly causing death is said to be homicide, although there be no intention or thought of killing; but an *omission* could not be regarded as a *cause* unless of such a nature as that it be reasonably known to tend directly to that result. As already said in connection with the subject of carelessness and negligence as supplying an intent (*ante*, p. 26), the law requires action only in cases where it is necessary to prevent injury from other acts or relations which might prove injurious, though done or entered into for another and proper purpose, and therefore not such as should be forbidden. So, negligence or omission to act will not constitute homicide unless there is a failure to act where there is a positive duty to do so, or, in acting, safeguards are omitted which the nature of the act done reasonably requires to prevent its being dangerous. Thus if one man who should see another drowning, should fail to throw to him a rope, which was available for that purpose, such omission would, aside from any question of guilt or innocence, clearly not be a homicide; while, if the man on shore should throw the rope to the other and in drawing him in, by accident, choke him to death, the act would be homicide, though of course perfectly innocent. In determining whether negligence or omission constitutes homicide, the intent is no more material than it is in reference to a direct act; the only question is whether there is the failure to do something which should be done and whether that failure, being something in its nature likely to cause death, did actually produce that result. What negligence will be considered sufficiently criminal to render death resulting therefrom imputable to the negligent party as a crime will be considered hereafter.

How soon Death must Occur.—As all men die sooner or later, and as it is often impossible to determine what remote causes may have contributed to the death, it is important that some limit of time be fixed within which the death must occur in order to be ascribed to the act to which it is sought to attribute

it. That limit is a year and a day; that is, an act or omission is not to be regarded as homicide unless the death attributed to it occurs on or before the day of corresponding date in the succeeding year. 2 Bish. Cr. L. (7th Ed.), Sec. 640; 1 Hawk. P. C., ch. 31, Sec. 9; *State v. Mayfield,* 66 Mo., 125.

Where the Death Must Occur.—The questions which arise where the death occurs in another jurisdiction from that where the wound is given, pertain to criminal procedure. The act constitutes a homicide irrespective of the place of death, if death follow within the requisite time.

Human Being.—Any living human being is the subject of homicide. In this sense a child in the mother's womb, even though quick, is not a living human being; it becomes such only when it is fully born and has an independent circulation. *State v. Winthrop,* 43 Iowa, 519; *Goff v. Anderson,* 15 S. W. R., 866; 2 Bish. Cr. L., Secs. 630–633; 3 Greenl. Ev., Sec. 136; *Rex v. Enoch,* 5 Car & P., 539; *Reg. v. Trilloe,* 1 Car. & M., 650; *Reg. v. West,* 2 Car. & K., 784; *Evans v. People,* 49 N. Y., 86.

Homicide of Three Kinds.—There are three kinds of homicide recognized in the books, at least by the English common law ; justifiable, excusable, and criminal or felonious.

Justifiable Homicide.—When the killing is done in compliance with a legal duty it is called justifiable, and is considered as wholly without blame. The common example is that of the execution of a prisoner by a sheriff in strict accordance with the forms of law, and under a valid judgment of death. (But if the judgment be one rendered by a court which has not jurisdiction, both the judge who renders it and the officer who executes it would be guilty of a crime. And the judgment, if valid, can only be executed by the proper officer and in the proper manner. Otherwise the execution will be murder. 4 Bl. Com., 178; 1 Hawk. P. C., Chap. 48, Secs. 4–10.) An officer whose duty it is to make an arrest may, if resisted, take life if necessary in the performance of that duty, or he may, to the same extent, resist an escape, or rescue, and so may a jailor having a prisoner in custody. (But it seems the right to take the life of a prisoner escaping by flight and not by resistance exists in case of felony only. 2 Hale P. C., 117; *Reneau v. State*, 2 Lea, 720, 31 Am. R., 626; *Head v. Martin*, 85 Ky., 480, 3 S. W. R., 622.) So an officer seeking to arrest a person guilty of felony (not misdemeanor) may kill if necessary to prevent escape before arrest, and a private person attempting to make an arrest in case of felony, under those circumstances in which a person is authorized so to act, may, it seems, go to the same extent as an officer. A killing necessarily done in any such cases will be justifiable. Again, as has been said under the head of "necessity" (*ante*, p. 33), one who attempts by force and surprise to commit a felony, or who takes part in a riot, or makes a murderous assault, should be resisted, and if in the resistance the assailant is necessarily killed, the homicide will be justifiable. 4 Bl. Com., 178–182; 2 Bish. Cr. L., Secs. 644–651; 1 ibid., Sec. 849; 1 Bish. Cr. Pr., Secs. 159–161; 1 Hawk. P. C., Chap. 28; Foster, 267; *Carr v. State*, 43 Ark., 99, 5 Am. Cr. R., 438; *Reg. v. Dadson*, 1 Eng. L. &. E., 566, and note; *Cooper's Case*, Cro. Car., 544; *People v. Payne*, 8 Cal., 341.

Killing Alien Enemy.—The old definitions of murder usually limited it to killing a person " within the King's peace," and the killing of an alien enemy was perhaps not punishable. But the justification which a soldier has for killing in battle is probably based on the idea that he is acting as an agent of the sovereign power and under its direct command; and therefore the killing of an alien enemy even in time of war, if not done in battle, is felonious. 1 Hale P. C., 433; 4 Bl. Com., 178; *State v. Gut*, 13 Minn., 341; 2 Bish. Cr. L., Sec. 631.

Excusable Homicide by Misadventure.—There are two classes of excusable homicides: 1. Those which occur through unforeseen misfortune or accident in doing a lawful act in a lawful manner. Here there is no criminal liability for there is no blame, the act being one which it was right to do, and the manner being

lawful, i. e., not criminally careless or negligent. Still this is less than justifiable homicide, and merely excusable because the party is not acting under command of the law, but simply for his own advantage. In the same class may be put cases of homicide happening in the course of due correction or chastisement of a child, pupil, servant, or prisoner by the parent, teacher, master, or officer respectively, where there is proper occasion for chastisement and no undue severity is used, but death results by casualty; also cases of death happening by misadventure in innocent and lawful games. Foster, 258, 262; 1 Hawk. P. C., Chap. 29, Secs. 1–8; 4 Bl. Com., 182, 183; *Levett's Case*, Cro. Car., 538; *Morris v. Platt*, 32 Conn., 75, 84; *Plummer v. State*, 4 Tex. Ct. App., 310, 30 Am. R., 165.

In Self-Defense.—II. Those in self-defense upon chance-medley, as they are called in the older books; that is, where a party under circumstances entitling him to make resistance, but not to resist to the full extent of taking life, does make resistance, and a conflict ensues and, after retreating to the wall (as explained *ante*, p. 34), he is obliged to kill in self-protection. This is said to be barely excusable for the party making resistance, when the law does not require resistance to be made, takes upon himself the consequences of his action, and even though he retreat as far as possible, is still looked upon as having in some measure caused the necessity under which the killing is done. *State v. Thompson*, 71 Iowa, 503; Foster, 275; 1 Hawk. P. C,. Chap. 29, Secs. 13–15; 4 Bl. Com., 184, 187. This self-defense is to be carefully distinguished from that in which a person is resisting a felony as explained in a preceding paragraph as to "justifiable homicide."

Distinction as to Penalty.—At common law some fault was attributed to the person causing the death in such cases, and although he was not considered guilty of felonious homicide he was, by early common law, subject to fine or forfeiture to some extent, though now, both in England and the United States, all such penalties are abolished, and the person committing an

9

excusable homicide, equally with one committing justifiable homicide, is exempt from punishment. 4 Bl. Com., 184–188; 1 Hawk. P. C., Chap. 29; 2 Bish. Cr. L., Secs. 617–622.

Distinction Falling into Disuse.--As the practical distinction between excusable and justifiable homicide no longer exists, American courts frequently ignore the difference entirely, and use the terms interchangeably, but in some cases it is preserved. It is a difference, however, which lies at the bottom of some other doctrines of homicide, and should be understood. *Com. v. Self-ridge*, Hor. & T. Ca., 1, and note, 16.

Felonious Homicide.—Every killing of a human being which is not justifiable or excusable is a felony (unless for some special reason, such as infancy, insanity, or necessity, there is no crime attributable to the person committing the act.) At common law a felonious homicide was either manslaughter or murder.

History of the Terms.—The term murder was first applied to a secret killing only. King Canute, it is said, for the protection of the Danes, against whom, as invaders, the English doubtless entertained deep animosity, enacted that in case of a secret killing, where the offender was not known or surrendered, the township or hundred within which the killing occurred should be fined or amerced unless it could be proven that the person killed was an Englishman (i. e., not a Dane), which proof was called making presentment of Englishery. The same law was revived by William the Conqueror, for the protection of the Normans. Thus an open killing, no matter with what violence or willfulness attended, was not murder, but voluntary homicide. The presentment of Englishery was abolished by statute of 14 Edw., 3. But the term murder, though it thus lost any definite significance, was extended apparently to all secret killings, and afterward to all such as involved willfulness. A later statute provided that " willful murder of malice prepensed" should be denied benefit of clergy. (23 Hen. 8, c. I.) As a felony to which benefit of clergy was not denied was practically but lightly punished, the effect was to create murder as a degree of felonious homicide, being

such as was done with malice aforethought (malice prepensed, or *malitia precogitata*). All felonious homicide not thus included in the term murder, is called manslaughter, which is therefore felonious homicide without malice aforethought. 1 Hale P. C., 447, 449; 1 Hawk. P. C., Chap. 31, Secs. 1–3; Foster, 302; 4 Bl. Com., 194; 1 Reeves Hist. Eng. Law (Am. Ed., 1880), 196; 2 ibid., 284; 5 ibid., 134; 2 Bish. Cr. L., Secs. 623–628; 3 Stephen Hist. Cr. L., Chap. 26; *Com. v. York*, 9 Met., 93, 117; 2 Green Cr. L. Rep., 392, note.

Malice Aforethought.—The distinguishing feature between murder and manslaughter is, therefore, malice aforethought, which is not to be limited in meaning to that of the general term "malice;" for malice toward a particular individual is not a necessary ingredient of the crime; nor is it necessary that it be premeditated or exist for any definite length of time. If it exist at the time of the act it is sufficient to characterize the act as murder. By the term "malice" in this connection the law means "that the fact hath been attended with such circumstances as are the ordinary symptoms of a wicked, depraved, malignant spirit." Foster, 256; 1 Hawk. P. C, Chap. 29, Sec. 12; *Com. v. Webster* 5 Cush., 295, 304; *Hopkins v. Com.*, 50 Penn. St., 9, 15; *Com. v Drum*, 58 Penn. St., 9. It is said that the term "malice aforethought" implies more than the mere willful doing of an unlawful act without excuse. 1 Bish. Cr. L. (7th Ed.), Sec. 429.

Express and Implied Malice.—The only method of proving malice is to show facts which the law regards as admissible to be considered in attempting to determine whether there was malice or not. If these circumstances show a direct intention to kill, without justification or excuse, the malice is called express; if the circumstances show an intent which is regarded as sufficiently wicked to render death resulting therefrom murder, although some other act be directly intended, then the malice is called implied, for the circumstances, it is said, "carry in them the plain indications of an heart regardless of social duty and fatally bent on mischief." Foster, 257; *State v. Moore*, 25 Iowa,

128 ; 2 Bish. Cr. L., Sec. 675; 1 Russ. Cr., 482; *Martinez v.* *State* (Tex. Ct. App.), 16 S. W. R., 767.

Malice Presumed.—In some cases it has been contended that the mere fact of killing, without more, gives rise to a presumption of malice aforethought, but this is doubted, and it seems unjust to presume the highest criminality when the fact shown (the killing alone) is equally consistent with the supposition of a killing under provocation, (that is, without malice) or in self-defense. The later cases generally hold that malice is only to be presumed when the killing appears to have been unaccompanied by circumstances showing alleviation, justification, or excuse. Foster, 255; 1 Russ. Cr., 483 ; *Com. v. Webster*, 5 Cush., 295, 305 (criticised in N. Am. Rev., Vol. 72, p. 178) ; *Com. v. York*, 9 Met., 93 ; *Com. v. Hawkins*, 3 Gray, 463 ; *Stokes v. People*, 53 N. Y., 164, 177 ; *State v. Shippey*, 10 Minn., 223 ; *Com. v. Drum*, 58 Penn. St., 9, 18 ; *State v. Holme*, 54 Mo., 153 ; *State v. Trivas*, 32 La. Ann., 1086, 36 Am. R., 293; *State v. Patterson*, 45 Vt., 308, 12 Am. R., 200 ; *State v. Evans*, 65 Mo., 574 ; *Kent v. People*, 8 Colo., 563, 5 Am. Cr. R., 406.

Presumption of Law.—The old rule was that malice was a question of law and that it was for the court to say whether, under certain facts, malice was presumed or not, but the present doctrine is to leave it for the jury to say whether from all the circumstances malice is to be presumed as a fact. Foster, 255, 257; 2 Bish. Cr. L., Secs. 673 a., 673 b.; *People v. Aro*, 6 Cal., 207 ; *Patterson v. State*, 85 Ga., 131, 11 S. E. R., 620.

Definitions Defective.—It is therefore evident that the term " malice aforethought " conveys, of itself, no meaning that can serve as a test, which, applied to a case of felonious homicide, will infallibly determine whether it is murder or manslaughter. But the law defines more specifically certain classes of homicides which shall be considered as done with malice aforethought and therefore constitute murder, and certain other classes which shall be considered as done without malice aforethought, and therefore constitute manslaughter. The line is, to some extent, arbitrary, uncertain, and undeniably hard to trace and fix.

Manslaughter.—Briefly, manslaughter is separated from justifiable and excusable homicide by the line which distinguishes the non-punishable from the punishable, and from murder by the line indicated by the expression, "malice aforethought." It occupies the intermediate ground, including on the one hand cases which are considered a little too aggravated to be excusable, and on the other, such as are imputed to the frailty of human nature, and are therefore looked upon as less than murder. The older books speak of involuntary and voluntary manslaughter, the former including, generally, those cases just referred to as akin to justifiable and excusable homicides, embracing for the most part unintentional killing, while the latter includes cases of intentional killing, where the circumstances palliate the offense. The distinction is not kept up and is of no value at present. It will be best, before going into details as to what cases constitute manslaughter, to consider what constitute murder, as we have already considered what are excusable, and then see what cases are left, on the one hand and the other, to fall into this middle class.

Murder.—The homicides which are regarded as murder may be roughly classed as follows : (a) those resulting from an attempt to kill the person killed ; (b) those resulting from an attempt to kill another than the one killed ; (c) those resulting from an attempt to cause great bodily injury to the one killed, or to some one else, or to any one in general, or from the doing of any act naturally endangering life, the intent to cause the natural result of the thing done being inferred ; (d) those resulting from the attempt to commit any felony not included in the foregoing classes ; (e) those resulting from resistance to lawful arrest. See classification in Stephen Dig. Br. L., Art. 223.

Intentional Killing.—An intentional killing will be murder unless, (a) it falls within those cases where it is justifiable or excusable (see *ante*), in which case it is not criminal ; or (b) is done in heat of blood, in which case it will be manslaughter. What is meant by heat of blood will be considered hereafter in discussing manslaughter more fully. But the intention need not have existed for any definite time ; it may have been premeditated or it may have been formed on the instant of its execution. A killing in heat of blood is not reduced to manslaughter because the killing is any less deliberate or intentional than would be sufficient to constitute murder, but because the intention is formed under circumstances which the law considers as relieving the act of that extreme degree of guilt. *People v. Clark,* 7 N. Y., 385, 393.

Suicide.—At common law suicide was looked upon as murder, and therefore the person taking his own life was a felon, punishable with forfeiture of goods, and a person advising or abetting the suicide, and being present, was a principal in the second degree, and punishable as for murder. If the adviser or abettor was not present, he was an accessory before the fact, and therefore not punishable at all, because the principal could not be convicted. Under some state statutes defining murder, suicide would not be included, and therefore, also, an attempt to commit suicide would not be punishable as an attempt to commit murder. An adviser and abettor would, however, probably still be, in most states, guilty of murder. 2 Bish. Cr. L, Sec. 1187 ; *Com. v. Bowen,* 13 Mass., 356 ; *Reg. v. Leadington,* 9 Car. & P., 79 ; *Reg. v. Alison,* 8 Car. & P., 418 ; *Com. v. Dennis,* 105 Mass , 162 ; *Com. v. Mink,* 123 Mass., 422, 25 Am. R., 109; *Blackburn v. State,* 23 Ohio St.,146 ; *Reg. v. Jessop,* 10 Cr. L. Mag., 862 ; 1 Hawk. P. C., Chap. 27 ; 4 Bl. Com., 189 ; 3 Stephen Hist. Cr. L., 104 ; note, 9 Cr. L. Mag., 376.

Attempt to Kill Another.—The older books all say that if A. shoot at B. with intent to kill him (in a case where such killing would be murder), but by accident hit and kill C., he is guilty of murdering C. The reasoning is, that as A. did the act with intent to kill, and as that result followed, the necessary elements of the crime, i. e., the act and the intent, are both present and the crime is complete. 1 Hale P. C., 466, and note (11) ; Foster, 261; *King v. Plummer,* 12 Mod , 627 ; *Rex v. Holt,* 7 Car. & P., 518 ; *Callahan v. State,* 21 Ohio St., 306; *Wareham v. State,* 25 Ohio St.,

601 ; *Barcus v. State*, 49 Miss., 17, 19 Am. R., 1, and note; *State v. Gilman*, 69 Maine, 163, 31 Am. R., 257. And in case of attempted suicide resulting in the death of another who interferes to prevent, the killing of such person is felonious homicide [in principle, murder, though that point may not be decided]. *Com· v. Mink*, 123 Mass., 422, 25 Am. R., 109.

Intent to Commit Great Bodily Harm.—The reasoning by which a person is said to be guilty of murder when death results from an attempt to do great bodily harm to the person killed, or any one else, either in particular or in general, is that, as death must be considered by any reasonable man as likely to result from such an act, and as the person doing the act must be conclusively presumed to have intended or contemplated what would likely result, he must have had "malice aforethought" which, uniting with the resulting death, constitutes murder. *Com. v. Webster*, 5 Cush., 295, 306; *State v. Moore*, 25 Iowa, 128; *Brennan v. People*, 15 Ills., 511 ; *Ruloff v. People*, 45 N. Y., 213.

Death in Attempt to Commit Felony.—Death caused in the commission of, or in the attempt to commit, any felony whatever, whether it be one likely to endanger life or not, is murder, however unintentional or accidental it may be. The reason alleged for the rule is that the intent to commit so grievous a crime as a felony is sufficient to constitute the malice aforethought, which, joined with the fatal result, will constitute the crime of murder. Foster, 258; 1 Hawk. P. C, Chap. 29, Sec. 11, Chap. 31, Secs. 41, 42; *Smith v. State*, 33 Maine, 48 ; *Wellar v. People*, 30 Mich., 16. . It matters not, it seems, whether the crime attempted is a felony at common law, or one expressly made so by statute. *State v. Smith*, 32 Maine, 370.

Resisting Legal Arrest.—The killing of an officer lawfully making an arrest is murder, irrespective of any proof of malice ; and so is the killing of a private person who is properly proceeding to make an arrest under circumstances authorizing him to do so. 2 Bish. Cr. L., Sec. 652 ; *MacKaley's Case*, Cro. Jac., 279 ; *Rex v. Edmeads*, 3 Car. & P., 390 ; *Reg. v. Price*, 8 Car. & P., 282 ;

Reg. v. Porter, 12 Cox C. C., 444, 5 Moak's Eng. R., 497, 1 Green's Cr. L. R., 155 ; *People v. Pool*, 27 Cal., 572 ; *Simmerman v. State*, 16 Neb., 615 ; *State v. Mowry*, 37 Kan., 369, 15 Pac. R., 282, 10 Cr. L., Mag., 23 ; Foster, 270.

Malice Inferred.—It is evident, therefore, that malice aforethought is a very different thing from intent to kill, and that a killing may be murder when death was wholly unintended, if it results from an act in pursuance of some other wrongful intent of such a criminal nature that the law deems it proper to infer malice aforethought.   Foster, 258-9; 1 Hawk. P. C., Chap. 29, Sec. 11.

Intent Presumed.   Use of Deadly Weapons.— Whether the act is to be regarded as dangerous to life so that death resulting therefrom, even by accident, will be murder, will depend often upon the character of the instrument or weapon employed.   A parent has the right to correct or chastise his child, but if he should use for that purpose a bar of iron, or a club, or even a suitable instrument in a violent or deadly manner, the intent to do great bodily harm would be presumed, and the resulting death of the child would be murder.   So as to all cases where some resistance or some chastisement is permitted, the manner in which it is done, and the weapon or instrument used must be such as are not calculated to produce more serious results than the law permits in such cases.   Death resulting from the use of a deadly weapon in defending property, or in resisting a mere assault and battery, would be murder.   Foster, 262; 1 Hale P. C., 454, 474; *Head v. State*, 44 Miss., 731, Hor. & T. Ca., 341 ; *Com v. Webster*, 5 Cush., 295, 306; *Rex v. Howlett*, 7 Car. & P., 274; *Stewart v. State*, 1 Ohio St., 66; *State v. Vance*, 17 Iowa, 138 ; *State v. Sullivan*, 51 Iowa, 142; *State v. Clifford*, 5 Cr. L. Mag., 241; 1 Greenl. Ev , Sec. 13; *People v. Rodrigo*, 69 Cal., 601, 8 Cr. L. Mag., 583.   And an assault which would not, in the case of an ordinarily strong person, endanger life, may give rise to the presumption of malice if the assailant knew or had reasonable cause to believe that the person assaulted was sick and in such condition that such an assault as was made would be dangerous.   *Com. v. Fox*, 7 Gray, 585.

Dueling.—To fight a duel is to fight by agreement with intent to kill, and of course, if death results, it is murder. So the seconds are principals in the second degree in the murder. The statutes of the respective states usually provide specifically that killing in a duel shall be murder in the first degree, and also provide punishment for fighting or aiding in a duel, although no death ensue. 4 Bl. Com., 185, 199, and note; 1 Hawk. P. C., Chap. 31, Sec. 21; *Reg. v. Young*, 8 Car. & P., 644; *Reg. v. Cuddy*, 1 Car. & K., 210; *Barker v. People*, 20 Johns., 457.

Classification of Cases of Manslaughter.—Cases of felonious homicide which the law considers manslaughter may be roughly divided into four classes. I. Those resulting from negligence, or omission of duty not implying a willful attempt to take or endanger life. II. Those resulting from the commission of an unlawful act not amounting to a felony or likely to endanger life. III. Those happening unintentionally in employing force in resisting or chastising another, where some force is allowable but not to the extent of taking life, including those committed in resisting unlawful arrest. IV. Those in which the killing is in heat of blood under what the law regards as provocation sufficient to make the offense less than murder.

I. **Negligence.**—Cases of this class are those in which the act is not in itself wrongful, but is accompanied by wrong in failing to use proper care ; also those in which there is omission of a legal duty ; but in either case in which the negligence or omission is not such as to imply an intent to endanger life or do great bodily harm. These cases of negligence are very numerous. They may be arranged, generally, under the following heads : (a) Neglect of a legal duty to provide necessaries of life, or otherwise properly care for a dependent person under the control of the person so neglecting. (b) Neglect of a special duty in regard to the use and management of appliances, or the performance of acts likely to prove dangerous. See, generally, *Rex v. Hull*, Kelyng, 40, 1 Lead. Cr. Ca., 50, and note ; 2 Bish. Cr. L., Secs. 659–671, 686–693 ; *State v. Merkley*, 74 Iowa, 695.

Failure to Provide Necessaries.—To bring a case under this head there must be, first, a legal duty to support, and secondly, such rightful dependence and helplessness that the death is attributable directly to such failure. The legal duty may arise from the natural relation of the parties, as that of parent to child, husband to wife, etc., or from an assumed relation, as where one should undertake to support another, or a prisoner should be put in the charge of an officer, or the like. The dependence may arise from infancy or old age, insanity, sickness, or other disability, which renders the person dependent. It is to be remembered that the negligence or omission must not be such as to imply an intent to take life, or do great bodily harm, otherwise the offense would be murder. *Rex v. Smith*, 2 Car. & P., 449 ; *Reg. v. Pelham*, 8 Q. B., 959 ; *Reg. v. Plummer*, 1 Car. & K., 600 ; *Reg. v. Hogan*, 5 Cox C. C., 255, 5 Eng. L. & E., 553 ; *Rex v. Saunders*, 7 Car. & P., 277, 611.

Management of Dangerous Appliances and doing of Dangerous Acts.—Here are included a mass of cases that cannot well be further classified. Those in charge of machinery, ships, railways, mines, light-houses, etc., etc., are held criminally accountable for neglect or omission of a special duty with respect thereto, when death results from such neglect or omission. But the death must be so connected with the neglect or omission that the latter may be said to be the cause of the death and not merely the condition under which it happened. *Reg. v. Haines*, 2 Car, & K., 368 ; *Reg. v. Barrett*, ibid., 343 ; *Rex v. Carr*, 8 Car. & P., 163 ; *Com. v. Metropolitan R. Co.*, 107 Mass., 236 ; *Reg. v. Lowe*, 3 Car. & K., 123, 1 Lead. Cr. Ca., 60, and note ; *Reg. v. Longbottom*, 3 Cox C. C., 439, 1 Lead. Cr. Ca., 66, and note ; *Reg. v. Pocock*, 17 Q. B., 34. And so the doing of any act in a manner which may reasonably be considered dangerous, will make the doer criminally responsible for death caused thereby ; as careless use of firearms, or negligently exposing or administering poison, or throwing timbers or snow or other articles down into a thoroughfare without warning. 1 Hale P. C., 473, 475 ; *Rex v. Mar-*

tin, 3 Car. & P., 211; *Rex v. Burton*, 1 Strange, 481; *Reg. v. Packard*, 1 Car. & M., 236; *Rex v. Sullivan*, 7 Car. & P., 641; *State v. Vance*, 17 Iowa, 138; *State v. Hardie*, 47 Iowa, 647; *State v. Justus*, 11 Oreg., 178, 6 Am. Cr. R., 551. The business of a physician and surgeon and that of preparing medicines so directly involve life that negligence therein, causing death, will be criminal. It seems to have been once held that a person who was not a regular physician was guilty at least of manslaughter if he administered medicine or prescribed treatment in case of disease, and death resulted, but the doctrine now is that he is not liable if he acts in good faith under an honest belief that his remedies will prove beneficial; but one who holds himself out to be a physician will be guilty of manslaughter if death occurs by reason of his not possessing the skill or exercising ·the care which a physician of ordinary skill and care in the same school of medicine would possess or apply under the circumstances. 4 Bl. Com., 197; 1 Hale P. C., 429; *Rex v. Spiller*, 5 Car. & P., 333; *Com. v. Thompson*, 6 Mass., 134; *Rice v. State*, 8 Mo., 561; *State v. Schulz*, 55 Iowa, 628; *Com. v. Pierce*, 138 Mass., 165, 6 Cr. L. Mag., 190, 5 Am. Cr. R., 391.

II **Doing an Unlawful Act.**—The law imposes upon any ⋅ one doing an unlawful act criminal liability in case such act causes death. If the act amounts to felony, or is calculated to cause great bodily harm, as has already been said, the killing is murder; if the act is less in degree, such as a misdemeanor, or a mere trespass, the killing is manslaughter. If one person going upon another's premises to shoot at game or a dog, should by accident hit and kill a human being it would be manslaughter. This is said only to apply to the doing of things *mala in se*, and not things merely *mala prohibita*, as, for instance, shooting at game in violation of game laws. 1 Hale P. C., 472–3, 475; Foster, 258–9, 261; *Com. v. McAfee*, 108 Mass., 458; *Rex v. Connor*, 7 Car. & P., 438; *Smith v. State*, 33 Maine, 48; *Yundt v. People*, 65 Ill., 372; *People v. Munn*, 65 Cal., 211, 6 Am. Cr. R., 431; 2 Bish. Cr. L., Sec. 694.

III. **Self-Defense: Chastisement: Arrest.**— One who employs improper force in self-defense, chastisement, or making arrest, under circumstances rendering the use of some force proper, will be guilty of manslaughter if death results from such improper force, in the absence of malice aforethought. *Com. v. Coffey*, 121 Mass., 66; *Rex v. Cheeseman*, 7 Car. & P., 455; *State v. Mizner*, 45 Iowa, 248.

Distinction.--Not many examples of this last class of cases are to be found. They lie intermediate between excusable homicide on one hand and murder on the other. Thus, as has already been indicated, there is a right to resist force with force in self-defense, also in many cases a right in one person to moderately chastise another, and also a right in an officer to use some force in arresting or stopping an escaping criminal, although guilty only of a trifling misdemeanor. (See 1 Hawk. P. C., Chap. 60, Sec. 23). If while keeping strictly within the limits of the force allowed, death result purely by misadventure, it will be excusable. If dangerous or deadly weapons are used it will be murder, for from such improper use of weapons malice aforethought will be presumed. But if undue force or violence is used, nevertheless not necessarily dangerous to life, death resulting therefrom, unintended, will be manslaughter. Foster criticises a statement of Hale to the effect that death caused by an officer in attempting to arrest a person on a civil process would be murder, and says that it would be murder or manslaughter according to circumstances, and adds that if the officer, merely to overtake the person fleeing, should trip up his heels, or give him a stroke with an ordinary cudgel, or other weapon not likely to kill, it would amount to no more than manslaughter, if in some cases even to that offense. 1 Hale P. C., 481; Foster, 271.

Resisting Unlawful Arrest.—On some principle, by no means clear, it is decided that killing in resisting an unlawful arrest, while it will not be justifiable or excusable, will be no more than manslaughter, though done deliberately. *Com. v. Carey*, 12 Cush., 246; *Rafferty v. People*, 69 Ill., 111; 1 Hale, P. C., 465,

and note (7); Foster, 312; *Reg. v. Tooley*, 11 Mod., 242; *Roberts v. State*, 14 Mo., 138, 146; 1 Bish. Cr. L. (7th Ed.), Sec. 868; *Reg. v. Chapman*, 12 Cox C. C., 4, 2 Moak's Eng. R.,160; *Noles v. State*, 26 Ala., 31, Hor. & T. Ca., 697; *Brooks v. Com.*, 61 Penn. St., 352; *Creighton v. Com*, 8 Cr. L. Mag., 98; *People v. Burt*, 51 Mich., 199. (The case of *Simmerman v. State*, 14 Neb., 568, hold-ing that causing death in resisting illegal arrest is not criminal, is opposed to the weight of authority). But, it seems, mere error in the process will not reduce the killing to manslaughter. *Mackaley's Case*, Cro. Jac., 279.

IV. **Killing in Heat of Blood.**—Killing done in actual heat of blood arising from what the law regards as sufficient provoca-tion, is manslaughter. It is not the absence of the intent to kill, but the circumstances under which the intent is formed and exe-cuted which are vital in determining the degree of criminality in such cases. *Erwin v. State*, 29 Ohio St., 186, 191; *Nye v. People*, 35 Mich., 16.

Provocation.—Whatever the law regards as adequate to cause heat of blood, the existence of which will reduce a felonious homicide from murder to manslaughter, may be classed under the head of provocation. What will be adjudged adequate provoca-tion, will vary with circumstances. 4 Bl. Com., 121; Foster, 291–296; 1 Hawk. P. C., Chap. 31, Secs. 21–45; 1 Hale, P. C., 486; 2 Bish. Cr. L., Secs. 697–718; 1 Russ. Cr., 580–592.

What Sufficient to Palliate use of Deadly Weapons.—As the use of a deadly weapon in a deadly manner implies intent to kill, only the most extreme provocation will be sufficient to reduce such an offense to manslaughter. The passion excited by mutual combat will be sufficient, irrespective of which party com-menced the affray; so will passion aroused by a beating, or even by an aggravated assault. But a slight blow from a woman or a child would not be sufficient. *Rex v. Taylor*, 5 Burr., 2793; *Reg. v. Smith*, 8 Car. and P., 160, Hor. & T. Ca., 130; *Com. v. Drum*, 58 Penn. St., 1, 18, Hor. & T. Ca., 183, 190; *Com. v. Mosler*, 4 Penn. St., 264; *State v. Shippey*, 10 Minn., 223, 230. The discovery by a husband of his wife in the act of adultery, will be sufficient provocation to reduce to manslaughter a killing of the wife or her paramour, committed by him in the passion naturally resulting, but if the killing be merely upon information or suspicion. or as the result of previous malice, or be done after an interval has elapsed, it will be murder. *Maddy's Case*, Ventris, 158; *Reg. v. Kelley*, 2 Car. & K., 814; *Reg. v. Fisher*, 8 Car. & P., 182; *Shufflin v. People*, 62 N. Y., 229, 20 Am. R., 483; *Maher v. People*, 10 Mich., 212; *State v. Holme*, 54 Mo., 153, 166; *Sawyer v. State*, 35 Ind., 80; *Lynch v. Com.*, 77 Penn. St., 205; note (c) Hor. & T. Ca., 755; *State v. Horton*, 4 Mich, 67, 83; *Price v. State*, 18 Tex. Ct. App., 474, 5 Am. Cr. R., 385; *State v. Adams*, 78 Iowa, 292.

What Sufficient to Palliate Unintentional Killing.--A less provocation will be sufficient to reduce to manslaughter a killing which is not committed in such way as to indicate anything more than intent to chastise in heat of blood for an insult or mild assault, where death results unintentionally. This is but another phase of the case where unintentional death results from doing an unlawful act less than felony and not essentially endangering life. 4 Bl. Com., 200.

Insulting Language as Provocation.—Mere language, no matter how threatening, insulting, or offensive will not be sufficient provocation to palliate an assault made in a manner to endanger life. But language may sometimes be shown to give color to accompany acts and thus become important. Foster, 290; 3 Greenl. Ev., Sec. 124; *Watts v. Brains*, Cro. Eliz., 778; *People v. Butler*, 8 Cal., 435, 441; *Com. v. Webster*, 5 Cush., 295, 305; *State v. Hill*, 4 Dev. & Batt., 491, Hor. & T. Ca., 199, 200; *Ray v. State*, 15 Ga., 244; Hor. & T. Ca., 523 (in note); *State v. Starr*, 38 Mo., 270; *Reg. v. Sherwood*, 1 Car. & K., 556.

Cooling Time.—Although the provocation be sufficient to produce heat of blood, yet if time enough has elapsed before the act for the passion to have subsided and come under control, in the case of a reasonable man, the provocation will no longer serve

to palliate, although the killing may, in fact, be in heat of blood. *Rex v Oneby*, 2 Stra., 766, 773; *Rex v. Hayward*, 6 Car. & P., 157; *Maher v. People*, 10 Mich., 212, 223; *Hurd v. People*, 25 Mich., 405; *State v. Yarborough*, 39 Kan., 581, 18 Pac. R, 474, 10 Cr. L. Mag., 698; Article, 29 Cent. L. J., 186.

Intentional Killing, Irrespective of Provocation.—Where the circumstances are such as to indicate intent to kill preceding the provocation, or where the quarrel is forced merely to produce an excuse to kill, or where a man enters a fight with an unfair advantage, he is guilty of murder if death ensues. *Mason's Case*, Foster, 132; 1 Hawk. P. C., Chap. 31, Secs. 23–27; *Stewart v. State*, 1 Ohio St., 66; *Reg. v. Smith*, 8 Car. & P., 160, Hor. & T. Ca., 130; *State v. Scott*, 4 Ired, 409, Hor. & T. Ca., 163; *People v. Robertson*, 67 Cal., 647, 6 Am. Cr. R., 519. Proof of willfulness, deliberation and premeditation, showing murder in the first degree as hereafter explained, precludes provocation or extenuation. *Clifford v. State*, 58 Wis., 477, 5 Cr. L. Mag. 241.

Questions of Law.—The question whether the provocation, when shown, is sufficient, and whether sufficient cooling time is shown, are questions of law and not of fact. *Reg. v. Fisher*, 8 Car. & P., 182; *Lynch v. Com.*, 77 Penn. St., 205, 212; *Rex v. Beeson*, 7 Car. & P., 142; *State v. Dunn*, 18 Mo., 419.

Degrees of Murder.—The statutes of most states divide murder into two or more degrees. In Pennsylvania it was early enacted (1794), that "all murder which shall be perpetrated by means of poison, or lying in wait, or by any other kind of willful, deliberate and premeditated killing ; or which shall be committed in the perpetration or attempt to perpetrate, any arson, rape, robbery, or burglary, shall be deemed murder in the first degree; and all other kinds of murder shall be deemed murder of the second degree." This statutory provision is substantially adopted in many other states. 2 Bish. Cr. L., Secs. 724–725.

First Degree.—Two classes of cases are thus included in murder in the first degree : (a) those in which the murder is committed by poison, or by lying in wait, or in the attempt to commit certain felonies; (b) those in which the murder is committed by willful, deliberate and premeditated killing. As to the first class, they stand as at common law; malice aforethought is inferred, and whenever a killing under the circumstances described, would be murder at common law, it will be murder in the first degree under the statute. In the second class of cases there must be something more than malice aforethought. There must be, it seems, a willful, deliberate and premeditated intent to take life. The implied malice, arising from doing an act threatening great bodily harm, or engaging in a riot, or committing a felony other than those specified in this connection, will not render a death resulting therefrom murder in the first degree. Nevertheless, it is not essential that the willful, deliberate and premeditated intent exist for any specified time. If at the instant of the commission of the act such intent has been formed, that is sufficient. The intent is to be inferred from the circumstances, but they must be such as to show that the intent was to kill, and that it was willful, deliberate and premeditated. 2 Bish. Cr. L., Secs. 726–730 ; *State v. Pike*, 49 N. H., 399, 6 Am. R., 533 ; *State v. Johnson*, 8 Iowa, 525 ; *People v. Bealoba*, 17 Cal., 389 ; *People v. Sanchez*, 24 Cal., 17, 30 ; *People v. Doyell*, 48 Cal., 85, 95 ; *Resp. v. Bob*, 4 Dall., 145 ; *Kelley v. Com.*, 1 Grant's Ca, 484 ; *Keenan v. Com.*, 44 Penn. St., 55 ; *State v. Dunn*, 18 Mo., 419 ; *State v. Phillips*, 24 Mo., 475, 486 ; *State v. Hicks*, 27 Mo., 588 ; *State v. Holme*, 54 Mo., 153 ; *Robbins v. State*, 8 Ohio St., 131, 168 ; *People v. Clark*, 7 N. Y., 385 ; *Hogan v. State*, 36 Wis., 226, 238 ; *Craft v. State*, 3 Kan., 450 ; *State v. Evans*, 65 Mo., 574 ; *State v. Hockett*, 70 Iowa, 442 ; *State v. Sopher*, ibid, 494.

Second Degree.—The common law definition of murder is not changed by the statutory provision above referred to. Its object is simply to divide the offense into two degrees. Therefore those cases which are within the definition of murder at common law and are not within the statutory definition of murder in the first degree, are murder in the second degree. *People v. Foren*, 25 Cal., 361 ; *Finn v. State*, 5 Ind., 400 ; *State v. Johnson*, 8 Iowa, 525. Proof of intentional killing, without proof of will-

fulness, premeditation and deliberation, will show only murder in the second degree. *McCue v. Com.*, 78 Penn. St., 185 ; *State v. Underwood*, 57 Mo., 40.

Manslaughter by Statute.—In some states manslaughter is also divided into degrees, but in many it is allowed to remain as at common law, and therefore those acts which would be manslaughter at common law will be manslaughter under the statute, and no others. *State v. Moore*, 25 Iowa, 128.

MAYHEM.

Definition.—Mayhem was, at common law, defined to be " a hurt of any part of a man's body whereby he is rendered less able in fighting, either to defend himself or annoy his enemy." 1 Hawk. P. C., Chap. 44. " If the injury be such as disfigures him only, without diminishing his corporal abilities, it does not fall within the crime of mayhem." East P. C. See 4 Bl. Com., 205 ; 2 Bish. Cr. L., Secs. 1001–1008 ; May Cr. L., Sec. 180.

Enlarged by Statute.—By statutes in England, one of which was the " Coventry Act " (22 & 23 Car. 2, c. 1), and by similar statutes in the various states of America, other forms of maiming or disfiguring are expressly made punishable. The language of these statutes is usually such that it is necessary, in order that an act shall constitute the offense, that it be done "with intent to maim or disfigure." Bish. Stat. Cr., Sec. 316 ; *Godfrey v. People,* 63 N. Y., 207 ; *Tully v. People,* 67 N. Y., 15 ; 3 Stephen's Hist. Cr. L., Chap. 27.

Punishment.—Originally the punishment was "member for member," but as this punishment fell into disuse, the offense was a high misdemeanor. Statutes usually, however, make it a felony. *Com. v. Newell,* 7 Mass., 245.

ROBBERY.

Defined.—Robbery is : " The felonious and forcible taking from the person of another of goods or money to any value, by violence or putting him in fear." (Blackstone.) " Larceny committed by violence from the person of one put in fear." (Bishop.)

II

"Larceny from the person or personal presence, by force and violence, and putting in fear." (May.) The essential elements of
larceny must be present, that is, the property taken must be such,
and the taking must be such, as to constitute larceny, if there was
nothing more. What these elements are will appear hereafter in
the proper connection. The additional elements now to be considered are "from the person or presence" and "by violence or
putting in fear." See generally, 4 Bl. Com., 242; 2 Bish., Cr. L.,
Secs. 1156, 1182; May Cr. L., Secs. 205–208; *Com. v. Humphries*,
7 Mass., 242; *State v. Hollyway*, 41 Iowa, 200, 20 Am. R., 586.

From the Person or Presence.—The property taken must
be from within the personal protection. So it may be committed
by driving away cattle from the presence of the owner, or by pick-
ing up a purse which has been thrown down, or a man's hat which
has fallen off in his flight, it being of course necessary that such
taking be preceded or accompanied by violence or putting in fear.
Turner v. State, 1 Ohio St., 422; *State v. Leighton*, 56 Iowa, 595;
State v. Calhoun, 72 Iowa, 432, 34 N. W. R., 194, 10 Cr. L. Mag.,
85; 1 Hale P. C., 533; 1 Hawk. P. C., Chap. 34, Sec. 5.

With Violence or by putting in Fear.—There must be actual
force or violence, or actual fear. If there is the former, the lttaer
is presumed. To snatch from the hand or person suddenly, without resistance being offered, is not sufficient to constitute the
offense at common law, but if the article is in any way attached
to the person so that resistance must be overcome, the taking of
it will be considered to be with force. If force or violence has
previously been exercised on the person to overcome resistance,
a mere taking will be sufficient. The fear must be of bodily harm
to oneself or those under his protection or, perhaps, to the habitation. Threats of prosecution, etc., or of damage to other property will not be sufficient; and the fear must be actual and reasonable, though it is said that in case of an inexperienced person,
the means used need not be such as to put in fear a man used to
the ways of the world. The violence or fear must precede or
accompany the taking. If subsequent, and merely resorted to in

order to retain possession already acquired, it will not suffice to make the taking robbery. That the taking must be against the will or consent of the owner is, of course, implied. *Com. v. Snelling*, 4 Binn., 379; *State v. Humphries*, 7 Mass., 242; *State v. Howerton*, 58 Mo., 581; *State v. Broderick*, 59 Mo., 318; *State v. Carr*, 43 Iowa, 418.; *Seymour v. State*, 15 Ind., 288; *Brennon v. State*, 25 Ind., 403; *Hope v. People*, 83 N. Y., 418, 38 Am. R., 460; *Shinn v. State*, 64 Ind., 13, 31 Am. R., 110; *Thomas v. State*, (Ala.), 9 So. R., 81; 1 Russ. Cr., 875–900.

RAPE.

Defined.—Rape is the offense of having unlawful carnal knowledge of a woman by force, without her consent. May Cr. L., Secs. 192–195; 2 Bish. Cr. L., Secs. 1107–1136; 1 Hale P. C., 626–636; Article, 32 Cent., L. J., 102.

Who may Commit.—A boy under fourteen years is presumed incapable of committing the offense; as to whether this presumption is conclusive, or may be rebutted by proof of capacity, is a point upon which the authorities are in conflict. Criminality in respect to such an act cannot be imputed to the husband. But a boy, or the husband, or a woman may be guilty as principal in the second degree, or as accessory to the commission of the act. *Reg. v. Phillips*, 8 Car. & P., 736; *Rex v. Groombridge*, 7 Car. & P., 582; *Williams v. State*, 14 Ohio, 222; *Hiltabiddle v. State*, 35 Ohio St., 52, 35 Am. R., 592; *Com. v. Green*, 2 Pick., 380; *State v. Comstock*, 46 Iowa, 265; *State v. Jones*, 83 N. C., 605, 35 Am. R., 586; *Williams v. State*, 20 Fla., 777, 5 Am. Cr. R., 612; *State v. Dowell*, 106 N. Car., 722, 11 S. E. R., 525; *State v. Jones*, (La.), 10 Cr. L., Mag., 89, 3 So. R., 57.

The Act.—There must be actual penetration by force, but the extent is immaterial, even the slightest being sufficient, and by statute, both in England and various states, emission is not essential; whether it was at common law, is a matter of doubt. *Reg. v. Hughes*, 9 Car. & P., 752; *Reg. v. Lines*, 1 Car. & K., 393; *Blackburn v. State*, 22 Ohio St., 102.

Without Consent.—The older definitions use the expression "against her will," but it is no longer deemed necessary to show actual resistance. That the act is without consent is sufficient. Thus if, with intent to accomplish the act forcibly if necessary, the connection is had with one who is insensible, or who is so overcome by fear as to be incapable of resisting, or who is, by reason of imbecility, or insanity, incapable of giving a valid consent, or, with a child under ten years, who is presumed not competent to give consent (though in this case perhaps actual consent of the child may be shown as a defense) the offense is complete; but in cases of consent secured by reason of imbecility or insanity, the act is not to be deemed criminal unless the culprit knew, or had reason to know the mental condition of the victim. The offense is not committed where actual consent is obtained, though it be by fraud. 19 Am. L. Rev., 860; *Com. v. Burke,* 105 Mass., 876; *People v. Dohring,* 59 N. Y., 374, 881; *Whittaker v. State,* 50 Wis., 518, 36 Am. R., 856, and note; *Oleson v. State,* 11 Neb., 276, 38 Am. R., 366; *State v. Atherton,* 50 Iowa, 189, 82 Am. R., 134; *State v. Tarr,* 28 Iowa, 397; *State v. Newton,* 44 Iowa, 45; *Reg. v. Barratt,* 12 Cox C. C., 498, 1 Green's Cr. L. R., 314; *Reg. v. Mayers,* 12 Cox C. C., 311; 1 Green Cr. L. R., 317; *People v. McDonald,* 9 Mich., 150; *O'Meara v. State,* 17 Ohio St., 516; *Hays v. People,* 1 Hill, 351; *Reg. v. Saunders,* 8 Car. & P., 265; 1 Hale P. C., 629; *Don Moran v. People,* 25 Mich., 356, 12 Am. R., 283, and note; *Murphy v. State,* 120 Ind., 115, 22 N. E. R., 106. That the injured party is a prostitute, or the mistress of the assailant, will not prevent the act being criminal, but will render the evidence of such person of less weight in establishing the crime. Rape may also constitute adultery or incest, the consent of the other party not being necessary in those crimes. *Mercer v. State,* 17 Tex. Ct. App., 452, 5 Am. Cr. R., 292; *contra, State v. Thomas,* 53 Iowa, 214.

ASSAULT AND BATTERY.

Assault Defined.—An assault is: "An attempt or offer, with force or violence, to do a corporal hurt to another."

(Hawkins.) "Any unlawful physical force, partly or fully put in motion, creating a reasonable apprehension of immediate physical injury to a human being." (Bishop.) "An attempt, with unlawful force, to inflict bodily injury upon another, accompanied with the apparent present ability to give effect to the attempt if not prevented." (Cooley.) 1 Hawk. P. C., Chap. 62; 2 Bish. Cr. L., Secs. 22–62; May Cr. L., Secs. 55–64; 3 Bl. Com., 120, and note; 4 ibid., 216; Cooley on Torts, 29, 160.

An Attempt.—Intent, preparation and attempt are not synonymous. Under the general subject of intent it has already been stated that mere intent alone, without any resulting act, is, in general, not punishable. Preparation for the doing of a criminal act, consisting of something done with a view to the consummation of such act, will not usually amount to an attempt to do it, in the eye of the law, if what is done by way of preparation is not inconsistent with lawful motives. But to procure dies for making counterfeit money is said to be an attempt toward committing the crime of counterfeiting, because not reasonably consistent with lawful intentions. Attempts to commit a felony will be considered particularly hereafter. But, in general, a criminal attempt is an intent to commit a specific crime, coupled with an act adapted to the commission of that crime which the law regards as sufficiently tending to its accomplishment to be a part of it, without, in itself, being the consummation of the crime. It seems it is not necessary, to constitute the criminal attempt, that under the circumstances the actor could have completed the crime. While all criminal attempts are not assaults, all assaults are in the nature of criminal attempts. The whole subject of attempts is elaborately treated by Bishop, and to some extent by other writers. 1 Bish. Cr. L. (7th Ed.), Secs. 435–441, 725–772; note, 1 Lead. Cr. Ca., 6; May Cr. L., Sec. 29; 2 Stephen's Hist. Cr. L., 221; *U. S. v. Stephens*, 3 Cr. L. Mag., 536; *Queen v. Goodman*, 2 Green's Cr. L. R., 83; *Kelley v. Com.*, 1 Grant's Ca., 484; *Barcus v. State*, 49 Miss., 17, 1 Am. Cr. R., 249; *Mullen v. State*, 45 Ala., 43, 6 Am. R., 691; *Hamilton v. State*, 36 Ind, 280,

10 Am. R., 22; *Com. v. Jacobs*, 9 Allen, 274; *Hicks v. Com*, 86 Va., 223, 9 S. E. R., 1024; *People v. Moran*, 123 N. Y., 254, 25 N. E. R., 412; Article, 41 Alb. L. J., 425; *Lamb v. State*, 67 Md., 524, 10 Atl. R., 208, 10 Cr. L. Mag., 92. As to abandonment of attempt, see *State v. Gray*, 19 Nev., 212, 8 Pac. R., 456; Whart. Cr. L., Sec. 187.

The Act.—To constitute an assault there must be an act, or some physical force set in motion which, if consummated, or allowed to proceed, will do violence to the person of another. The degree of force used, or of injury threatened, is immaterial. If the act is of such character as to cause reasonable apprehension of danger on the part of the person toward whom it is directed, it will constitute an assault, but if the danger is merely apparent to the person menaced, but, for reasons which he does not know, is not real, nor intended, it is questioned whether it constitutes an assault. But mere words, however threatening, insulting, or aggravating, without any act in connection therewith which is, at least apparently, done with purpose to do bodily harm, will not constitute an assault. *People v. Yslas*, 27 Cal., 630; *Kirland v. State*, 43 Ind., 146, 2 Green's Cr. L. R., 706; 22 Cent. L. Jour., 123; *Chapman v. State*, 78 Ala., 463, 6 Am. Cr. R., 37; *Com. v. Stratton*, 114 Mass., 303; *Com. v. White*, 110 Mass., 407, 2 Green's Cr. L. R., 269, and note; *State v. Shepard*, 10 Iowa, 126; *Reg. v. St. George*, 9 Car. & P., 483; *Hayes v. People*, 1 Hill, 351.

Unlawful.—The act threatened must be unlawful or the attempt will not constitute a criminal assault. A parent has the right, under proper circumstances, to use force in restraining or chastising a child; a teacher may have a similar right as to a pupil, an officer as to one under arrest, or whom he is attempting to arrest, etc. But it seems that such right is not now recognized in the husband as to the wife, nor, in general, in a master as to his servant. Also, the conductor of a railway train, the sexton of a church, and other persons acting in a *quasi* official capacity have the right to use sufficient force to eject disorderly persons or persons attempting to gain admittance to, or remain in, places

where they have no right to be. So, as already mentioned under the head of "necessity," every person has a right to protect person and property with force. In all such cases where force is lawful, the attempt to use it will not constitute a criminal assault, but no more force must be used than necessary. So, where by accident, in doing á lawful act in a lawful manner, personal harm results to another, it does not constitute an assault. *Com. v. Randall*, 4 Gray, 36; *Com. v. McAfee*, 108 Mass., 458; note in 2 Green's Cr. L. R., 287; *Matthews v. Terry*, 10 Conn., 455; *Com. v. Dougherty*, 107 Mass., 243; *State v. Goold*, 53 Maine, 279; *State v. Hull*, 34 Conn., 132; *Gallagher v. State*, 3 Minn., 270; *State v. Dowell*, 106 N. Car., 722, 11 S. E. R., 525.

Consent.—There can be no criminal assault where the force used or act done is with the consent of the person toward whom it is directed, unless, perhaps, it tends to a breach of the peace which no one can rightfully consent to. But the attempt may be so far without consent that it constitutes a criminal assault, although its completion, being with consent, does not constitute the crime threatened. But submission by one who has not a mind competent to give intelligent assent, by reason of being unconscious, or imbecile, or overcome by fear, or deceived as to the nature of the act threatened, does not deprive the wrongful act of its criminality. *People v. Bransby*, 32 N. Y., 525; *Champer v. State*, 14 Ohio St., 437; *Com. v. Collberg*, 119 Mass., 350; *Reg. v. Mayers*, 1 Green's Cr. L. R., 317; *Com. v. Burke*, 105 Mass., 376; *State v. Cross*, 12 Iowa, 66.

Battery.—"A battery is any unlawful beating or other wrongful physical violence or constraint inflicted on a human being without his consent." (Bishop.) "A successful assault becomes a battery." (Cooley.) 2 Bish. Cr. L., Secs. 70–72; 1 Hawk. P. C. Chap., 62, Sec. 2; 3 Bl. Com., 120 and note; Cooley on Torts, 162.

Illustrations.—A battery is simply the completion of an assault, and if the assault is carried out until some other crime of a higher nature than battery is completed, then a battery is necessarily included. The slightest unlawful touching of another, either directly, by striking or seizing with the hand, or indirectly through some other means which interferes with the inviolability of the person, such as spitting upon him, throwing water upon him, striking his clothing, etc., etc., constitutes a battery. *Resp. v. De Longchamps*, 1 Dall., 111, 113; 1 Russ. Cr., 751; *Com. v. Ordway*, 12 Cush., 270; *Kirland v. State*, 43 Ind., 146.

FELONIOUS ASSAULTS.

Statutory Provisions.—At common law an attempt to commit a felony was punishable as a misdemeanor. But the statutes of many states provide for the punishment of attempts to commit or assaults with intent to commit, certain felonies, or any felony whatever. Thus the statutes usually designate as specific offenses, assault with intent to commit murder, with intent to commit rape, with intent to maim, rob, or steal, or to commit arson or burglary, with intent to inflict great bodily injury, and with intent to commit any felony not otherwise designated. It will be noticed that under such provisions no kind of attempt is punishable unless it constitutes an assault, although the punishment of some other acts in the nature of attempts may be also provided for (as for instance, setting fire to a building with intent to burn. See *State v. Johnson*, 19 Iowa, 230.) But in other states any attempt to commit an offense is made punishable, whether it constitutes an assault or not. What has already been said in relation to assaults and attempts will furnish all the guidance necessary in interpreting these provisions. *State v. Newberry*, 26 Iowa, 467; *State v. White*, 45 Iowa, 325; *State v. Hagerman*, 47 Iowa, 151; *State v. Atherton*, 50 Iowa, 189; *State v. Malcom*, 8 Iowa, 413.

OFFENSES AGAINST THE HABITATION.

Habitation Specially Protected.—It has already appeared, in various connections, that the law looks upon the habitation as peculiarly sacred and entitled to special protection. It therefore punishes certain criminal acts interfering with the security of the habitation, more severely than similar acts directed against other property, although greater in value.

House: Dwelling: Mansion.—The "house" is a building fitted for habitation, and in some sense, occupied for that purpose. It must be finished and suitable for such use, but it is not necessary that the building shall have been originally intended for such occupancy. It includes not only the main building, or all under the main roof, but all out-buildings, such as stable, wood-house, smoke-house, etc., used in connection therewith, as constituting the habitation, and not for a distinct purpose. 1 Hale P. C., 558; Bish. Stat. Cr., Secs., 278–286; *State v. Shaw*, 31 Maine, 523; *Pond v. People*, 8 Mich., 150; *Pitcher v. People*, 16 Mich., 142; *Brown's Case*, 2 East P. C., Chap. 15, Sec. 10; *State v. Sampson*, 12 S. C., 567; 32 Am. R., 513.

The requirement that the buildings be within the curtilage or common enclosure seems not now to be insisted upon, if they are in fact near to and used in connection with the house. *People v. Taylor*, 2 Mich., 250; *Reg. v. Gilbert*, 1 Car. & K., 84.

Not all that is under the same roof with the dwelling is necessarily a part of it. If one portion of the building is separated from the part used as a dwelling and occupied for another purpose, it may lose its right to special protection, but all parts of the building connected with the part used as a dwelling by inner openings or passages are portions thereof, whatever the use to which they are put. Bish. Stat. Cr., Secs. 280–282; *Stedman v. Crane*, 11 Met , 295; *State v. Toole*, 29 Conn., 342; *Quinn v. People*, 71 N. Y., 561, 27 Am. R., 87; *State v. Clark*, 89 Mo., 423, 8 Cr. L. Mag., 537.

The occupant is the person occupying as a habitation. A guest, or a lodger, is not an occupant of the building, but where the whole building is let to lodgers, or separate families, each is the occupant of the portion so let. Rented rooms may constitute a dwelling when occupied as such. *Smith v. People*, 115 Ill., 17, 6 Am. Cr. R., 80.

The "dwelling" or "mansion-house" (the terms being synonymous) is the house, but implies, perhaps, a more positive requirement as to actual occupancy. It must be used, not merely as a place for eating meals and doing business, but as a lodging place for the person occupying it, his family, or servant. The mere fact, however, that some one sleeps in a building will not render it a dwelling, if such occupancy be merely for the protection of property. *State v. Potts*, 75 N. C., 129, 1 Am. Cr. R., 363; *Reg. v. England*, 1 Car. & K., 533; *State v. Reid*, 20 Iowa, 413; *Com. v. Barney*, 10 Cush., 478; *State v. Meerchouse*, 34 Mo., 844; *State v. McGowan*, 20 Conn., 45.

A temporary absence from the habitation will not destroy its character, there being an intention to return, and it retaining its character as a habitation; but vacation for repairs renders it no longer a habitation, although the occupant leaves his property there. *Nutbrown's Case*, Foster, 76; 1 Hale P. C., 556; *Reg. v. Labadie*, 1 Green's Cr. L. R., 204, and note; *Com. v. Brown*, 3 Rawle, 207.

ARSON.

Defined.—Arson is the malicious burning of the house of another. 2 Bish. Cr. L., Secs. 8–21; 4 Bl. Com., 220; May Cr. L., Secs., 49–54; 1 Hawk. P. C., Chap. 39; 3 Greenl. Ev., Secs. 51–57. It seems that at common law the burning of a barn with hay or grain in it was also arson. *Sampson v. Com.*, 5 Watts & S., 385.

The Burning.—It is sufficient to constitute a burning, within the definition, if some part, no matter how small, of the fiber of the portion sought to be ignited, is wasted. There need be no blaze; an extinguishment of the fire before it has gone further will not prevent the crime being complete. The burning must be of something which is part of the realty. Bish. Stat. Cr., Sec. 310; *Com v. Tucker*, 110 Mass., 403, 2 Green's Cr. L. R., 266; *People v. Haggerty*, 46 Cal., 354, 2 Green's Cr. L. R., 431; *People v. Butler*, 16 Johns., 203; *Com. v. Van Shaack*, 16 Mass., 105; *Com. v. Betton*, 5 Cush., 427; *Reg. v. Parker*, 9 Car. & P., 45.

The House.—The meaning of the term "house" has been already stated. It must be, however, the house of another; the burning of one's own house would not be within the definition.

Neither would the burning by the husband, or the wife, of the habitation of the family, be arson, although the other was the legal owner. In each of these cases, however, statutes have either made the act a specific crime, or extended the crime of arson so as to cover it. But ownership in the occupant is not necessary to constitute the habitation his "house;" occupation as a tenant for years, or at will, or otherwise under a right to occupy, is sufficient. Thus a landlord who should burn a building owned by him, but leased to and occupied by a tenant, would be guilty of the crime. A servant, however, is not the "occupant" of his master's habitation, and a burning by him would be arson. *Snyder v. People*, 26 Mich., 106, 1 Green's Cr. L. R., 547, 12 Am. R., 302; *Case of Harris*, Foster, 113, 115; *Holmes' Case*, Cro. Car., 376; *Allen v. State*, 10 Ohio St., 287, 302; *People v. Van Blarcum*, 2 Johns., 105; *State v. Taylor*, 45 Maine, 322; *State v. Toole*, 29 Conn., 342; *State v. Gailor*, 71 N. C., 88, 17 Am. R., 3.

Malice.—If the burning be by mischance or negligence, it will not constitute the crime, even though resulting from a trespass; but the malice need not be express. It is not a case where a specific intent is made requisite; and if the intent is to do a criminal act, and the burning results therefrom, the crime is complete. It seems a person will be held to have intended the natural consequences of his own act, even though he had an ulterior motive and the object sought was something quite distinct from the burning. Again, if a person incautiously sets fire to his own property in such way that it is likely to communicate and in fact does communicate to his neighbor's property, he is presumed to have so intended. *Holmes' Case*, Cro. Car., 376; *State v. Toole*, 29 Conn., 342; *People v. Cotteral*, 18 Johns., 115; *Luke v. State*, 49 Ala., 30, 20 Am. R., 269; *Jenkins v. State*, 53 Ga. 33, 21 Am. R., 255, and note; *Rex v. Cooper*, 5 Car. & P., 535; *Reg v. Price*, 9 Car. & P., 729.

Similar Statutory Crimes.—The statutes of the various states provide for the punishment of other burnings not technically arson, and also sometimes of attempts.

BURGLARY.

Defined.—Burglary is the breaking and entry of the dwelling, or mansion house of another, in the night time, with intent to commit a felony. 2 Bish. Cr. L., Secs. 90–120; 1 Hawk. P. C. Chap. 38; 1 Hale P. C., 547; 4 Bl Com., 223; May Cr. L., Secs. 71–81.

Time.—The breaking and entry must both be in the night time. The night time, aside from statutory definition, means that portion of the time between sunset and sunrise, when it is too dark to reasonably discern a man's features, no account being taken of moonlight. Bish. Stat. Cr., Sec. 276; *Lewis v. State*, 16 Conn., 32; *People v. Griffin*, 19 Cal., 578.

The Place.—What constitutes the dwelling, within the meaning of the definition, has already been considered. It must be that of another, so that an inn-keeper breaking into his guest's room to steal would not be guilty of burglary, and the same would probably be true as to a person who let his house to lodgers, but if one guest at an inn break into the room of another it will constitute the crime. If the entire building is let to lodgers or families, the portion occupied by each becomes a separate habitation. It is also said by old writers to be burglary at common law to break and enter either a church or a walled town, with felonious intent. 1 Hale, P. C., 554–6, and notes.

The Act.—Both the breaking and the entering must be at night; and it is not necessary that the breaking precede the entry; but they must both be accomplished to complete the crime. It was doubted whether, at common law, a breaking in order to escape from the house was a sufficient breaking, but it is so declared by statute, both in England and in most, if not all, the states. *State v. McPherson*, 70 N. C., 239, 2 Green's Cr. L. R., 737 and note, 739, 16 Am. R., 769; *Rolland v. Com.*, 82 Penn. St., 306, 324, 22 Am. R., 758; *State v. Ward*, 43 Conn., 489, 21 Am. R., 665; *Rex v. Wheeldon*, 8 Car. & P., 747; *Rex v. McKearney*, Jebb. C. C., 99, 2 Lead. Cr. Ca., 62 and note.

The Breaking.—If the dwelling is secured in the ordinary way, any entry by force will constite a breaking. Opening a door

or window, by raising a latch, turning a lock, shoving˙ back a bolt, or by raising or lowering a window sash, or even the cutting a twine netting out of a window, will be a breaking. But leaving a window or door ajar, even to a slight extent, is such an invitation as would prevent an entry thereat from being a breaking, though the door must be further opened, or the window further raised, to admit the person. It not being usual to cl᎐se a chimney in any way, an entry by the chimney will be considered a breaking, though there be no breaking in fact. Moreover, if entry is effected by means of threats, or by fraud, as by conspiring with a person within, or under color of legal process fraudently obtained, or by enticing the owner to open the door or otherwise, the act will be considered a constructive breaking. But if the burglar is admitted by one whom he supposes to be an accomplice, but who is, in fact, acting under the instructions of the occupant for the purpose of apprehending the wrong-doer, then burglary is not committed. The breaking must be of some part of the building; to break into the enclosure will not be sufficient. But it need not be a breaking of the exterior; any breaking of an inner door or other division, after entry, will be sufficient, but a breaking of chattles, such as a chest or trunk, will not suffice, nor it seems, will the breaking into a cupboard or closet. *State v. Reid*, 20 Iowa, 413, 421; *Dennis v. People*, 27 Mich., 151, 2 Green's Cr. L. R., 565; *Speiden v. State*, 3 Tex. Ct. App., 156, 30 Am. R., 126, and note; *Johnson v. Com.*, 85 Penn. St., 54, 27 Am. R., 622; *Brown v. State*, 55 Ala., 123, 28 Am. R., 693; *Adkinson v. State*, 5 Baxt., 569, 30 Am. R., 69; *Rolland v. Com.*, 82 Penn. St., 306, 323, 22 Am. R., 758; S. C., 85 Penn. St., 66; *Timmons v. State*, 34 Ohio St., 426, 32 Am. R., 376; *Com. v. Strupney*, 105 Mass., 588; *Rex v. Russell*, 1 Moody C. C., 377, 2 Lead. Cr. Ca., 44 and note; *Neiderheck v. State*, 23 Tex. Ct. App., 38, 3 S. W. R., 573; *Nichols v. State*, 68 Wis., 416, 32 N. W. R., 543; *Walker v. State*, 52 Ala., 376, 1 Am. Cr. R., 362.

The Entry.—An entry by any part of the person, however slight, or by a tool with which is sought to accomplish the ultimate felony intended, will be sufficient; but an entry of the tool used for the purpose of breaking, or to complete the breaking so as to admit the person, will not be enough. *State v. Whitby*, 15 Kan., 402; *Walker v. State*, 63 Ala., 49, 35 Am. R., 1; *State v. McCall*, 4 Ala., 643, 39 Am. D., 314.

The Intent.—The act must be with specific intent to commit a felony (though statutes sometimes make an intent to commit any public offense sufficient). It is not necessary, to render the offense complete, that this specific intent be carried out; the breaking and entering with·such intent completes the offense. The fact that a felony is actually committed, though not intended, will not render the previous breaking and entry burglary. But the presumption is that the intent was to do whatever was done, and proof of the commission of a felony will make out a *prima facie* case as to the intent, and so, too, the fact that, for reasons not known to the person having the intent, it was impossible to execute it, will not, it seems, make the breaking and entry less than burglary. *State v. Bell*, 29 Iowa, 316; *Com v. Newell*, 7 Mass., 245; *People v. Jenkins*, 16 Cal., 431; *Com. v. Brown*, 3 Rawle, 207; *Robinson v. State*, 53 Md., 151, 36 Am. R., 399; *Lowden v. State*, 63 Ala., 143, 35 Am. R., 9; *State v. Teeter*, 69 Iowa, 717; *State v. Fox*, 80 Iowa, 312, 45 N. W. R., 874.

Similar Statutory Offenses.—The breaking and entering in the day time, or the entry without breaking in the night time, of a dwelling, or the breaking and entry of any other building, etc., where goods are kept, etc., are also usually made offenses by statute, as also the attempt to commit burglary, or any of these kindred offenses, and the possession of burglars' tools.

OFFENSES AGAINST PROPERTY.

LARCENY.

Defined.—Larceny is: " The felonious taking and carrying away of the personal goods of another." (Blackstone). " The willfully wrongful taking possession of the goods of another with intent to deprive the owner of his property in them." (Stephen).

And see 4 Bl. Com., 229; 2 Bish. Cr. L., Secs. 757 – 891; May Cr. L., Secs. 148 – 168; 3 Stephen's Hist. Cr. L , Chap. 28.

Essentials.—Three elements at least must be considered. I. The property in relation to which the crime may be committed. II. The acts necessary to constitute the crime. III. The intent with which the act must be done.

I. The Property: Personalty.—The first essential is that the property be personalty — "personal goods." Therefore it is not larceny to take away a portion of the realty, which has not, by severance, become personalty in the possession of the. owner. Thus to cut and carry away trees, or growing crops, or mineral ores, even a nugget of gold washed out by natural agencies, is not larceny, nor to tear loose and remove those things which have been artificially attached to the freehold, although as to fixtures merely constructively attached, the rule is different, so that the taking of a key or a window screen might be larceny. (But deeds, etc., savor of the realty and are not subjects of larceny). Therefore it is the common law rule that if things which are attached to, or a part of, the realty are severed and carried away by one continuous act, the act cannot be larceny, for the property never, as personalty, belonged to the owner of the realty; but if the severance is by one act and the carrying away by another, so the acts be distinct, with no matter how short an interval, during which the trespasser relinquishes his possession, then, during that interval, the property is personalty in the owner and the carrying away may be larceny. The courts now regard this distinction as unnecessary and absurd, but they still observe it, for the reason that it is too well settled to be disregarded. *State v. Berryman*, 8 Nev., 262, 1 Green's Cr. L. R., 335 and note; *People v. Williams*, 35 Cal., 673; *Jackson v. State*, 11 Ohio St., 104; *King v. Westbeer*, 2 Stra., 1133, 1 Lead. Cr. Ca., 543; *Emmerson v. Annison*, 1 Mod., 89; *Ward v. People*, 6 Hill, 144, 146; *Lee v. Risdon*, 7 Taunt., 188; *People v. Williams*, 35 Cal., 671; *Harberger v. State*, 4 Tex. Ct. App., 26, 30 Am. R., 157; *Smith v. Com.*, 14 Bush, 31, 29 Am. R., 402.

Things in which there is no Property.—The thing must be something in which the law recognizes a right of ownership. Wild animals, even running in a park, or the like, are not regarded as property, though when reclaimed, as by training, they become property if their flesh is fit for food, not otherwise, and the same rule applies to fish. Bees may be made personal property by reason of the value of their honey for food. A wild animal becomes reclaimed, i. e., reduced to control, by being killed, hence, if the flesh is good for food, the carcass is personal property. Fish in a tank and oysters planted in a bed, are considered as sufficiently reduced to control. But dogs, cats, singing birds, etc., etc., with many other animals which are sometimes tamed, are not regarded as subjects of property in such sense that larceny can be committed by taking them, although there may be rights as to them which will be recognized in a civil action as of value. *Queen v. Steer*, 6 Mod., 183; *Findley v. Bear*, 8 S. & R., 571; *Warren v. State*, 1 G. Greene, 106, 111; *State v. Lymus*, 26 Ohio St., 400, 20 Am. R., 772; *Ward v. State*, 48 Ala., 161, 17 Am. R., 31; *Harrington v. Miles*, 11 Kan., 480, 15 Am. R., 355, and note; *State v. House*, 65 N. C., 315, 6 Am. R., 744; *People v. Campbell*, 4 Park. Cr. R., 386; *Mullaly v. People*, 86 N. Y., 365; *State v. Yates*, 10 Cr. L. Mag., 439.

Things without Value: Choses in Action.—The thing to be subject of larceny must be something of value, though the most insignificant value will be sufficient. A mere piece of paper has sufficient value to make the taking of it criminal. But if the paper contains writing evidencing a chose in action, as, for example, a promissory note, a written contract, or the like, then it is no longer a piece of paper merely, but is an instrument of evidence, and as the chose in action will still exist though that instrument of evidence be destroyed, the paper containing the writing was said, at common law, to be without pecuniary value and not the subject of larceny. This rule is, however, quite generally, if not universally, changed by statute. *Payne v. People*, 6 Johns., 103; *Rex v. Bingley*, 5 Car. & P., 600; *People v. Loomis*, 4 Denio, 381; *R. v. Mead*, 4 Car. P., & 535.

The Property of Another.—While the person from whom the thing is taken must have some ownership in it, it is not necessary that he have more than a special ownership. A bailee has sufficient property in the thing bailed, so that a taking from him by the bailor may be larceny ; and even a thief has, in the thing stolen, such ownership that a stealing from him will be criminal. But a servant to whom property is entrusted, does not become the special owner, and a taking from him must be looked upon as a taking from the master. *Ward v. People*, 3 Hill, 395 ; S. C., 6 ibid., 144 ; *State v. Mullen*, 30 Iowa, 203 ; *Com. v. Sullivan*, 104 Mass., 552 ; *People v. McDonald*, 43 N. Y., 61 ; *People v. Long*, 50 Mich., 249 ; *State v. Somerville*, 21 Maine, 14 ; *People v. Thompson*, 34 Cal., 671 ; *Palmer v. People*, 10 Wend., 166 ; *Bruley v. Rose*, 57 Iowa, 657.

II. **The Act.**—The older books say there must be a "taking and carrying away," a "trespass and asportation," but the essential element is that there shall have been a willful taking from the possession of the owner (i. e., the person having, as against the wrong-doer, the right to possession) into that of the wrong-doer. Such possession in the wrong-doer need only continue for an instant, if it is full and complete. Thus, lifting a pocket-book in the pocket of another, though it is not completely removed, or lifting a bag, which is let fall again upon detection, will be a sufficient taking into possession, but where a bale was raised on end, without being completely lifted, it was held the possession was not complete. There must be a complete severance from the person of the owner, if the property is on his person, and the control over the thing must be, for an instant, perfect in the wrong-doer. But to tole or entice an animal away by food held before it, or otherwise, so complete control is exercised over it, will be sufficient. Also, to wrongfully conduct gas or water from a main by means of a pipe may be larceny. The wrongful act may be done through an agent, as well as personally. *Harrison v. People*, 50 N. Y., 518, 10 Am. R., 517 ; *People v. Smith*, 15 Cal., 408 ; *Com. v. Shaw*, 4 Allen, 308 ; *Rex v. Frith*, L. R. 1 C. C.,

172; *Ferens v. O'Brien*, 11 Q. B. D., 21; *Rex v. Pitman*, 2 Car. & P., 423; Article 11, Cr. L. Mag., 170; Broom Com., 946.

From the Possession of the Owner.—Remembering that only special ownership is required to constitute the person, in whose possession the property is, the owner thereof, as that term is used in this connection, the taking must be from his possession. As to third persons, the possession of the servant may be considered as that of the master, for a man may exercise through another whatever control he might exercise for himself. So, even as to a servant who has the mere custody of his master's property while engaged about his master's business, the possession may be considered as still in the master, and the servant may commit larceny by taking the property and appropriating it to his own use, and the doing with it what he has no authority to do will be a taking. Mere manual control in such cases will not amount to possessions, and in general, custody may be distinguished from possession. But if the servant or agent has not only custody, but also a possession vesting in him special ownership, no matter for how limited a time or purpose, then an appropriation by him will not be a taking from the possession of the master, although a taking from him by another may be so considered. Thus a misappropriation by bailees, carriers, etc., is not larceny, they having a qualified ownership. But where this rightful possession has been terminated, as by the property reaching its destination, or being wrongfully opened or improperly used by the person having a possession for the purpose of transportation only, or other limited use, then the taking is larceny. Again, if delivery be made to a servant with intent that he shall transport to the master, the actual possession not having yet been in the master, a misappropriation by the servant will not be larceny. But if the property has reached its destination, a subsequent taking by the servant will be a taking from the master's possession. The whole question is, has the wrong-doer committed trespass? *Com. v. James*, 1 Pick., 375, 2 Lead. Cr. Ca., 181 and note, 190; *Krause v. Com.*, 93 Penn. St., 418, 39 Am. R.,

762; *Johnson v. People*, 113 Ill., 99, 5 Am. Cr. R., 350; *Jenkins v. State*, 62 Wis., 49; *Reg. v. De Banks*, 13 Q. B. D., 29, 5 Cr. L. Mag., 844; *Com. v. O'Mally*, 97 Mass., 586; *R. v. Prince*, L. R. 1 C. C., 150; *R. v. Matthews*, 1 Green Cr. L. R., 32; *R. v. Howell*, 8 Car. & P., 325; *R. v. Jenkins*, 9 id., 38.

Wrongful Taking: Consent: Fraud: Mistake.—To constitute a trespass, the taking must be wrongful. If it be with consent, there is no larceny. But the consent must be to change of possession, not to a mere custody not inconsistent with possession continuing in the owner.

Moreover, a consent procured by fraud, or fear, or under mistake, is void. Thus to fraudently procure possession with consent, but with the intent to steal or misappropriate the property, as where a bill is taken and there is a refusal to return an amount due as change, is a sufficient wrongful taking. *People v. Abbott*, 53 Cal., 284, 31 Am. R., 59; *State v. Anderson*, 25 Minn., 66, 33 Am. R., 455; *Zink v. People*, 77 N. Y., 114, 33 Am. R., 589, *Hildebrant v. People*, 56 N. Y., 394; 15 Am. R., 435.

It is also larceny to receive and retain a bill or coin given by mistake for a bill or coin of smaller denomination. *Queen v. Ashwell*, 16 Q. B. D., 190, 7 Cr. L. Mag., 485, 6 Am. Cr. R., 355, 23 Cent. L. J., 87; *Queen v. Flower*, 6 Am. Cr. R., 388; *State v. Ducker*, 8 Oreg., 394, 34 Am. R., 590; *Queen v. Middleton*, L. R. 2 C. C., 38.

It is larceny to procure possession of property or money with intent to deprive the owner of it, though by consent, if such consent is procured by trick or artifice; *Smith v. People*, 53 N. Y., 111, 13 Am. R., 474; *Loomis v. People*, 67 N. Y., 322, 23 Am. R., 123; *Defrese v. State*, 3 Heisk., 53, 8 Am. R., 1; *Miller v. Com.*, 78 Ky. 15, 39 Am. R., 194; *State v. Brown*, 25 Iowa, 561; *State v. Fenn.*, 41 Conn., 590; *U. S. v. Murphy*, 5 Cr. L. Mag., 847; *Grunson v. State*, 89 Ind., 533, 46 Am. R., 178; *People v. Shaw*, 57 Mich., 403, 6 Am. Cr. R., 403; *State v. Hall*, 76 Iowa, 85, 14 Am. St. R., 204.

But where the intent of the party making delivery is that not the mere possession, but the general ownership of the property shall pass by the delivery, then the fraud will not render the transaction larceny, but it will be a case of procuring property by false pretenses.

It is only the wrongful taking into possession with which the law deals in larceny. And so, if the person from whom the property is obtained has no title, or but merely a possession- for qualified purpose, the right obtained from him can be to no greater extent than possession, and therefore the fraudulent procuring may be larceny; and so it will be where the delivery is coupled with a condition precedent which is to be performed before title passes.

Custody by the Wife.—The wife has, at common law, such right of possession of the husband's property that she cannot commit larceny thereof, and it seems that there could not be larceny in taking the husband's property from her with her consent, unless the taker knew that it was without the consent of the husband, his consent being presumed from hers unless in some way negatived. But a paramour is presumed to know that a transfer to him from the wife is without the husband's consent, and such a taking, even of the wife's clothing, is larceny; but in such case the property must come into the actual possession of the paramour. 2 Lead. Cr. Ca., 197, 358–370; *People v. Cole*, 43 N. Y., 508; *Reg. v. Taylor*, 12 Cox C. C., 627, 10 Moak's Eng. R., 509; *People v. Swalm*, 80 Cal., 46, 22 Pac. R., 67.

Title to Property.—The essential difference between those cases where the *possession* only is obtained by fraud and larceny is committed, and those wherein the *title* is obtained by fraud and larceny is not committed, appears in considering the effect of the two transactions in regard to subsequent purchasers of the property from the wrong-doer. It is a rule without exception (save in case of negotiable instruments), based on the character of the crime, that if the transaction amounts to larceny, the title of the property does not pass from the owner and he may follow and retake it wherever it can be found, even in the hands of an

innocent purchaser for value, while if the title passes, no matter how fraudulent the transaction, the innocent purchaser from the wrong-doer will be protected, the right to rescind the transaction for fraud being only available as against the wrong-doer and those affected with knowledge thereof. *Bassett v. Spofford*, 45 N. Y., 387; *Zink v. People*, 77 N. Y., 114, 33 Am. R., 589; *State v. Anderson*, 47 Iowa, 142; *Dows v. Greene*, 24 N. Y., 638, 643; *People v. Morse*, 99 N. Y., 662, 7 Cr. L. Mag., 211.

III. **The Intent.**—There must be, in doing the act, a specific wrongful intent, beyond the mere intent to commit trespass. The books usually call this a "felonious intent." The intent must be to deprive the owner of his entire ownership. So that to wrongfully take property for a temporary use, not meaning to acquire and retain its ownership, is not larceny. But if the intent is to deprive the owner of his property, it is immaterial that the use for which it is taken is merely temporary. *State v. Davis*, 38 N. J. Law, 176, 20 Am. R., 367, 1 Am. Cr. R., 398; *Reg. v. Holloway*, 2 Car. & K., 942; *Johnson v. State*, 36 Tex., 375, 1 Green's Cr. L. R., 347; *U. S. v. Wight*, 38 Fed. R., 106.

If the intent is to deprive the owner of a portion of the article or its value, it is felonious. Thus if property is taken with intent to sell it back again to the owner, or claim a lien upon it, the act will constitute larceny. Broom's Com., 958; *Berry v. State*, 31 Ohio St., 219, 27 Am. R., 506; *Fort v. State*, 82 Ala., 50, 2 So. R., 477, 9 Cr. L. Mag., 935 and note; 2 East P. C., 662; *Com. v. Mason*, 105 Mass., 163, 7 Am. R., 507.

It is not necessary that the taking be for the purpose of acquiring pecuniary advantage (or *lucri causa*). It is sufficient if the intent be to deprive the owner of his property. *State v. Slingerland*, 19 Nev., 135, 6 Cr. L. Mag., 686.

But if the intent is only to do malicious mischief and injure the owner without taking his property, the act will not be larceny.

The felonious intent must exist at the time of taking; if the taking be by mistake, or ignorance, or unintentional, or with some intent not felonious, a subsequent appropriation, even intentional, will not make the act larceny.

Lost Goods.—Thus a person who finds lost goods, and does not know the owner, is not guilty of larceny in not returning them, or even in afterwards concealing them with the intent to appropriate (see *ante* p. 23), but if he knows or could reasonably ascertain the owner, and immediately appropriates to his own use, it will be larceny. So articles left by mistake do not cease to be the property nor in the possession of the owner, and a taking with the intent to appropriate may be larceny. *Bailey v. State*, 52 Ind., 462, 21 Am. R , 182 and note; *Baker v. State*, 29 Ohio St., 184, 23 Am. R., 731; *State v. Levy*, 23 Minn., 104, 23 Am. R., 678; *Com. v. Titus*, 116 Mass., 42, 17 Am. R., 138 and note; *Griggs v. State*, 58 Ala., 425, 29 Am. R., 762 and note; *State v. Clifford*, 14 Nev., 72, 33 Am. R., 526; *State v Taylor*, 25 Iowa, 273; *State v. Dean*, 49 Iowa, 73, 31 Am. R., 143; *Starck v. State*, 63 Ind., 285, 30 Am. R., 214.

Punishment: Grand and Petit.—At common law, larceny was divided into grand and petit, the former including those cases where the goods stolen were over twelve pence in value, the latter where they were of the value of twelve pence or under. Both were felonies, the former punishable capitally, the latter by some corporal punishment such as whipping, or imprisonment, and by the forfeiture usual in cases of felony. The distinction between grand and petit larceny is now abolished in England and in many of the states. It is usual to provide by statute that there shall be two grades of punishment depending upon whether the value of the property does or does not exceed a certain amount. But it is held that there are not different degrees of larceny but that the value of the property stolen simply determining the punishment. 1. Bish. Cr. L. (7th Ed.), Secs. 679, 680 ; *State v. Murray*, 55 Iowa, 530.

Simple and Compound.—The foregoing discussion has referred to simple larceny alone. Compound larceny is larceny aggravated by some attendant fact, increasing its enormity. Robbery, already considered, is one compound larceny. Statutes usually create other compounds, such as larceny from the person,

from a building on fire, from any building by night or by day, etc. *State v. Gleason,* 56 Iowa, 203; 2 Bish. Cr. L., Secs. 892-904.

EMBEZZLEMENT.

What Constitutes.—It has already been shown that one who is entrusted with the possession—not the mere custody—of property, is not guilty of larceny in appropriating it to his own use, for the reason that there can be no technical taking of possession from the owner, the possession already being in the one having the custody; also that property or money coming into the possession of a servant from another, for the master, is not subject of larceny by such clerk until delivered into the possession of the master, even in cases where such custody, if originally derived from the master, would not constitute possession in the servant so as to defeat a prosecution for larceny by him. And it was seen that the same principles were applied in case of bailees, such as common carriers, etc., etc. In England, by statutes (the first being 39 Geo , 3, c. 85), it was provided that if persons standing in such relation to property as described above, embezzle the same, they shall be deemed to have feloniously stolen it; and a punishment similar to that for larceny is provided. Some such statute is in force in every state and the crime therein described is called embezzlement, and is usually made punishable in like manner as larceny; embezzlemeet by public officers being sometimes made an aggravated form of such offense, in the nature of a compound larceny. In general, it is necessary that all the elements of larceny be present except the technical "taking." *State v. Bryan,* 40 Iowa, 379; *State v. Johnson,* 49 Iowa, 141; 2 Bish. Cr. L., Secs. 318-383, May Cr. L., Secs., 96-102; articles, 13 Cent. L. J., 462, and 8 Cr. L. Mag., 131.

FALSE PRETENSES.

What Constitutes.—To obtain the title to property by falsehood, fraud, or misrepresentation, as has already been shown, does not constitute larceny. To reach this class of cases statutes were enacted in England (30 Geo. 2, Chap. 24, Sec. 1, and 52 Geo. 2, Chap. 64, Sec. 1), making it a crime to knowingly and designedly, by false pretense or pretenses, obtain from another money, goods, notes, securities, etc., with intent to defraud any person of the same. Similar statutes are found in the various states. A false pretense is defined as "such a fraudulent representation of an existing or past fact, by one who knows it not to be true, as is adapted to induce the person to whom it is made to part with something of value." There must be a false representation; a mere promise, or statement of opinion will not suffice. It must be knowingly false; not merely erroneous or mistaken. It must be as to something past or present; a representation as to the future would be either in the nature of a promise or an opinion and therefore insufficient. It must be made with intent to defraud and it must be the direct means of accomplishing the fraud. 2 Bish. Cr. L., Secs. 409–488; May Cr. L., Secs. 107–120; *State v. Neimeier*, 66 Iowa, 634.

MALICIOUS MISCHIEF.

What Constitutes.—Willful and malicious destruction of personal property constituted an offense at common law. Statutes have, however, superceded the common law and extended the scope of the punishment. It is sometimes difficult to draw the line between cases of larceny and of malicious mischief. There must be a trespass in the latter case, as well as the former, but in general the offenses are distinguishable. Mere trespass, however, will not constitute malicious mischief. Willfulness and malice must appear, and the malice must be something more than a mere wrongful intent inferred from the act itself. It seems malice and ill-will toward some particular individual is not necessary, but malice toward the owner of the property, whoever he be, will suffice; and this malice may be inferred from circumstances. *State v. Linde*, 54 Iowa, 139; 2 Bish. Cr. L., Secs. 983–1000; May Cr. L., Secs. 177–179; 4 Bl. Com., 235; 3 Stephen's Hist. Cr. L., 187.

FORGERY.

Defined.—Forgery is: "The fraudulent making or alteration of a writing to the prejudice of another man's right." (Black-

stone.) "The fraudulent making of a false writing, which, if genuine, would be apparently of some legal efficacy." (Bishop. 4 Bl. Com., 247; 2 Bish. Cr. L., Secs. 521–612; May Cr. L., Secs. 121–125; 3 Stephen's Hist. Cr. L., Chap. 29.

The Fraudulent Making.—The act, constituting forgery, may be a fraudulent writing of an entire instrument, or a false signature to one already written or printed, or it may be a material alteration of a genuine instrument. In the case of an alteration, it must be as to some material part, but if so, the slightest will be sufficient. The name fraudulently signed may be that of a fictitious person, or of one deceased, or of a corporation which has expired. Even the signing of one's own name with fraudulent intent to have it taken for the signature of another person of the same name may be forgery. Nor is it necessary that the signature bear any similarity to that of the person whose name it purports to be. *Com. v. Baldwin,* 11 Gray, 197; *Mead v. Young,* 4 Term R., 28; *State v. Stratton.* 27 Iowa, 420; *Caulkins v. Whisler,* 29 Iowa, 495; *State v. Shurtliff,* 18 Maine, 368; *Com. v. Stephenson,* 11 Cush., 481; *State v. Farrell* (Iowa), 48 N. W. R., 940.

The Writing.—It matters not what the writing is, so it be of apparent legal efficacy. If upon its face it would be of no pecuniary value, or void, even if genuine, the falsification of it will not be criminal. But it will be sufficient that it be of such form as to create an apparent pecuniary liability on the part of him whose instrument it purports to be, or calculated to cause pecuniary loss to others. *Com. v. Ray,* 3 Gray, 441; *Case of Ames,* 2 Maine, 365; *Waterman v. People,* 67 Ill., 91; *People v. Shall,* 9 Cow., 778; *State v. Wheeler,* 19 Minn., 98; *State v. Pierce,* 8 Iowa, 231; *People v. Tomlinson,* 35 Cal., 503.

The Intent.—There must be an intent to defraud, but it is not necessary that actual fraud shall result, nor need the intent be to defraud any specific person. *Com. v. Ladd,* 15 Mass., 526; *Pauli v. Com.,* 89 Penn. St., 432; *Reg. v. Parish,* 8 Car. & P., 94.

COUNTERFEITING.

What Constitutes.—" Counterfeiting is making false coin in the similitude of the genuine with intent to defraud. It is a species of forgery and its distinguishing characteristic is that there must be some appearance of similitude to the thing counterfeited." (May). But whether this similitude exists is a question of fact. The federal government is expressly given power for the punishment of counterfeiting the securities and coin of the U. S. (Const. of U. S., Art. 1, Sec. 8), and it has done so by statute. (U. S. Rev. Stat., Secs. 5413–5415, 5457–5462). State statutes provide for the punishment of the acts of similar nature relating to the public securities of the states, evidences of debt issued by corporations, such as bank bills, etc., etc., also the counterfeiting or having in possession any current coin. 4 Bl. Com., 84, 88, 100; 2 Bish. Cr. L., Secs. 275–300; May Cr. L., Sec. 94. A state can punish an act of counterfeiting as a crime against itself although the same act is an offense under the laws of the United States. *Ex Parte Houghton*, 8 Fed. R., 897; *State v. McPherson*, 9 Iowa, 53; *Dashing v. State*, 78 Ind.. 357; *Fox v. State*, 5 How. (U. S.), 410; *U. S. v. Marigold*, 9 ibid., 560; *People v. White*, 34 Cal., 183.

OFFENSES AGAINST PUBLIC JUSTICE.

PERJURY.

Defined.—"Perjury, by the common law, seemeth to be a willful false oath, by one who being lawfully required to depose the truth, in any proceeding in a course of justice, swears absolutely in a matter of some consequence, to the point in question, whether he be believed or not." 1 Hawk. P. C., Chap. 69; 4 Bl. Com., 137, and notes; 2 Bish. Cr. L., Secs. 1014–1056; May Cr. L., Secs. 184–190; 3 Stephen's Hist. Cr. L., 240–250.

The Oath.—Either an oath or affirmation such as provided for by law will support a prosecution for perjury, but it must appear that it was administered by one authorized to administer oaths, in a proper proceeding, and in one in which he may be required to be sworn.

The Statement Under Oath.—The statement made under oath must, to constitute perjury, be in a judicial proceeding or in a case where an oath is required by statute. It must be willfully false, though if the witness states as a matter of belief what he knows to be false, the statement is as willfully false, as if he had made a positive assertion. But a statement which is merely careless and negligent, when the witness might have known it was false but did not, is not perjury. If the witness believes his statement to be false he is guilty of perjury, although in fact it is true. The statement must be one which is material in the proceeding in which it is made, but it is not necessary that it shall have had any effect. *The King v. Crossley*, 7 Term R., 311, 315; *Com. v. Brady*, 5 Gray, 78; *O'Bryan v. State*, 27 Tex. Ct. App., 339, 11 S. W. R., 443.

Subornation.—Subornation of perjury is procuring witnesses to commit perjury.

CRIMINAL PROCEDURE.

GENERAL NATURE AND HISTORY.

EMBRACES WHAT.—Criminal law, as the term is used in its more restricted sense, determines whether as an abstract proposition a given act or omission is punishable as a crime, and prescribes what punishment may be inflicted. Criminal procedure is the method provided for determining whether a certain person is guilty of a specified crime, and for inflicting the prescribed punishment upon him if found guilty. In other words, criminal procedure is the method of applying the general principles of criminal law to the particular case, just as civil procedure is the method provided for protecting and enforcing in the concrete those rights and duties which in the abstract are recognized by civil, or private, law as proper to be protected and enforced.

HISTORY.—The earliest accounts accessible as to the punishment of acts such as are now considered crimes, indicate the existence of a recognized right of private vengeance on the part of the injured person, or his representatives, against the wrong-doer. And the earliest indications of an effort to supersede this right of private war by some other remedy, is to be found in laws fixing the price to be paid by the wrong-doer to the injured party and to the king for each specific wrong, upon the payment of which the right of private vengeance was to terminate; but a second offence could not thus be atoned for. A somewhat nearer approach to the idea of a criminal procedure is to be found in the law of infangthief, which may briefly be designated as the right of summary execution for theft; which was considered by the law as allowable, under certain circumstances, to the person injured and was generally granted as a franchise to the lords of townships (1 Stephen, Hist. Cr. L., 59–64). Criminal procedure proper, however, can only exist when there is some recognized method of trial for determining the guilt of the accused; and such a trial necessarily involves an accusation. The earliest form of accusation seems to have been by the injured party as a private accuser in what was called an appeal, whereby the accused was put upon trial of battle as to his guilt. Failure of accused to submit to this ordeal, when tendered according to the strict requirements of law, resulted in outlawry. Accusation by public report corresponded to, and was the origin of, the present indictment by grand jury; and put the accused upon trial by ordeal, or, afterwards, by jury (1 Stephen, Hist. Cr. L., 244–254; 2 Reeves, Hist. Eng. L., 286–299; 4 id., 214).

PRESENT FORM OF PROCEEDING.—The appeal by private accuser finally merged into the action of tort to recover damages for the private injuries sustained, while the accusation by public report, together with accusation by information in behalf of the king by a public officer, became the criminal prosecution as we now have it. Bearing in mind the distinction between the crime and the tort, it will be readily understood that the criminal prosecution is primarily in behalf of the public, and not for the benefit of the injured party. But the public can, in the nature of things, act only through some agency. The agency representing the public in such cases is the sovereign power, and the criminal prosecution, as it exists, is a proceeding by the sovereign power as plaintiff, against the accused as defendant, in which the commission of the specified crime of defendant is charged, and it is asked that he be found guilty thereof, and the prescribed penalty be inflicted. In this country the sovereign power acts directly through a prosecuting officer as its representative in the more important prosecutions, while minor ones are left to be carried on by a private complainant who is, however, also the representative of the sovereign power, the proceedings being as in the other case in its name, and the costs being paid by it unless taxed to the prosecutor as a penalty for acting in bad faith, or without reasonable grounds.

At common law there was no prosecuting officer and the institution of proceedings was left in the charge of the private prosecutor as above indicated. But the whole proceeding shows that he acted in behalf of the public, and not as the accuser, as in case of the ancient appeal. It is still true that criminal proceedings will seldom be commenced or carried on without the active agency of some person feeling an interest, from some cause, in the punishment of the accused; but the state, and not the person thus interested, is the actual party plaintiff in the proceeding.

COMMON AND STATUTORY — The law regulating criminal procedure is like other divisions of the law in being either unwritten or written, and as fully as any other branch it had its origin in customs and usages crystallized into precedents preserved in the reports. As statutes are usually looked upon as additions to the common law except in so far as they repeal it, the rules of criminal procedure in general might be said to be what they were at common law, with such modifications as have been made by statute. However, in some states the whole ground has been covered by statutory codification and it may be considered that it was intended thereby to supercede the common law procedure; although the common law will still be looked to as supplying definitions of terms and showing the principles on which the statutes are based. As there is no common law for the United States, the rules of criminal procedure therein are such as existed in the states when the federal courts were organized, except as modified by acts of congress. See *post*.

LEGISLATIVE MODIFICATIONS AND CONSTITUTIONAL LIMITATIONS. — The general power of prescribing the forms and methods of criminal procedure being inherent in the legislative branches of our state and federal governments, it is competent for the legislative power to make any changes therein which it may see fit, subject, however, to the limitations found in the constitutions, which preserve to the accused certain rights deemed fundamental and necessary to his proper protection, such as the right to counsel, to have a copy of the accusation, to have compulsory process for witnesses, to a trial by jury, etc., which are enumerated in the various bills of rights. So far as such provisons are contained in the federal constitution they are applicable only to proceedings in the federal courts, unless expressly declared to be limitations upon state power. Cooley, Cost. Law, 19; *Twitchell v. Com.*, 7 Wall. 321; *Prescott v. State*, 19 Ohio St., 184, 2 Am. Rep. 388.

EX POST FACTO LAWS.—The only provisions of the federal constitution which are designated as limitations on the power of the state governments, as affecting the regulation of criminal procedure, are those providing respectively that no state shall pass any *ex post facto* law (U. S. Const. article 1, sec. 10) or deprive any person of life, liberty, or property without due process of law (U. S. Const. 14 Amendment, sec. 1). Similar provisions are to be found in the federal and most of the state constitutions as limitations upon the legislative authority of the United States and the states respectively. As to *ex post facto* laws, see *ante*, page 13. It may be added that these provisions protect the defendant from any changes in procedure to his disadvantage, as fully as from a change in the definition of the crime or the increase of punishment. *Kring v. State* (U. S. S. C.) 15 Rep. 769, 4 Cr. L. Mag. 550; *Garvey v. People*, 4 Cr. L. Mag., 715.

DUE PROCESS OF LAW.—The fifth amendment to the federal constitution contains a provision that no person shall "be deprived of life, liberty or property without due process of law," and a similar clause is found in most state constitutions. Furthermore, by the fourteenth amendment to the federal constitution the same provision is directly imposed as a limitation upon the power of the states.

MEANING OF THE PHRASE.—The term is general in its meaning, and synonymous with "law of the land" used in Magna Charta. In general, proceedings which are in conformity with the established rules and principles of the common law as it existed at the time of the independence of the United States must be considered as conforming to the constitutional requirement. It does not follow, however, that modifications

in the common law made by statute will be in derogation of the constitutional guaranty, for a right to make such modifications was itself a part of the common law. Yet the fact that a proceeding is expressly authorized by statute does not necessarily render it "due process of law," otherwise the constitutional guaranties would furnish no security against improper legislation. No general definition covering all cases can be given, but as to criminal procedure it is well settled that to constitute due process of law there must be a formal and specific charge of the offence and a trial thereof in a court of justice in which the defendant is found guilty, before the punishment provided for the offence can properly be inflcted. Cooley, Const. Lim., 351; Cooley, Const. Law, 221–225, 298; 2 Kent, Com. 13; *State v. Doherty*, 60 Maine, 504, 509; *Wynehamer v. People*, 13 N. Y., 378, 432; *Taylor v. Porter*, 4 Hill, 140, 145.

APPLICABLE AT ALL STAGES. — The provision is applicable, of course, at every stage of the proeeeding and no step is be taken in restraining or punishing, without conformity to the safeguards which the common law has thrown around such step for the protection of the subject; but the safeguards are very different under differing circumstances. The safeguards provided at different stages will be considered from time to time in their proper connection. Many of them are preserved by express constitutional provisions. The following cases contain discussions of the principle as it is sought to be applied under particular circumstances: *Portland v. Bangor*, 65 Maine, 120, 20 Am. Rep. 681; *Milwaukee v. Supervisors*, 40 Wis. 328, 22 Am. Rep. 702; *Prescott v. State*, 19 Ohio St., 884, 2 Am. Rep. 388; *Jones v. Robbins*, 8 Gray, 329.

THE MACHINERY.

CLASSES OF AGENCIES. — The agencies employed in criminal procedure may be divided into two distinct classes. The first class comprise what may be designated as conservators of the peace, whose duties pertain, either to the prevention of an anticipated crime, or the arrest and detention of the supposed criminal preparatory to his trial. The other class consists of the various courts provided for the trial of offenders, and officers authorized to assist in their proceedings or in carrying out their judgments. The second class of agencies is similar to, and frequently the same as, the agencies provided by the sovereign power for the protection of private rights and the redress of private wrongs. The first class of agencies has no parallel in civil procedure. It may be added that the same person may be authorized to act at one time as a conservator of the peace, at another, as a judge, but his functions in the two capacities are nevertheless entirely different.

FEDERAL AND STATE. — Owing to the dual form of our government we have two complete systems of agencies for the administration of the criminal law, one system existing under the state government dealing with crimes against the laws of the state, the other existing under the federal government dealing with crimes against the laws of the United States The two systems are similar, but entirely distinct and independent, and must be separately described.

In States.

CONSERVATORS OF THE PEACE. — By the common law the king and certain great officers, including the chancellor and the judges of the king's bench, were conservators of the peace throughout England, while minor officers were intrusted with the same authority within more limited jurisdictions, among these being the sheriff, the coroner, the constable, justices of the peace, etc., (1 Stephen, Hist. Cr. L. 185). These officers are now divided into two classes with somewhat different functions, to-wit: magistrates and peace officers; judges, justices of the peace, police magistrates and mayors of cities belonging to the first, and sheriffs, constables, marshals, and policemen, to the second.

MAGISTRATES. — The distinction between the duties of the magistrate and those of a peace officer is, briefly, that the former acts in some sense in a judicial capacity, while the latter is merely an executive officer. It is only desirable here to

describe the various officers of each class, leaving their powers and duties to be more fully detailed hereafter.

JUDGES—At the common law, judges of the king's bench, as well as other judicial officers, had authority to act as magistrates anywhere within the kingdom, and it is generally provided in a similar manner by statute as to the judges of the various State courts within the State. Judges do not, however, in practice, often act in this capacity.

JUSTICES OF THE PEACE.—The office of justice of the peace dates from the reign of Edward the Third, when it was provided by statute "That for the better maintaining and keeping of the peace in their county, good men and lawful, which were no maintainers of evil or barrators in the country, should be assigned to keep the peace." By subsequent statutes of the same reign these conservators of the peace were given certain judicial powers, which powers were variously enlarged and added to from time to time until they became very complicated; but were finally classified in the revised commission prepared by Lord Chief Justice Wrey, in the reign of Elizabeth, and adopted by the Lord Chancellor as the form of all subsequent commissions; and which remained subsequently unaltered in England until very recently. Without express statutory modifications the common law powers and duties of the justice of the peace were very essentially changed. While at first he acted in his own person in making arrests and otherwise conserving the peace, he subsequently came to act in a judicial capacity, entertaining complaints, signing warrants for arrest or commitment, etc. In our modern forms of procedure, the justice of the peace is the officer most generally exercising the powers of a magistrate. 1 Bish. Cr. Pr. (3d Ed.), § 174

CORONERS.—The office of coroner is one of great antiquity, originating, it seems, as early as 1194. The duties of the office remain practically the same as they were in early times. In cases of death under circumstances raising suspicion of criminality, the coroner is required to attend and summon a jury to hold an inquest over the body as to the cause of the death, and as to whether any one be culpable in connection therewith.

If it appears from such inquest that the death is the result of crime, he should issue a warrant for the arrest of the supposed criminal, if known, and bind over the witnesses to appear upon the trial. Minutes of the evidence of witnesses examined at the inquest are to be kept and returned to the court. In these respects the coroner acts in a magisterial capacity. He is further authorized to act as a substitute for the sheriff in certain circumstances, and in so doing he is a ministerial officer. 1 Bl. Com., 346; 1 Stephen, Hist. Crim. L., 217; 2 Reeves, Hist. Eng. L., 275–277.

POLICE MAGISTRATES, MAYORS, ETC.—As to other officers authorized by statute to act as magistrates, nothing need be said. They are of modern origin, creatures of statute, and derive all their authority from express enactment.

PEACE OFFICERS.—The duties of these officers are in general to act under the command of magistrates in making arrests and detaining the arrested person in custody; also, in certain circumstances, to make arrests without warrant, as will be explained hereafter in treating of arrest. They were, like justices, originally conservators of the peace, but as the justices assumed *quasi* judicial functions, the peace officers retained merely ministerial duties.

SHERIFFS.—The sheriff is the principal peace officer. The office is one of the most ancient, having existed among the Anglo-Saxons as that of shire reeve or keeper of the shire or county. Under the Normans the same officer was designated as the vice-comes, or deputy of the earl, who was the lord of the county. Next to the earl, who was nominal rather than real chief, the sheriff was the head man of his county, outranking therein by virtue of his office all others. He had charge of the king's business within his jurisdiction, and therefore as representative of the king, who was the great keeper of the peace, it was his especial duty to see that the law was administered and the subject was protected. Not only was he the king's chief executive officer, but he had some judicial and military authority. 1 Bl. Com., 339; 1 Stubbs, Const. Hist., 113. In this country he has few judicial functions, but remains the chief

ministerial officer of the courts of justice for his county in civil as well as in criminal proceedings.

CONSTABLES. — Standing in somewhat the same relations to the township that the sheriff does to the county, the constable is in general the executive officer of the courts of justices of the peace in both civil and criminal matters. Originally his duties pertained more especially to the preservation of the peace. 1 Stephen, Hist. Cr., L. 194; 1 Bl. Com., 355.

MARSHALS, POLICEMEN, ETC. — The municipal officers being purely creatures of statute, and depending upon municipal charters and regulations for their power, need not be further referred to.

THE MILITIA; POSSE COMITATUS; HUE AND CRY. — A remnant of the military authority of the sheriff may be found in his power to call upon the militia of the state to assist him when resisted in the exercise of the duties of his office. The whole military power of the state is placed at the disposal of the civil authorities for the maintainance of peace, and the execution of the law; but when so called upon, the military must act under the direction of the civil authorities. Not only may the sheriff call upon the militia, he may in general call to his aid bystanders, even the whole posse comitatus, or power of the county, consisting at common law of all persons over 15 years of age; and any one failing to obey such summons is liable to punishment. This provision is a relic of the "hue and cry" which was to be raised by a constable when advised of the commission of a crime and the flight of the criminal, in which hue and cry the sheriff with the power of his county was to join, and which was to be kept up from township to township until the criminal was captured or had made good his escape. 1 Bl. Com., 343; 4 id., 122, 293; 1 Stephen, Hist. Cr. L., 186; 2 Hawk. P. C., ch. 12, sec. 5.

COURTS. — The system of courts of criminal jurisdiction in England, as it existed when the common law was brought to this country, was quite complex, and having been entirely changed with us, it is useless to give its details. It is fully explained in 4 Bl. Com., ch. 19; 1 Stephen, Hist. Cr. L., ch's 4–

6. Courts having criminal jurisdiction in the various states may be divided into three classes: first, those for the trial of minor offences as to which the constitution or statutes of the state do not require trial by jury, and the proceedings in which are somewhat summary in their nature; second, courts of general original jurisdiction in criminal cases; third, courts having jurisdiction in such cases by appeal.

COURTS OF SUMMARY JURISDICTION. — It is usually provided that prosecutions for minor offences, the punishment for which does not exceed a specified limit, may be tried by justices of the peace, police magistrates, mayors of cities and towns, etc. The procedure is either without a jury, or with a jury of less than twelve. It is usually provided that from a conviction in such summary proceeding the defendant may take an appeal to the court having general criminal jurisdiction, where he can have another trial before a regularly constituted jury, and such provision prevents summary convictions from being in violation of the general constitutional guaranty of right of trial by jury. *Jones v. Robbins*, 8 Gray, 329; *Zelle v. McHenry*, 51 Iowa, 572. The history of the modern English courts of summary jurisdiction may be found in 1 Stephen, Hist. Cr. L., 122–5; and will illustrate the nature of similar courts as variously constituted in this country.

ON WHAT THIS JURISDICTION DEPENDS. — It is usual to limit this summary jurisdiction to crimes punishable not to exceed a specified limit. If the jurisdiction over these is made exclusive, a crime of that degree cannot be originally prosecuted in the higher court. A crime of higher degree cannot, of course, be prosecuted in the lower court; and even if the defendant appeal from such a conviction to the higher court the latter does not get jurisdiction, although it would have had jurisdiction if the prosecution had been first commenced there. *State v. Carpenter*, 23 Iowa, 506. The jurisdiction is determined, however, by the offence charged. If that is of such degree as to give the higher court jurisdiction, it may sentence for a lower degree of the same offence or for any included offence of which defendant is found guilty although such

offence or degree of the offence is, itself, cognizable exclusively by summary proceedings. *State v. Jarvis*, 21 Iowa, 44; *State v. Dolby*, 49 N. H., 483, 6 Am. Rep., 588.

COURTS OF GENERAL ORIGINAL JURISDICTION.—The court of King's Bench (or Queen's Bench as the case may be) in England had, at common law, general criminal jurisdiction as to all cases where not expressly otherwise provided; it had all the jurisdiction of the *curia regis* which was not given to the common pleas, or exchequer, neither of which was given criminal jurisdiction. This *curia regis* was the medium through which the king acted, not only in administering justice but in affairs of state; and as the king was looked upon as the fountain of all justice, this court, which was simply the king and council sitting for the administration of justice, had all the powers and jurisdiction which a criminal court could have. 1 Stephen, Hist. Cr. L., 85-94. In each of the states there is some one court which exercises the same general powers. It is the procedure in such court which is generally referred to when criminal procedure is spoken of, unless otherwise specified.

APPELLATE COURTS. — The right of appeal by writ of error from this court of original jurisdiction to a higher court is provided for in nearly all the states. The appeal from the court of summary jurisdiction to that of general original jurisdiction has already been referred to. In England, as will be pointed out in speaking of appeals hereafter, there is not such complete provision for the review of the proceedings of a trial court in a criminal case by a higher court, as is found in civil cases.

In the United States.

MAGISTRATES. — By the Revised Statutes of the United States (Secs. 1014, 727), judges of the United States courts, and United States commissioners, as also, judges, justices of the peace, and other magistrates of the state, are authorized to act in regard to crimes triable in the federal courts in a manner similar to that of magistrates of the state. Conkling's Treatise, United States Courts (4th Ed.), 570. The United

States commissioners have, in other respects, some of the powers of a justice of the peace, but in neither civil nor criminal cases do they have authority to act as a court in the trial of actions.

PEACE OFFICERS. — The executive officer of the United States courts is the marshal, who has, in the district in which he is appointed, the same power in executing the laws of the United States as the sheriff in such state may have within his county; and in a similar manner he may summon the posse comitatus. R. S., §§ 787, 788. Whether when a state magistrate issues a warrant as contemplated in R. S., § 1014, it may be directed to a state officer, and executed by him, seems a matter of doubt. Conkling's Treatise, *supra*.

SUMMARY PROCEEDINGS. — The only provision under the laws of the United States for trial by summary proceedings, is in case of offences not capital or otherwise infamous, committed by a master, officer, or seaman of a vessel of the United States, against the laws of the United States made for the protection of persons or property engaged in commerce or navigation. Such proceeding is to be had by a judge of the district court of the United States on complaint, without a jury, unless a jury is demanded at the time of pleading or answering; and the punishment inflicted for such offences is limited to imprisonment of one year, or fine of five hundred dollars, or both. R. S., §§ 4300–4305.

DISTRICT AND CIRCUIT COURTS. — The district court of the United States has general original criminal jurisdiction as to all crimes cognizable under the authority of the United States not capital; and the circuit court has exclusive cognizance of capital offences and concurrent jurisdiction with the district court of all crimes triable therein. R. S., §§ 563, 629. There are provisions also for the removal of prosecutions from the district to the circuit court and *vice versa*; and when a prosecution is commenced in the district court for a capital offence, it must be removed to the circuit court. R. S., §§ 1037–9. There are further provisions for the removal from the state courts to the United States circuit court of criminal prosecu-

tions against a revenue officer for acts done by authority of his office, or against a United States officer for acts done in enforcement of the election laws. R. S., § 643; *Tennessee v. Davis*, 100 U. S. 257.

WRIT OF ERROR FROM DISTRICT TO CIRCUIT COURT. — Provision is made for a review in the circuit court, by writ of error, of criminal cases tried in the district court, when the sentence imposed by the latter includes imprisonment, or a fine is imposed exceeding three hundred dollars. United States Stat's, of 1878-9, p, 354 (Act of Mar. 3, 1879); *Brand v. United States*, 4 Fed. Rep., 394.

THE SUPREME COURT. — There is no provision for direct appeal to the supreme court of the United States from the judgment of the circuit court in criminal cases; but if upon trial of the case in the circuit court before two judges, there is a difference of opinion upon any material point, they may send to the supreme court a certificate of such division, and the latter will determine the question. R. S., §§ 651,697. Appeal by writ of error may be taken from the judgment of the highest court of the state to the supreme court of the United States where the decision involves what is called a federal question. R. S., § 709.

JURISDICTION OF THE FEDERAL COURTS. — As has been stated (*ante*, pp. 11-13) the federal government has but limited, or delegated power to punish acts as crimes, and as a consequence its courts are courts of limited criminal jurisdiction. But Congress has given to the United States district and circuit courts general jurisdiction to punish all acts which are crimes under the United States law, and their powers and procedure are those of courts of general criminal jurisdiction in the state where the court is held, as they existed when the judiciary act of 1789 was passed, except as Congress has otherwise provided. Conkling's Treatise, U. S. Courts, 167; 1 Abbott's U. S. Prac., 197; 2 id., 171; *United States v. Reid*, 12 How. 361.

JURISDICTION.

WHAT NECESSARY TO GIVE. — In order that the court or magistrate may have jurisdiction in any proceeding, the subject matter must be such that the law in general authorizes such a proceeding with reference thereto, by such a magistrate or court, and the person to be affected thereby must be subject to the authority of the magistrate or court in such manner as the law requires. As is generally stated, in brief, there must be jurisdiction of the subject matter and the person.

SUBJECT MATTER; JURISDICTION OF SOVEREIGN. — Whether an act is of such nature that under the laws of a sovereignty it is made a crime within the cognizance of the sovereign power to punish, will depend upon whether the act was done within the limits over which it assumes criminal jurisdiction, and by a person amenable to its laws. These questions are to be determined by what is called international law, which consists, in this instance, of those principles which the sovereignty recognizes as regulating in this respect its relations with other nations, and which are generally, but not necessarily, such as are recognized by other nations. In other words, while each nation considers itself bound, in its relations with other nations, to follow the principles of international law, it determines for itself what these principles are. 2 Stephen, Hist. Cr. L., 34–38.

SUBJECT MATTER; JURISDICTION OF COURT. — If the crime is one which the sovereignty has jurisdiction to punish, the question will still arise whether it has conferred that jurisdiction upon any of its courts, and it will be found that the jurisdiction conferred upon any particular court by the sovereign power is made to depend, among other things, upon the territorial subdivision within which the crime was committed, which is spoken of as the venue of the crime.

JURISDICTION OF THE PERSON. — Finally, even when it appears that the location of the crime and the status of the criminal are such as to bring the case within the general jurisdiction of the court, it cannot proceed with it to trial until, by proper steps, the particular person charged is brought within

its power in the manner provided by law.   It is apparent,
therefore, that it is necessary to consider how far the power of
the sovereignty to punish extends, and also how this power is
divided among different courts.

TERRITORIAL LIMITS OF THE UNITED STATES. — Where
the territory of a sovereignty is bounded by the sea, its exclusive jurisdiction extends not only to low water mark, which is
the strict boundary line, but the distance of a cannon-shot
beyond such line, which distance is considered to be a marine
league (about three and a half miles).   An island so near the
mainland that the water between is not, under the above rule,
common sea, is deemed part of the shore.   Where inland seas,
gulfs, bays, etc., are within the territory of one nation and have
a narrow inlet, all within the headland is deemed a part of the
territory of that nation.   1 Bish Cr. L. (6th Ed.), §§ 102–105; 1
Kent Com., 28–31.   Where the territory of two nations is separated by lakes, rivers, etc., a line through the center is deemed
the boundary.   *People v. Tyler*, 7 Mich., 161, 208; 1 Bish., Cr.
L. (6th Ed.) § 108.

SHIPS ON THE HIGH SEAS; FOREIGN SHIPS. — While a
nation cannot exercise exclusive jurisdiction over any portion
of the high seas except as above specified, its ships, public or
private, while on the high seas, are deemed a part of its territory;   and offences committed thereon are looked upon as
committed within its jurisdiction.   And although while a
private vessel is within the ports of a foreign nation, those on
board are, temporarily, subject to the laws of that nation, it
does not follow that they cease to be within the jurisdiction of
the nation to which the vessel belongs.   The jurisdiction extends also to all acts of piracy on the high seas, the pirate being
deemed an enemy of all mankind and punishable by whatever
nation seizes him.   As to the whole subject of the jurisdiction
of a sovereign over acts committed on the high sea, see 2
Stephen, Hist. Cr. L. 16–61; 1 Bish., Cr. L. (6th Ed.), §§ 117–
120; Wheat., Int. Law, §§ 105–108.

TERRITORIAL LIMITS OF STATES. — Where states of the
United States border on the high seas, their territorial limits

extend outward as far as those of the United States. As between states, the territorial boundaries are determined by the acts of admission to the Union. Usually, when separated by a river or lake, the central line is the boundary, but sometimes the whole of the river is in one state, and in the case of states formed from the northwestern territory bordering on the Mississippi, it was provided in the acts for their admission, as well as in their state constitutions, that they should have concurrent jurisdiction over the whole of the river adjacent to their respective territories. 1 Bish. Cr. L. (6th Ed.), §§ 145–150; *Gilbert v. Moline &c. Co.*, 19 Iowa, 319.

JURISDICTION OF SOVEREIGN AS TO PERSONS. — It is said that the laws of a sovereignty can have no extra territorial force. *The Apollon*, 9 Wheat., 362, 370. It is better, however, to say that the laws of the sovereignty are binding only on those who owe allegiance to it. All persons within its territorial jurisdiction owe at least temporary allegiance, even though not citizens, for they are entitled to the protection of its laws. 1 Kent Com., 36; 1 Bish. Cr. L., § 134; 1 East, P. C., 52; *People v. McLeod*, 1 Hill, 377, 406, 423; *Adams v. People*, 1 N. Y., 173. Thus aliens on board a nation's ships on the high seas are amenable to the laws of that nation as fully as its own subjects. 2 Stephen, Hist. Cr. L., 4–9.

FOREIGN SOVEREIGNS, AMBASSADORS, ETC. — An exception to the foregoing general principle is to be found in a rule that a foreign friendly sovereign visiting in person the territory of another sovereignty, is exempt, with his attendants, from the jurisdiction of the latter. The same exemption extends to the ambassadors and public ministers (not including consuls) of a foreign friendly sovereign; and to the ships of war and armies of such sovereign so long as they are within the waters or upon the territory of the other by express or implied permission. This exception, however, is said not to apply as to acts directed against the sovereignty itself. 1 Bish. Cr. L., §§ 124–130; 2 Stephen, Hist. Cr. L., 3; Wheat. Int. Law, §§ 97–105.

CITIZENS ABROAD. — The allegiance of a citizen to his government does not terminate upon his passing beyond its

territorial limits; and for acts committed by him while abroad he may be amenable to its laws. *Rex v. Speke,* 3 Salk. 358; *Rex v. Helsham* (4 Car. & P. 394) 19 E. C. L. 570; *Rex v. Sawyer,* (2 Car. & K.) 61 E. C. L. 101, 111,; *Reg v. Azzopardi,* (1 Car. & K.) 47 E. C. L. 203. As the sovereignty cannot, however, administer its laws within a foreign jurisdiction, and the foreign government within whose territory the act was committed would not recognize such laws, he could only be punished therefor upon coming within the territorial limits of his own country. However, by express treaty between different nations, it is sometime provided that certain officers of the one, residing within the territory of the other, may, within such territory, to some extent, administer the laws of the former as to its own citizens. Thus by treaty of the United States with China, consuls and diplomatic agents of the United States in that country, are authorized to administer justice as between citizens of the United States residing there. 1 Bish. Cr. L. (6th Ed.) §§ 121–123; 2 Stephen, Hist. Cr. L. 12–16.

JURISDICTION OF STATES BEYOND BOUNDARIES. — It is doubtful whether a citizen of a state passing beyond the limits of such state continues to be in any sense a citizen thereof. If he passes into another state, he doubtless becomes at once a citizen of that state; if he does not go within the limits of another state, he perhaps is only a citizen of the United States. Cooley, Const. Law, 242-4; 1 Bish. Cr. L. (6th Ed.) § 152; *Tyler v. People,* 8 Mich. 320, 342. Therefore it would seem that the courts of a state can have no jurisdiction over offences committed beyond its boundaries.

AS BETWEEN THE UNITED STATES AND THE STATES. — Neither the United States nor the state has jurisdiction to punish acts as crimes against the laws of the other. The jurisdiction of the federal courts over offences against the United States is exclusive, but when an act is of such nature that it may be treated by both the state and the United States as a crime, and it is made criminal by the laws of each, it seems it may punished by either. R. S. § 711; *Ross v. State,* 55

Ga. 192, 21 Am. Rep. 278; *Ex Parte Houghton*, 8 Fed. Rep. 897; *State v. McPherson*, 9 Iowa, 53; *Moore v. Illinois*, 14 How. 13; *Fox v. Ohio*, How. 410; *United States v. Marigold*, 9 How. 560; *State v. Tuller*, 34 Conn. 280; *Com. v. Felton*, 101 Mass. 204; *Dashing v. State*, 78 Ind. 357, 14 Cent. Law Jour., 351; *People v. White*, 34 Cal. 183.

CRIME WITHIN BY PERSON BEYOND. — When a person who is beyond the jurisdiction of a sovereignty commits a complete crime within the territorial limits by force set in motion from without (as by shooting across the boundary line, or by an innocent agent, or by representations made in a letter through the mails), he is guilty of a crime within the jurisdiction of such sovereignty; that is, the sovereignty has jurisdiction of the subject matter and may proceed to punish the offender whenever it can get jurisdiction of his person. 1 Bish. Cr. L. (6th Ed.), § 110; 1 Bish. Cr. Pr. (3d Ed.) § 53; *People v. Adams*, 3 Denio, 190; *Adams v. People*, 1 N. Y. 173; *Barkhamsted v. Parsons*, 3 Conn., 1, 8; *Com. v. Blunding*, 3 Pick. 304; *Com. v. Gillespie*, 7 S. & R. 469, 478; 2 Stephen, Hist. Cr. L. 9; *Reg. v. Keyn*, 19 Eng. Rep., 366.

ACTS BEYOND THE JURISDICTION.— In the cases just specified, the sovereignty in which the offender was at the time he set in motion the agency through which the crime was committed in the territory of the other sovereignty, might doubtless punish him for his act within its limits if it had before made it a crime. But as to the crime itself, it is a general principle of the common law, though otherwise in other systems, that a criminal act is to be regarded as local, and punishable only within the jurisdiction where committed; therefore the sovereignty would not consider itself as having jurisdiction of the subject matter, in case of a crime in another jurisdiction, committed by a person within its limits. That this rule is varied sometimes, by statute, as to citizens abroad, we have already seen. It might, doubtless, be varied as to such cases as those referred to in the preceding paragraph, but unless there were some explicit provision for such cases, it would be considered that the criminal quality of the act was to

be determined by the laws of the place where it was committed, not by those of the place where the offender was, and it would not be considered as covered by the latter, although within their general terms. Wheat. Int. Law, (8th Ed.) § 113; 1 Bish. Cr. L. (6th Ed.) §§ 109–112; *Rex. v. Hooker*, 7 Mod. 193; *Rex. v. Munton*, 1 Esp. 62; *Attorney General v. Kwok-a-Sing*, (L. R. 5 P. C. 179) 8 Eng. Rep. 143, 160.

ACTS PARTLY IN ONE JURISDICTION AND PARTLY IN ANOTHER. — It follows that in order that a sovereignty can have jurisdiction of a crime, there must have been sufficient acts within its jurisdiction, irrespective of what was done outside, to constitute a crime against its laws.

DEATH WITHIN FROM MURDEROUS BLOW WITHOUT. — Thus it is perhaps the better doctrine, that death within the jurisdiction of the sovereignty, resulting from a murderous blow inflicted without, does not properly constitute murder within the jurisdiction where the death occurs, and a statute making it murder, and punishable as such, ought to be confined in its application to citizens of the sovereignty, and not applied to foreigners, as to whom such sovereignty has, by the law of nations, no right to legislate. 1 Bish. Cr. L. (6th Ed.) §§ 112–115, *State v. Carter*, 27 N. J. Law, 499. *Contra*, Whart. Cr. Ev. § 110; *Com. v. Macloon*, 101 Mass. 1; *Tyler v. People*, 8 Mich. 320 (but see dissenting opinion of Campbell, J.). The point is discussed in *Reg. v. Keyn*, 19 Eng. Rep. 366, briefly referred to in 2 Stephen, Hist. Cr. L. 10. On the other hand, that a state may punish for a blow within its jurisdiction, resulting in death in another state, is decided in *Hunter v. State*, 40 N. J. Law, 495, 1 Cr. L. Mag. 64; *Green v. State*, 66 Ala. 40, 41 Am. Rep. 744.. This question is not to be confounded with the one as to venue when death results in one county from a blow struck in another, but within the territory of the same sovereignty, a point discussed hereafter under the head of venue.

LARCENY. — Where larceny is committed within the territory of one sovereignty, and the thief carries the goods thus wrongfully taken from the owner into the territory of another sovereignty, still acting in pursuance of the intent to steal them, he is, by perhaps the better view, guilty of larceny in the latter jurisdiction; not that any of the acts committed out of such jurisdiction are to be considered as aiding in making up the crime, but because each new removal of the property thus wrongfully in possession, made in pursuance of the intent to steal, constitutes a new larceny, entirely distinct from the first one.   1 Bish. Cr. L. (6th Ed.) §§ 137–142; 4 Bl. Com. 305; 1 Hale, P. C. 507; 1 Stephen, Hist. Cr. L. 278; *State v. Bennett,* 14 Iowa, 479; *Worthington v. State* 58 Md. 403, 42 Am. Rep. 338, 4 Cr. L. Mag. 219; *Com. v. White,* 123 Mass. 430, 25 Am. Rep. 116; *State v. Newman,* 9 Nev. 48, 16 Am. Rep. 3; *Com. v. Andrews,* 2 Mass. 14; *State v. Underwood,* 49 Maine, 181; *State v. Ellis,* 3 Conn. 185; Whart. Cr. Ev. § 111.   *Contra, Lee v. State,* 64 Ga. 203, 37 Am. Rep. 67; *Stanley v. State,* 24 Ohio St. 166, 15 Am. Rep. 604; *State v. Le Blanch,* 31 N. J. Law, 82; *State v. Loughridge,* 1 Neb. 11, and see opinions of divided court in *Morissey v. People,* 11 Mich. 327.   Whether the rule above stated be the common law rule or not, it is within the power of the legislature to enact it as a statutory rule, which has been done in several states.   *People v. Williams,* 24 Mich. 156, 9 Am. Rep. 119; *People v. Burke,* 11 Wend. 129; *McFarland v. State,* 4 Kan. 68; *State v. Williams,* 35 Mo., 229.

BIGAMY. — Similarly, in case of bigamy, it is commonly provided that although the bigamous marriage be contracted beyond the jurisdiction, yet the continuing to live in such connection within the jurisdiction, shall constitute the crime. *State v. Sloan,* 55 Iowa, 217; *Com. v. Bradley,* 2 Cush. 553; Bish. Stat. Cr. § 588.

ACCESSORIES IN FELONY. — One who incites to the commission of a felony within another jurisdiction, and therefore stands to the crime in the relation of accessory before the fact, is not, probably, to be held amenable in the jurisdiction where the crime is committed, for the wrongful act is done elsewhere. *State v. Wyckoff,* 31 N. J. Law, 65; *State v. Moore,* 26 N. H. 448; *Johns v. State,* 19 Ind. 421.   If the act is procured

through an innocent agent, the procurer is punishable within the jurisdiction of the crime (*ante* p. 123) because he is principal; and Bishop suggests that his character as accessory, even when the agency was a responsible one, might be disregarded, in view of the fact that, as such, he could not be punishable by the common law in the jurisdiction of the procurement, and he might be punishable as principal where the crime is committed. 1 Bish. Cr. L. (6th Ed.) § 111; and see *State v. Grady*, 34 Conn. 118. This idea is, in some states, embodied in a statutory provision. Code of Iowa, (1873) § 4157; Pub. Stat's. of Mass. (1882) p. 1179.

CONSPIRACY. — If a conspiracy be participated in by a resident of one jurisdiction, to commit a crime against the laws of another, perhaps such conspirator may be punished in the latter. *Com. v. Gillespie*, 7 S. & R. 469, 478. But, on the other hand, a conspiracy in one jurisdiction to commit a crime in another, but accompanied by some act in the former in execution of such conspiracy, is punishable where entered into, although the contemplated crime is not carried out. *Ex parte Rogers*, 10 Tex. Ct. App. 655, 38 Am. Rep. 654.

VENUE, OR LOCAL JURISDICTION. — So far as the sovereignty has jurisdiction to take cognizance of an offence at all, it may do so in whatever manner it may have provided; and the question whether any particular court has jurisdiction of an offence, properly punishable by the sovereignty, will depend upon whether such jurisdiction has been given to it. It was a principle of the common law, however, that one charged with a crime should be indicted and tried in the county in which the crime was committed. This rule arose probably from the original functions of grand and trial juries, they being supposed to act as witnesses, and base their findings rather upon their own knowledge, than upon the testimony of others. Therefore it was necessary that they come from the vicinity of the supposed crime in order that they should be cognizant of the facts. Under our present system of procedure in criminal prosecutions, in which the function of the trial jury is that of judges of the evidence, acting irrespective of any previous knowledge, and an acquaintance with the facts leading to an opinion of guilt or innocence is a disqualification, there is no such reason for the rule. It is, of course, desirable that the place of trial be the one most accessible to the witnesses and the defendant; but the point insisted upon most strenuously by the common law rule was, that the *jury* should come from the county of the offence, and this requirement was observed, even when the trial was allowed to be had in an adjoining county, or when it was taken by certiorari to the court of King's Bench at Westminster. 2 Hawk. P. C. ch. 5, § 19; 1 Stephen, Hist. Cr. L. 276.

IN FEDERAL COURTS. — The rule of the common law is substantially preserved by the constitution of the United States as to criminal trials in the federal courts, by the provisions of the federal constitution that they shall be " held in the state where the crimes shall have been committed, but when not committed within any state the trial shall be at such place or places as congress shall by law have designated," (Const. Art. III, § 2) and that accused shall have the right to trial by " jury of the state and district wherein the crime shall have been committed, which district shall have been previously ascertained by law.". (Am. to Const. Art. VI). It is further provided by statute, that trial of capital offences " shall be had in the county where the offence was committed, where that can be done without great inconvenience," (R. S. § 729); and accordingly provision is made for the holding of a circuit court for the trial of such cases, at a " convenient place within the district, nearer the place where the offenses are said to be committed, than the place appointed by law for the stated sessions." (R. S. §§ 661, 662). As to crimes committed on the high seas, or elsewhere, out of the jurisdiction of any particular state or district, it is provided that the trial shall be " in the district where the offender is first found, or into which he is first brought." (R. S. § 730, and see *U. S. v. Arwo,* 19 Wall. 486; *U. S. v. Dawson,* 15 How. 467.)

IN STATE COURTS; COUNTIES. — The state court to which criminal jurisdiction is given, is usually a court holding sessions in each county, and authorized to try offences committed in

that county. The limits of the county are such as may be prescribed in their organization. Where they are bounded by the
sea it is doubtful whether they extend further than the water's
edge unless there is statutory provision that they cover the
adjoining sea so far as the state jurisdiction extends. (But see
Mahler v. Transportation Co. 35 N. Y. 352; *State v. Mullen*,
35 Iowa, 199.) Where an arm of the sea extends into the land,
it will be part of the county or counties adjoining, if it lies
within headlands or islands, or between lands, so near together
that a person on one shore may clearly discern with the naked
eye objects and acts on the opposite shore. 1 Bish. Cr. L.
(6th Ed.) §§ 146–149; *Manley v. People*, 7 N. Y. 295; *Com. v.
Peters*, 12 Met. 387. Where the state is bounded by a river
over which it has concurrent jurisdiction, it may give such
jurisdiction to the courts for the adjacent counties, and possibly
they would have such jurisdiction without special legislation.
State v. Mullen, 35 Iowa, 199.

SPECIAL PROVISIONS. — There are usually special statutory
provisions, modifying the general rule as to place of trial, in
particular classes of cases, corresponding to statutory modifications of similar character in England, some of the more
important of which are the following:

OFFENCES NEAR BOUNDARY BETWEEN COUNTIES. — For
practical convenience, it is generally provided that the court in
either county may take jurisdiction of any offence committed
within a certain distance of the boundary line between them.

OFFENCES PARTLY IN EACH OF TWO COUNTIES. — If an
offence is committed in one county and completed in another, it
may usually be tried in either. Such a provision is found in
the federal statutes, R. S. §§ 731.

OFFENCES COMMITTED IN TRANSIT. — It is often provided
that if a crime is committed against a person or property while
being conveyed from one place to another, by means of a vessel, coach, or other conveyance employed in a voyage or
journey, the offender may be tried in any county into or through
which said conveyance passed in the course of such voyage or
journey.

DEATH IN ONE COUNTY FROM WOUND GIVEN IN ANOTHER.
— So rigid was the common law as to local jurisdiction, that if
a man was wounded in one county, and died in another, it was
doubted whether the criminal could be indicted in either, for
the reason that the grand jury of the former could have no
knowledge of the death, and that of the latter could not take
cognizance of the act.   1 Stephen, Hist. C. L. 277; 1 Hale, P.
C. 426; 1 East, P. C. 361; 1 Hawk. P. C. ch. 31, § 13.   By
statute which is common law in this country (2 and 3 Edw. 6, ch.
24) the crime was made cognizable in the county where the
death occurred, but it long remained a disputed question
whether the offence could be considered completed in the
county where the wound was inflicted, so that the offender
could be tried there for the murder.   The weight of later authority is to the effect that the inflicting of the blow, from
which death results within a year and a day, is a complete offence in the county (or the country) where it is inflicted, without regard to the place of death.   1 Bish. Cr. Pr. (3d Ed.) §§
50–52; *State v. Gessert*, 21 Minn. 369; *State v. Bowen*, 16 Kan.
475; *United States v. Guiteau*, 13 Rep. 138; *People v. Gill*, 6
Cal. 637; *Green v. State*, 66 Ala. 40, 41 Am. Rep., 744, 2 Cr.
L., Mag. 804.   (On a similar point, see *State v. Hollenbeck*, 36
Iowa, 12.)   The question as to jurisdiction in such case, as between two sovereignties, has already been referred to (*ante* p.
124).

OTHER CASES. — Exceptional provisions are also sometimes
made for larceny, bigamy, kidnapping, abduction, and other
offences.

CHANGE OF VENUE. — By statutory provision, a right to
change of venue is generally given to defendant upon showing
that some fact, recognized by the statute, exists which will
prevent his having a fair trial in the county where the prosecution is commenced, but such change is not allowed to the
state.   1 Bish. Cr. Pr. (3d Ed.) §§ 68–76; Whart. Cr. Pl. &
Pr. 602.

PREVENTION OF OFFENCES.

RESISTANCE BY THE PERSON ABOUT TO BE INJURED AND OTHERS. — The prevention of offences was, by the common law, left mainly to the party about to be injured, and others who should come to his aid, and they were considered by the law as justified in using whatever force was necessary for that purpose (*ante*, p. 31). This right of private resistance is sometimes recognized by statutes. Penal Code of Cal. (1872), §§ 692–694; Code of Iowa (1873), §§ 4112–4114.

SURETIES TO KEEP THE PEACE. — Where it is made to appear to a magistrate that there is reasonable ground to believe that a suspected person is about to commit a public offence, he may require such suspected person to give bond to keep the peace, as against the person threatened, or the public in general, and on failure to give such security, may commit him to prison until such security is furnished; and the same thing may be done in case of affrays or threats in the presence of the magistrate. 4 Bl. Com. 251; Whart. Cr. Pl. & Pr. § 80; 1 Hawk. P. C., ch. 60; *Ritchey v. Davis*, 11 Iowa, 124, 128. In the statutory regulations upon the subject, it is usually provided that the party can only be bound to the next term of court; *Com v. Morey*, 8 Mass. 78, but at common law it might be for a term of years. *King v. Bowes*, 1 Term R. 696; *Resp. v. Donagan*, 2 Yeates, 437. It must be, however, for a time certain; *Prickett v. Gratrex* (8 Q. B.), 55 E. C. L. 1020.

SECURITY FOR GOOD BEHAVIOR. — It was held at common law, that if it appeared to the court upon the trial of an accused person, whether he was convicted or acquitted, that there was danger of the repetition of that same offense or the commission of some other, it might, in general, cause him to furnish bond for his good behavior in the future, either for life or a definite period. 1 Bish. Cr. L. (6th ed.), § 945; 1 Bish. Cr. Pr. (3d ed.), § 229; *Page's Case*, Cro. Car. 332; *Holmes' Case*, id. 376, 378; *Rex v. Woolston*, 2 Stra. 834; 2 Hawk. P. C. ch. 47, § 11; 1 Hawk. P. C. ch. 61; *O'Connell v. The Queen*, 11 Cl. & Fin. 155, 251; *Bamber v. Com.* 10 Penn. St. 339. Such was definitely decided by the court of England to be the rule in case of conviction of misdemeanor; *Dunn v. The Queen* (12 Q. B.), 64 E. C. L. 1032 and note.

VAGRANTS, ETC. — It was provided by statute in England (34 Edw. III, ch. 1) that persons not of good fame, vagrants, vagabonds, etc., might be arrested and put under bond to keep the peace, and such provisions, more or less elaborate, are found in nearly all states. 4 Bl. Com. 256; 2 Hale, P. C. 136 and note [2].

WHAT IS A BREACH OF SUCH BONDS. — There is little certainty as to what is to be regarded as a breach of such bonds. The term "breach of the peace" used in a statute of different import was held to cover all indictable offences; *Rawlins v. Ellis*, 16 M. & W. 172, and see *Pearce v. Atwood*, 13 Mass. 324, 347; 1 Bish. Cr. Pr. (3d ed.) § 264, n. In one case a libel was held to be a breach of the bond for good behavior; *Resp. v Cobbet*, 3 Yeates, 93; see also 1 Hawk. P. C. ch. 60, §§ 20-27. Punishment for a breach of the peace while under bond does not bar an action for the forfeiture; *Com. v. Braynard*, 6 Pick. 113.

BY FEDERAL AUTHORITY. — The statutes of the United States contain a provision authorizing United States judges and commissioners, and the various magistrates of the state, acting in behalf of the United States, to hold to security of the peace and good behavior in cases arising under the constitution and laws of the United States in the same manner as magistrates may do under the laws of the state. R. S. § 727.

SUPPRESSION OF RIOTS. — Under the same head of preventive regulations may be mentioned the provisions for suppressing and dispersing riots and tumultuous assemblies, it being generally enacted that it shall be the duty of magistrates and peace officers to go as near as may be to such gatherings and command the persons assembled to disperse, and on their failure to do so may arrest them, and for that purpose command the aid of those present, or the whole power of the county. 4 Bl. Com. 142.

PROCEEDINGS IN THE PUNISHMENT OF PAST OFFENCES.

How Divided. — The whole proceeding from first to last, by which the penalty of the law is enforced against a person who has committed a crime, may be divided into five steps: First, the proceedings by which the accused is taken and held in custody, for the purpose of bring him within the jurisdiction of the court, which may be all considered under Arrest and Preliminary Examination. Second, the Method of Accusation. Third, the form of the allegations by which the charge is made and denied, or The Pleadings. Fourth, the proceedings in court for the determination of the question thus raised, or The Trial; and Fifth, the proceedings for the infliction of whatever punishment, if any, may be adjudged upon the trial, or, in a general sense, The Execution.

ARREST AND PRELIMINARY EXAMINATION.

Object of Preliminary Proceedings. — The arrest of a person charged with crime may be made, either before formal proceedings in court are commenced for his trial, and for the purpose of preventing his escape until time for trial, or after such proceedings are commenced, and for the purpose of giving the court jurisdiction over him. In the latter case the fact that proceedings for trial are commenced in due form is sufficient ground for his arrest and detention in custody during the pendency of the proceedings. In the former case, there must be some formal action by a magistrate upon complaint made and evidence in support thereof showing reasonable ground to believe that the person charged has committed some offence for which he may, in due course of law, be put upon trial. The proceeding to determine whether a person shall be held, or bound over, as it is called, to await trial, is a preliminary examination and is before a magistrate, while the trial itself is an entirely separate proceeding and is before a court, although as to minor offences it may happen that the final trial is before the same officer as a court, who, as a magistrate, has already conducted the preliminary examination in the same case.   In other words, the term magistrate is one applied to various officers, such as judges, justices of the peace, mayors, etc., while acting in relation to the arrest and preliminary examination of those charged with crime.   This whole preliminary proceeding is merely auxiliary, to secure the presence of defendant when a prosecution may be regularly commenced in court, and therefore is not essential in any way to the regularity or validity of a prosecution, which may be commenced without such preliminary examination (unless, possibly, in a few states the statutes may render a preliminary proceeding essential).   On the last point, see 1 Bish. Cr. Pr. (3d Ed.) § 239, a.

Information and Warrant.

PRELIMINARY INFORMATION OR COMPLAINT. — To authorize the magistrate to proceed to a preliminary examination, there must be laid before him a sworn statement, in such form as the statutes or practice of the particular state may require, charging the person accused with the commission of a crime, specifying it with sufficient particularity.   How specific this charge must be, it is not easy to say.   Perhaps it is not subject to the strict rules applying to indictments, which are to be hereafter considered.   The requirements under various statutes may be different; but it ought to state facts showing the commission of some offence and also state, at least a belief on the part of the complainant that the accused committed it.   1 Bish. Cr. Pr. (3d Ed.) § 230; *Housh v. People*, 75 Ill. 487.

It may be quite important to the magistrate that the complaint be sufficiently specific, otherwise he may be civilly liable in damages for proceeding thereon, but a defect therein could hardly affect the legality of subsequent proceedings if the magistrate should find sufficient ground to bind the accused over.   The magistrate may also be required to have other evidence, aside from this sworn statement, to authorize him to act thereon, but this is not usual.

This preliminary information or complaint is not to be confounded with an information or complaint upon which an accused is put upon trial.

It may be provided in special cases that the complaint can only be made by a person bearing some particular relation to the crime (e. g. see *State v. Wilson*, 22 Iowa, 364) but in general the information or complaint may be sworn to, either by the injured person, or any one else conversant with the facts. The person swearing to it is called the informer, or prosecuting witness, but has no other control over the proceeding than to set it in motion.

WARRANT OF ARREST. Upon the presentation of a sufficient preliminary information or complaint to the magistrate, he issues a written order, technically call a warrant, to a peace officer (or, at common law, it may be to any person by name) commanding him to arrest the person against whom the charge is made, and this warrant is the legal authority to the officer to proceed. As we shall see, however, arrests may, under some circumstances, be made by an officer or even a private person, on his own motion, without a warrant and before any complaint is filed. In such cases information or complaint must be made as soon as practicable and before further proceedings, but a warrant need not issue, as its purpose, the arrest of accused, has already been accomplished. By common law, and usually by statute, a magistrate may, by warrant or even by verbal order, command the arrest of a person committing an offence in his presence or within his personal knowledge, but probably an information or complaint ought to be filed in most states before the preliminary examination is proceeded with. For history of warrant, see 1 Stephen, Hist. Cr. L. 190.

JURISDICTION TO ISSUE OR SERVE WARRANT. — The warrant of arrest may be issued by any magistrate of the state or United States, as the case may be, irrespective of the place of commission of the crime (so it be within the jurisdiction of the state or United States, respectively), but at common law it could only be served within the territorial jurisdiction of such magistrate (in case of a justice of the peace, within his county), and the officer serving it could act only within his jurisdiction. *State v. Thompson*, 20 N. H. 250; *Blatcher v. Kemp*, 1 H. Bl. 15, n.

But a custom grew up of having a warrant issued by a justice in one county "backed" by a justice in another county where it was desired to make the arrest, and then acting upon it as though it were a new warrant issued by the justice backing it.   4 Bl. Com. 291.   This is now authorized by statute in England.   However, a provision is now often found in state statutes that the warrant of any magistrate may be served anywhere within the state without any intermediate proceeding and that any peace officer of the state may serve it, regardless of his local jursidiction.

The Arrest.

METHODS. — The following methods of arrest are recognized as lawful, under the circumstances hereafter specified: 1. By a peace officer under the authority of a warrant directed to him or to such officers in general; 2. By a peace officer without a warrant, on his own motion; 3. By any person not a peace officer, without a warrant, on his own motion; 4. By a peace officer, or person not a peace officer, on the oral command of a magistrate.   1 Bish. Cr. Pr. (3d Ed.) §§ 155-218; Whart. Cr. Pl. & Pr. §§ 1-27; 4 Bl. Com. 289-295; 2 Hawk. P. C. ch's 12, 13, and 14; 1 Stephen, Hist. Cr. L. 193.

BY PEACE OFFICER, ON WARRANT. — The ordinary method of procuring an arrest is upon preliminary information or complaint before a magistrate and warrant issued by him thereon, as above specified.   If the warrant is in regular form and issued by one of the officers having authority to issue warrants in such cases, the proper officer will be authorized to act under it and will not be responsible for anything done in its due execution, even though he may know that it was procured for an improper purpose.   Neither will the officer be liable for acting under a warrant which is merely irregular, not void; but, if the warrant is void, for instance, if the person issuing it is not duly authorized to issue warrants, or the like, it will be no authority or protection to the officer for acts done under it, even in good faith.   *State v. Weed*, 21 N. H. 262, 1 Lead. Cr. Cas. 202 and note, 220; *Rafferty v. People*, 69 Ill. 111, 18 Am. Rep. 601; *Cooper v. Adams*, 2 Blackf. 294.

By Officer Without Warrant. — A peace officer without a warrant, may arrest any person committing in his presence any felony, or breach of the peace, or any person whom he has *good reason to believe* guilty of a *felony. Com. v. Carey*, 12 Cush., 246; *State v. Underwood* (Mo.), 13 Rep. 726; *Doering v. State*, 49 Ind. 56, 19 Am. Rep. 669; *Ledwith v. Catchpole*, 1 Lead. Cr. Cas. 195 and note, 197; 1 Albany Law Jour. 86, 149; *Kindred v. Stitt*, 51 Ill. 401; *Davis v. Russell*, (5 Bing. 354) 15 E. C. L. 618; *Rohan v. Sawin*, 5 Cush. 281; *Hobbs v. Branscomb*, 3 Campb. 420; *McLennon v. Richardson*, 15 Gray, 74; *Danovan v. Jones*, 36 N. H. 246.

By Private Person. — The rule at common law as to arrests by persons not peace officers and not acting under a warrant or the authority of an officer, seems to have been that such a person might arrest any one committing *in his presence* any felony or breach of the peace, and perhaps this right extended to any offences committed in the presence, though this is not clear. Further, such person might, in case of a *previous felony actually committed,* arrest one whom he had reasonable ground to believe guilty thereof. *Handcock v. Baker*, 2 Bos. & P. 260; *Brooks v. Com.* 61 Penn. St. 352; *Keenan v. State*, 8 Wis. 132; *Price v. Seeley*, 10 Cl. & Fin. 28, 1 Lead. Cr. Cas. 177, and note 183; 1 Albany Law Jour. 28; *Wrexford v. Smith*, 2 Root, 171.

In case of a past felony, to justify a person for acting without a warrant it must be shown that a felony was *actually* committed, and that the person arresting had reasonable ground for believing that the person arrested was guilty thereof. *Holley v. Mix*, 3 Wend. 350; *Burns v. Erben*, 40 N. Y. 463; *Reuch v. McGregor*, 32 N. J. Law, 70; *Allen v. Wright*, (8 Carr. & P. 522) 34 E. C. L. 870.

It is only in case of a felony that an arrest without warrant is justifiable after the offence is over. In case of affray or breach of the peace, the arrest without a warrant by an officer or private person present must be made at once or on quick pursuit. *Phillips v. Trull*, 11 Johns. 486; *Fox v. Gaunt*, (3 Barn. & Ad. 798) 23 E. C. L. 349; *Shanley v. Wells*, 71 Ill. 78; *Hanway v. Boultbee*, (4 Carr. & P. 350) 19 E. C. L. 549.

Where the proper ground for an arrest without warrant for a past felony exists, the right to make such arrest does not depend upon whether there is danger of escape of the person to be arrested before a warrant can be procured. *Wade v Chaffee*, 8 R. I. 224, 5 Am. Rep. 572; *Halley v. Mix*, 3 Wend. 350.

By statutory provision in England and in the several states, and also by municipal ordinances, the authority of officers and private persons to make arrests on view, without warrant, is much enlarged. For example, see *White v. Kent*, 11 Ohio St. 550; *Roberts v. State*, 14 Mo. 138; *Main v. McCarty*, 15 Ill. 441; *Danovan v. Jones*, 36 N. H. 246; *Wolf v. State*, 19 Ohio St. 248, 258.

ARREST WITHOUT WARRANT IN GENERAL. — It has been expressly decided that an arrest as above specified by a private individual or an officer, is not in violation of constitutional guaranties. *Mayo v. Wilson*, 1 N. H. 54; *Wakely v. Hart*, 6 Binn. 316; *Rohan v. Sawin*, 5 Cush. 281.

BY VERBAL ORDER OF MAGISTRATE. — For any offence committed in his presence, the magistrate may, on view, by oral command, direct any peace officer or other person to arrest the offender, and such command dispenses with with the necessity for a warrant, and the proceedings preliminary thereto; for a warrant would be useless after the arrest is effected; but aside from express statutory provisions it seems the magistrate cannot proceed to try or bind over without information or complaint being filed. *O'Brien v. State*, 12 Ind. 369; *Tracy v. Williams*, 4 Conn. 107; *Holcomb v. Cornish*, 8 Conn. 375; *Lancaster v. Lane*, 19 Ill. 242; *Com. v. McGahey*, 11 Gray 194; 2 Hale, P. C. 86.

DISPOSITION OF PRISONER. — When the arrest is by warrant, the officer should, as soon as practicable, take the prisoner before the magistrate, and a failure to do so will render the arrest a trespass. *Tubbs v. Tukey*, 3 Cush. 438. If the arrest is by an officer without a warrant, he may detain the prisoner for such time as is necessary to bring him before a magistrate and allow a complaint to be filed; and may in the

meantime put him in jail (*Com. v. Deacon*, 8 S. & R. 47); any unnecessary delay, however, will render the officer a trespasser *Burke v. Bell*, 36 Maine 317. If the arrest is by a private person, he should proceed at once with him before a magistrate, or he may give him into the custody of a peace officer, to be taken before a magistrate, but in either case must make complaint.

SEIZING PROPERTY. — A person making a lawful arrest is authorized to take, not only the person, but also any articles of personal property found in his possession which are the fruits of the crime, or which have been used in its commission, that they may be used as evidence against the prisoner, and, if taken from the rightful owner, may be restored. Such property is to be put in the custody of the court or magistrate, to be disposed of as directed. 1 Bish. Cr. Pr. (3d Ed.) §§ 210–212.

SEARCH WARRANT. — As an assistance in procuring evidence of the commission of a crime, or recovering property taken in the commission of such crime, magistrates have authority to issue search warrants, authorizing the officer to whom they are directed to search a certain place for certain property, the place and the property being specifically described. General warrants were illegal, even at common law, and the federal and most state constitutions specially forbid them and provide that the people shall be secure against unreasonable searches and seizures, and that search warrants shall issue only upon probable cause, supported by oath. (U. S. Const. Am. IV.) The practice, therefore, is to issue them only upon a sworn affidavit or complaint, specifying the crime committed, the place to be searched, and, the property to be seized. 1 Bish. Cr. Pr. (3d Ed.) §§ 240–246; Whart. Cr. Pl. & Pr. §§ 22–26; 2 Hawk. P. C. ch. 13, §§ 10, 17, notes (2) & (6); 2 Hale, P. C. 150; *Robinson v. Richardson*, 13 Gray, 454.

WHEN ARREST MAY BE MADE. — The arrest may be made on any day, and at any hour of the day or night. *State v. Smith*, 1 N. H. 346; 1 Lead. Cr. Cas. 225.

WHERE ARREST MAY BE MADE. — The maxim that every man's house is his castle has no application to criminal arrests.

The officer or private person, under circumsances justifying an arrest by him, may break and enter any building, even a dwelling, for the purpose of arresting a person whom he has good reason to believe therein, even though the person sought is not there, provided he act in good faith and first demand admittance, stating his object. A person called upon by the officer to assist him has the same power as the officer while so engaged. *Barnard v. Bartlett,* 10 Cush. 501; *Com. v. Irwin,* 1 Allen, 587; *Com. v. Tobin,* 108 Mass. 426; 1 East P. C. 322.

WHAT CONSTITUTES ARREST. — The rule is that in order to constitute an arrest there must be some act on the part of the officer or person arresting which, if he were not making a lawful arrest, would amount to a trespass upon the person of the one arrested. Mere words will not constitute an arrest. But a touch of the finger may be sufficient. *Genner v. Sparks,* 1 Salk. 79; S. C. 6 Mod. 173.

It is often important to determine whether what the law regards as a technical arrest has been effected or not. If once effected, the officer may thereafter prevent escape by whatever force is necessary, even to the extent of taking life; but up to the point of effecting arrest he can only proceed to such extremity in case of felony. (See *ante,* p. 63.) Further, it is a crime in itself to escape after arrest, but not to escape from an officer seeking to make an arrest. The arrest is considered effected when the person seeking to make it lays his hand upon the person to be arrested, for the purpose of arresting him, though he may not succeed in stopping and holding him. *Whithead v. Keyes,* 3 Allen, 495.

But no force, nor even touching, is necessary if the officer have the present purpose and ability to effect the arrest, and the other party, knowing these facts, submits thereto. *Emery v. Chesley,* 18 N. H. 198; *Pike v. Hanson,* 9 N. H. 491; *Mowry v. Chase,* 100 Mass. 79.

METHOD OF ARREST. — The person proceeding to make an arrest must inform the one to be arrested of his intention, the cause of the arrest, and his authority, if he is acting under warrant or in official capacity. If under a warrant he must have it in his possession and show it if demanded. But the production and examination of the warrant need not precede the exercise of official authority to compel submission. *Com. v. Cooley*, 6 Gray, 350.

All that seems necessary to entitle the person attempting an arrest to the protection of the law is that he is proceeding upon a proper occasion and with no more force than necessary for the purpose, and that the person to be arrested know, or have reasonable ground to know, the intention with which he is acting. *Roberts v. State*, 14 Mo. 138, 144. This knowledge may be brought home to the person to be arrested in various ways. If the person attempting the arrest is a private person he must in some manner have announced his intention, but if the person sought to be arrested has committed a crime and is fleeing from fresh pursuit he may well be held to understand that the object of his pursuers, even though not announced, is to effect arrest. *People v. Pool*, 27 Cal. 572.

If the person seeking to make the arrest is an officer, the knowledge of that fact by the person to be arrested, either from general repute, or from his wearing a well known uniform or badge of office, will be sufficient without any formal announcement by him of that fact. *Wolf v. State*, 19 Ohio St. 248, 259; *Com. v. Tobin*, 108 Mass. 426; 1 Hale. P. C. 465, note.

The question whether the person arresting was properly acting in making the arrest, is often very important. Resistance to lawful arrest, in proper manner, is a crime, and death caused in making such resistance is murder (*ante*, p. 71); but resistance to unlawful arrest is justifiable to any extent short of taking life, and death caused thereby is only manslaughter (*ante*, p. 78). On the other hand, one making a lawful arrest may overcome resistance with any necessary force, even to taking life, though in pursuit he can only take life in case of felony (*ante*, p. 63), while if he take life in unlawful arrest, it is murder; and manslaughter if the arrest be lawful but the manner of making it is unlawful (*ante*, p. 77). Hor. & T. Cas. 713.

PURSUIT AFTER ESCAPE. — If the prisoner escape after arrest upon warrant, he may be re-arrested upon the same warrant at any time, but if the escape be from arrest without warrant, pursuit must be made at once or a re-arrest cannot be lawfully made where the original arrest without warrant was for an offence less than felony.   If pursuit be made at once, the same authority which justified the original arrest will warrant the re-arrest: *Com. v. McGahey*, 11 Gray 194; *Cooper v. Adams*, 2 Blackf. 294.

AMOUNT OF FORCE. — The force to be used is all that is necessary to effect the purpose and overcome any resistance that may be made; but if more force is used than necessary the person arresting will be guilty of trespass.   *Wright v. Keith*, 24 Maine 158; *Murdock v. Ripley*, 35 Maine 472.

PERSONS EXEMPT FROM ARREST. — In the constitution of the United States and those of most states are found provisions exempting members of congress or the legislature from arrest during the sessions of their respective houses, and in going to or returning from the same, except in cases of treason, felony, and breach of the peace.   But these exceptions are considered to include all criminal offences, so that the exemption amounts only to a privilege from arrest in civil cases.   1 Story, Const. § 865; *Coffin v. Coffin*, 4 Mass. 1, 29.   And the provisions of the federal statutes exempting United States officers from arrest or detention while in the discharge of their duties (as in case of persons transporting the mail) go no further.   *U. S. v. Kirby*, 7 Wall. 482; *Penny v. Walker*, 64 Maine 430.

Foreign ambassadors and ministers, with the persons composing their families and suits are entirely exempt even from criminal arrest.   Wheat. Int. Law §§ 224–226.

EFFECT OF ILLEGAL ARREST. — The difference in the positions of the parties in case of legal and illegal arrest has already been pointed out.   Moreover, for an illegal arrest the magistrate issuing the warrant, if wrongfully issued, and the officer serving it, if wrongfully served, and the person causing the arrest, if it be without a warrant and without proper grounds, are each liable to an action for tort.   But the fact that the method of arrest is illegal will not entitle the prisoner to release if any ground appear upon which he might lawfully have

been arrested and held in custody. The defect in the preliminary proceedings does not render the whole action erroneous and the proceedings void from the beginning as in a civil case. Whart. Cr. Pl. & Pr. § 27; *In re Noyes,* 17 Alb. L. Jour. 407.

Fugitives from Justice.

EXTRADITION OF OFFENDERS. — As by the law of nations a person committing a crime within the territorial jurisdiction of one sovereignty and escaping into that of another cannot be followed up and arrested by the sovereignty under which the crime was committed, and cannot be tried by that to which he has escaped, justice would frequently, in this era of rapid transit, be balked if there were not some arrangement among nations by which offenders escaping from one to the other might be returned by the latter to the former for trial. The right of one sovereignty to demand back an escaped criminal from another sovereignty was not recognized, perhaps, at common law, and is now secured among most civilized nations by extradition treaties, which provide, as may be agreed, in what cases such surrender shall be made, and what steps shall be pursued to secure the surrender. In general, however, extradition is not provided for in case of political offences. 2 Stephen, Hist. Cr. L. 65; 17 Am. L. Rev. 315; Wheat. Int. Law §§ 115–120; 1 Bish. Cr. Pr. (3d Ed.) § 224; Whart. Cr. Pl. & Pr. §§ 38–58.

The question whether an offender having been surrendered under one criminal charge, may rightfully be tried for a different one, has been somewhat discussed. The answer must be found usually in a construction of the provisions of the particular treaty under which the surrender is made; but in general it seems to be considered that he cannot be tried for another offence, at least, not for one which would not have been a ground on which his surrender could have been secured under the treaty, and the right not to be be tried for such an offence is a privilege which may be insisted upon by the prisoner and will be recognized by the courts. 10 Am. L. Rev.

617; *U. S. v. Watts*, 4 Cr. L. Mag. 64; *Com. v. Hawes*, 13 Bush. (Ky) 697, 6 Cent. L. Jour. 350; *Adriance v. Lagrave*, 59 N. Y. 110, 17 Am. Rep. 317; *State v. Ross*, 21 Iowa, 467; 1 Kent Com. 38; 1 Bish. Cr. Pr. (3d Ed.) § 224 b.

Congress has the sole power to provide for and regulate the demand for and surrender of fugitives from justice as between this and foreign countries, and the states have no power to make such provisions nor surrender persons found within their limits. *People v. Curtis*, 50 N. Y. 321, 10 Am. Rep. 483; *Holmes v. Jennison*, 14 Pet. 540.

FUGITIVES FROM JUSTICE AS BETWEEN STATES. — As the states stand toward each other in regard to their jurisdiction in the relation of foreign nations, the ends of justice would often be defeated if there were not, as between them, some method of extradition. In place of extradition treaties between each other, which they would have no power to make, there is a provision of the federal constitution to the same end, applicable to all. "A person charged in any state with treason, felony, or other crime, who shall flee from justice and be found in another state, shall, on demand of the executive authority of the state from which he fled, be delivered up, to be removed to the state having jurisdiction of the crime." U. S. Const. Art. IV, § 2. On the general subject, see 1 Bish. Cr. Pr. (3d Ed.) §§ 219–224; Whart. Cr. Pl. & Pr. §§ 28–38.

FOR WHAT CRIME. — The expression "other crime" in the above provision is held to mean any act which is a crime by the laws of the state from which the person has fled, whether it is a crime by the laws of the state from which he is demanded or not. *Brown's Case*, 112 Mass. 409, 17 Am. Rep. 114; *Kentucky v. Dennison*, 24 How. 66, 99–103; *In re Clark*, 9 Wend. 212, 222; *People v. Brady*, 56 N. Y. 182, 188; *In re Voorhees*, 32 N. J. Law, 141.

WHAT CONSTITUTES A "FLEEING." — Merely to depart from the state where the crime is committed, and go to another state, even though the latter be the place of domicil, constitutes a fleeing within the constitutional provision. *Kingsbury's Case*, 116 Mass. 223; *In re Voorhees*, 32 N. J. Law, 141. But a person cannot be said to have fled from a state where he has committed a crime, if he was never in such state, as in a case of crime committed by means of a letter, or an agent, and in such case he cannot be demanded by the state where the crime was committed. *Jones v. Leonard*, 50 Iowa, 106, 32 Am. Rep. 116; *Hartman v. Aveline*, 63 Ind. 344, 30 Am. Rep. 217.

How CHARGED. — The constitutional provision contemplates a surrender only in case of a "crime charged" in the state where committed. Hence before the demand can be made proceedings must have been commenced whereby the offender is charged with the commission of the crime. The method provided by common law, and in most of the states, for charging a person with a crime, is either by indictment, or by sworn information or affidavit. If the charge is by information or affidavit, it must be actually filed as a step in the proceedings for trial of the person charged, in a court having jurisdiction to try the offence charged, upon such complaint. A preliminary information or complaint which merely charges a crime for the purpose of securing the offender's arrest and detention to await proceedings for his trial, is not sufficient. 3 Cr. L. Mag. 792.

METHOD OF PROCEDURE. — Congress has by statute provided that upon demand made upon the executive authority of one state to which a criminal has fled, by the executive authority of another state, for the surrender of a fugitive from justice from that state, and the production of a copy of an indictment found or an affidavit made before a magistrate of such latter state, charging such person with a crime, and certified as authentic by the governor thereof, it shall be the duty of the executive authority of the state to which the offender has fled, to cause him to be arrested and delivered up to the agent of the executive authority making demand; and such agent is empowered to transport him to the state from which he fled. U. S. Rev. Stats. §§ 5278, 279. This demand by the one governor upon the other is called a requisition. There is nothing in the federal constitution or statutes specifying that a governor shall issue a requisition when requested or when the proper steps have been taken, and it would seem that this is a matter which, as between the governor and any one asking a requisition, may be regulated by state statute. As to the general procedure, see 3 Cr. L. Mag. 787.

ACTION UPON THE DEMAND. — It is the duty of the governor upon whom demand is made to look into the indictment or affidavit which accompanies the requisition, far enough to see whether a crime is substantially charged therein, but he is not to determine judicially whether such indictment or affidavit would be technically sufficient to put the party on his defence in the state from which demand is made; and he cannot hear evidence as to whether the party is guilty or not of the crime charged. *In re Perry*, 2 Cr. L. Mag. 84 and note; *In re Voorhees*, 32 N. J. Law 141; *In re Manchester*, 5 Cal. 237; *Kingsbury's Case*, 106 Mass. 223; *Com. v. Dennison*, 24 How. 66, 106.

It is sometimes provided by state statutes, or assumed without express provision, that the governor may, before surrendering the alleged fugitive, require some proof outside of the requisition and the accompanying certified copy of proceedings in the other state, such as that the person demanded actually fled from the state where the crime was committed (*i. e.* was in the state and fled therefrom, instead of committing the crime from without the state by an agent or otherwise), or that the demand was for the good faith purpose of trying the offender, and not of securing his return to the state for some other purpose, or that proceedings were commenced with due diligence. But the better opinion seems to be that no discretion is given to the governor by the federal constitution and statutes, and that the facts required to be shown by the requisition and accompanying certified copy of the indictment or affidavit charging the crime, are all the facts which he can consider, and that as to these facts the statements of such documents, if genuine, are conclusive. If the federal constitution and statutory provisions enacted auxiliary thereto do not give the executive any discretion, of course a state statute cannot confer it upon him. 13 Am. Law Rev. 181; 2 Kent. Com. 32, note; Cooley Const. Law, 191; *Work v. Cor-*

rington, 34 Ohio St. 64, 32 Am. Rep. 345. But the last case holds that if it appears to the governor granting the surrender that it was asked for improper purposes, or in an improper case, he may revoke it at any time before the person surrendered is taken out of the state.

The surrender will not be made if the person demanded is already under arrest in the state from which he is demanded, for some crime against such state, or the United States. *In re Troutman*, 24 N. J. Law, 634; *Taylor v. Taintor*, 16 Wall. 366; *Taintor v. Taylor*, 36 Conn. 242.

WHETHER THE SURRENDER CAN BE ENFORCED. — As the governor of a state is not an officer of, nor amenable to, the federal government, congress has no authority to impose duties upon him; and therefore there is no method by which a governor can be compelled to act in obedience to the directions of congress in case of a demand upon him. *Kentucky v. Dennison*, 24 How. 66. But possibly it would be proper for congress to provide that the surrender be made by some officer of the United States, and that he could therefore be compelled to act. *In re Voorhees*, 32 N. J. Law, 141; *Prigg v. Com.* 16 Pet. 539.

Moreover, the state statutes sometimes direct that upon demand properly made, the governor shall cause the person demanded to be arrested and surrendered; and there seems to be no reason why, under such legislation, the governor might not be compelled to act.

METHOD OF SURRENDER. — It is not provided in the federal statute how the surrender shall be made, but the method usually provided by state legislation is a warrant issued by the governor to the agent of the state making the demand authorizing him to arrest the person mentioned and transport him from the state.

HABEAS CORPUS. — The legality of the arrest may of course be inquired into upon *habeas corpus*, but it would seem that, if the warrant recites a proper demand, in compliance with the federal statute, the court or judge hearing the case should not go behind it and inquire into the facts upon which the governor acted. His warrant ought to be as conclusive as a bench warrant in case of indictment. *Davis' case*, 122 Mass. 324; *Robinson v. Flanders*, 39 Ind. 10; *People v. Donohue*, 84 N. Y. 438; *People v. Pinkerton*, 77 N. Y. 245. Contra, *Jones v. Leonard*, 50 Iowa, 106, 32 Am. Rep. 116. If the warrant sets out the documents upon which the governor acted, the correctness of his action thereon is generally held to be subject of review by the court. *People v. Brady*, 56 N. Y. 182.

AUXILIARY STATE LEGISLATION. — The fact that there is, in many of the states, legislation supplementing the act of congress by providing when the governor shall issue a requisition and what method he shall pursue in making the surrender in a proper case, has already been suggested. Provision is also made in many states by which, before a requisition has been secured, the fugitive may be arrested and bound over before a magistrate to await a requisition, upon a showing that he is already charged in another state with a crime and that he is a fugitive from justice from that state; and such legislation is constitutional. Indeed it is claimed that the right to arrest and hold a person to await a requisition exists without statute. 18 Albany Law Jour. 166; 32 Am. Rep. 355, note; *In re Fetter*, 23 N. J. Law, 311; *In re Cubreth*, 49 Cal. 435.

It must appear, however, to warrant such detention, that proceedings have been actually commenced in the state from which the person has fled. *State v. Hufford*, 28 Iowa, 391; *Ex parte White*, 49 Cal. 433.

TRIAL FOR ANOTHER OFFENCE. — Whether the fugitive, when brought back to the state from which he fled, may be tried for any other offence than that upon which his surrender was procured, is not settled. See, however, to the effect that he may be tried for another offence, *In re Noyes*, 17 Alb. L. Jour. 407. But it seems that he cannot properly be detained under arrest in another proceeding of such nature (e. g. a bastardy proceeding) that it would not be a ground for demanding him in the first instance. *In re Cannon*, 47 Mich. 481. On same point see cases under national extradition, (*ante* p. 143).

Preliminary Examination.

OBJECT. — The prisoner having been, in some of the methods specified under the head of Arrest, brought before the magistrate and an information or complaint charging him with the commission of a crime having been filed (either before or after the arrest), it is the duty of the magistrate to proceed with an investigation to determine whether there is sufficient probability of the guilt of the prisoner to justify his being held in custody (or under bail as hereafter explained) until he can be tried. On the one hand, no person should be imprisoned, even for such length -of time as is necessary to commence a criminal action against him and bring it to trial, unless there is a probability of his guilt. On the other hand, where such probability does exist, he ought to be held to prevent escape until a trial can be had. 1 Bish. Cr. Pr. (3d Ed.) §§ 225-239; Whart. Cr. Pl. & Pr. §§ 70-79; 4 Bl. Com. 296.

HOW SOON. — The examination, therefore, should be held speedily (it was said in an old case, within three days. *Scavage v. Tateham*, Cro. Eliz. 829). It is usually provided by statute that for good cause the examination may be adjourned for a limited time, and in the meantime the prisoner may be held in custody. *Davis v. Capper*, (10 Barn. & C. 28) 21 E. C. L. 22; *Hamilton v. People*, 29 Mich. 173. Provision is sometimes made, also, for a change of venue on application of the prisoner, that is, a transfer of the case to another magistrate for hearing. The proceedings on such application being similar to those on a similar application when the prisoner is put upon trial, need not be here described.

METHOD OF CONDUCTING. — The proceedings on the examination are almost entirely regulated by statute. It is usually provided that the prisoner shall be informed of the charge against him, that he may have the services of counsel, that he may have witnesses summoned in his behalf, etc., etc. However, the constitutional provisions as to trial do not apply to such an examination. It is conducted by the magistrate without a jury. Witnesses are sworn and examined as to the facts concerning the charge made, and minutes of their testimony are kept by the magistrate or a clerk appointed by him. The prisoner usually is given the right to have witnesses examined in his behalf also, though it was not perhaps his right at common law, and it is generally provided that he may himself be sworn and testify as a witness, or may at least make a statement not under oath, but he cannot be compelled to do so.

Although the examination can only be had upon some specific crime being charged, yet it is not to be strictly limited to that particular charge. The information or complaint may be amended to charge a different crime, and if upon the whole evidence there is probable cause to believe the prisoner guilty of any crime for which he may be held for trial, the magistrate should order his detention.

It is difficult to suggest any rule as to how much evidence is necessary to show probable cause, but it need not be enough to prove guilt beyond a reasonable doubt; perhaps it need not be even sufficient in technical requirements to warrant a convction on the trial, if uncontradicted. *Cox v. Coleridge* (1 Barn. & Cress. 37), 8 E. C. L. 17; *Anonymous* (2 Car. & K.), 61 E. C. L. 845; *State v. Hartwell*, 35 Maine 129; *Linhart v. Buiff*, 11 Cal. 280; *Redmond v. State*, 12 Kan. 172; *Yaner v. People*, 34 Mich. 286; *People v. Smith*, 1 Cal. 9; *State v. Shaw*, 4 Ind. 428; *Rex v. Fagg* (4 Car. & P., 566), 19 E. C. L. 652; *Reg. v. Johnson* (2 Car. & K.), 61 E. C. L. 394; *Rex v. Green* (5 Car. & P. 312), 24 E. C. L. 581.

EFFECT OF THE PROCEEDING. — A finding by the magistrate that there is probable cause to believe the prisoner guilty, is sometimes called a binding over for trial. It is of no effect except to warrant his detention. He may, if he sees fit, refuse on such examination to make any statement or offer any evidence, or may even waive the examination entirely, and consent to commitment without a hearing, without in any way admitting guilt. A discharge on one preliminary hearing does not prevent a new complaint and hearing for the same alleged offence. *Templeton v. People*, 27 Mich. 501; *State v. Ritty*, 23 Ohio St. 562; *State v. Jones*, 16 Kan. 608; *Ex parte Walsh*, 39 Cal. 705; *Cowell v. Patterson*, 49 Iowa 514.

WARRANT OF COMMITMENT. — If the magistrate determines that the prisoner should be held for trial, he issues a warrant of commitment directing the proper officer to detain him in custody to await further proceedings according to law.

COMMITMENT OR RECOGNIZANCE OF WITNESSES. — It being important for the administration of justice, not only that the prisoner be held to await a trial if there is reasonable probability of his guilt, but also that the material witnesses for the prosecution be on hand at the trial to testify against him, it is usually provided that the magistrate, on binding the prisoner over, shall require each material witness for the prosecution to enter into a written undertaking to appear and testify at the trial; and he may even require such undertaking to be with sureties, and commit the witness to jail to await such trial on failure to give sureties. *Markwell v. Warren Co.*, 53 Iowa 422.

HABEAS CORPUS. — Upon a writ of *habeas corpus* the warrant of commitment is not conclusive, as is a bench warrant issued on the indictment by a grand jury, or the final warrant for imprisonment upon conviction, but the regularity of the proceedings, and even the sufficiency of the evidence to warrant a commitment, may be inquired into. On the hearing upon *habeas corpus* the written minutes of evidence before the committing magistrate may be looked into, but aside from statutory provision (which is sometimes made), new evidence cannot be heard. If it appears that there is probable cause to believe prisoner guilty of any crime authorizing his detention, he will not be discharged. *People v. Smith*, 1 Cal. 9; *Ex parte Granice*, 51 Cal. 375; *Snowden v. State*, 8 Mo. 483; *State v. Best*, 7 Blackf. 611; *People v. McLeod*, 1 Hill, 377; *Cowell v. Patterson*, 49 Iowa, 514.

Bail.

WHAT IT IS. — The sole object of imprisonment preliminary to, and during, a trial, being to prevent the escape of the prisoner, and not as a punishment, it is evidently in harmony with the humane policy of the law toward those accused, but not yet proved guilty of crime, to substitute some other means to secure the same end which shall be accompanied with less hardship to the accused. This end is attained by "bailing" the prisoner, that is, by delivering him into the custody of persons not officers who shall be responsible for his presence at any time required (the word "bail" being derived from a French verb meaning "to deliver"). Originally, perhaps, the responsibility of the bailors or sureties was corporal (*corpus pro corpore*), but now it is pecuniary, by virtue of a penal bond entered into by them, by which they become absolutely liable in a fixed penalty in case the prisoner bailed fails to appear at the time when his presence is required.

HISTORY. — The practice of taking bail existed at the earliest period of the common law of which we have any records, and as Sir James Stephen points out it was out of the attempt made by statute (1 & 2 Phil. & M. ch. 13) to check the improper or secret bailing of offenders, by requiring the justices admitting to bail to take and return to court the depositions of witnesses as to the offence charged, that the preliminary examination arose. Another method of releasing on security practiced at early common law, was by mainprize, so called, which has become entirely obsolete. By that method the sureties became liable for failure of the prisoner to appear as required, but they acquired no custody over him. On the whole subject, see 1 Stephen, Hist. Cr. L. 233-239; 1 Bish. Cr. P. (3d Ed.) §§ 247-264; Whart. Cr. Pl. & Pr. §§ 74-82; 2 Hawk. P. C. ch. 15; 2 Hale, P. C. 124-135; 4 Bl. Com. 296-300.

EFFECT OF BAIL. — After release on bail the prisoner is considered still in the custody of the law and may be re-arrested by the officers in case of failure to appear as required. But he is especially in the custody of his bail, and they may arrest and return him to the custody of the officers after such failure to appear, or on attempt to escape, or even on fear or suspicion of such attempt, and this arrest may be made at any time or place, even out of the state. The details of such arrest and surrender are usually fully specified by statute, and must be followed. *Nicolls v. Ingersoll*, 7 Johns. 145; *Com. v. Brickett*, 8 Pick. 137; *Read v. Case*, 4 Conn. 166; *Harp v. Osgood*, 2 Hill, 216; *State v. Beebe*, 13 Kan. 589.

WHEN BAIL ALLOWED. — In almost every state will be found constitutional provisions guaranteeing the right of bail before conviction upon sufficient sureties, except for capital offences where the proof is evident or the presumption great, and a somewhat similar provision as to persons arrested under process of federal courts is found in the acts of congress, (R. S. §§ 1015, 1016). The general rule at common law was that the prisoner had a right to bail in all cases not felonies, and that even in those cases it was discretionary with the court. *U. S. v. Hamilton*, 3 Dall. 17; *Moore v. Com.* 6 Watts & S. 314; *Lynch v. People*, 38 Ill. 494; *Ex parte Baronnet*, 16 Eng. L. & E. 361; *Anon.* 3 Salk. 58; *People v. Tinder*, 19 Cal. 540; *Reg. v. Chapman*, (8 Car. & P. 558), 34 E. C. L. 890; *Ex parte Tayloe*, 5 Cow. 39, 1 Lead. Cr. Cas. 228 and note, 256.

There are three stages at which bail may be granted. 1. After commitment; 2. After indictment or other commencement of proceedings for trial and before conviction; 3. After conviction, pending an appeal. It will be readily seen that the probability of guilt is greater at each succeeding step. Bail upon commitment is the only branch of the subject that is pertinent in the present connection, but the general doctrines are stated here and the particular points under the other two branches will be referred to in the proper connection. Before commitment on preliminary examination there was no common law right to bail, but it is sometimes provided for, in case of a continuance or other delay in the examination, and it is even provided in many states, in case of misdemeanors at least, that upon arrest in another county than that of the magistrate issuing the warrant, the prisoner shall have the right, on demand, to be taken before a magistrate of the county where arrested and be admitted to bail by him. *State v. Kruise*, 32 N. J. Law, 313.

AMOUNT AND FORM OF BAIL. — The constitution of the United States provides, as to persons arrested for crimes under federal laws, that "excessive bail shall not be required" (Am. Art. 8) and a similar provision is common in the state constitutions; but the officer or magistrate authorized to take bail must determine, in the exercise of his discretion, what amount shall be required, and the amount so fixed is the amount of the bond which must be given, with satisfactory sureties, to secure the release of the prisoner. It is sometimes provided that money to the amount of bail required may be deposited, in lieu of other security. *Evans v. Foster*, 1 N. H. 374.

WHO MAY ADMIT TO BAIL. — The question who may admit to bail must be answered by reference to statutory provisions. At common law the power was originally in the sheriffs, but afterwards confided to the justices of the peace. The rule will be different, also, at different stages of the proceeding. After the prosecution is commenced the power of letting to bail is often only in the court in which the prosecution is pending, or a judge thereof; at least in cases of felony. *State v. Walker*, 1 Mo. 389; *Com. v. Otis*, 16 Mass. 198; *State v. Nelson*, 28 Mo. 13; *Ex parte Ryan*, 44 Cal. 555; *State v. Dawson*, 6 Ohio 251.

HOW ALLOWANCE SECURED; HABEAS CORPUS. — The right to be released on reasonable bail upon commitment is one which may be secured by writ of *habeas corpus*, and in such proceeding it may be determined, irrespective of the action of a magistrate, whether the case is a proper one for bail, and if so, the proper amount, and the prisoner may secure his release accordingly. In determining the question as to whether bail should be allowed, and the amount, the court or judge can, in the *habeas corpus* proceeding, look into the evidence before the magistrate, but after indictment this cannot be done. *People v. McLeod*, 1 Hill 377, 392; *Mohun's case*, 1 Salk. 104.

At subsequent stages in the prosecution the matter may rest entirely with the court itself, or may be confided also in some higher tribunal to be exercised on *habeas corpus*. In general, the action in allowing or refusing bail is not reviewable on appeal, unless from a *habeas corpus* proceeding. *Lynch v. People*, 38 Ill. 494; *Lumm v. State*, 3 Ind. 293; *Ex parte Tayloe*, 5 Cow. 39.

FORFEITURE. — Mere failure to appear at the proper time amounts to a technical forfeiture of bail, that is, renders the

sureties absolutely liable on the bond. It is sometimes provided that if good excuse be shown for such failure the court may remit the forfeiture, and also that the same may be done if the prisoner is afterwards re-arrested, but this is usually discretionary with the court. The forfeiture of bail and recovery of the amount of the bond has no effect whatever upon the criminal proceedings, which will go on, if the defendant is re-captured or in any manner brought again into custody, just as if no forfeiture had occurred. *State v. Meyers*, 61 Mo. 414; *State v. Rollins*, 52 Ind. 168.

Method of Accusation.

INDISPENSIBLE. — There can be no legal trial without some form of accusation. A proceeding looking to final punishment as its result not founded upon an accusation would not be due process of law. Consent of the person to be tried will not give the court jurisdiction, without accusation properly made, and therefore the absence of essential requisites in the accusation is a defect which cannot be waived. Thus, an indictment presented by a grand jury cannot be amended as to substantial defects without the action of the grand jury, even by consent of the accused. (See as to amendment, *post.*). 1 Bish. Cr. Pr. (3d Ed.) §§ 79, 96–112.

The common law looks upon a criminal prosecution as a contention, and not an inquisition, although the state itself is a party; while in those nations where the civil law prevails, the inquisitorial view is taken, and the proceeding does not have so fully the characteristics of a civil action.

FORMS OF ACCUSATION. — At common law three forms of accusation on which a person could be put on trial for a crime were recognized. 1. By Appeal. 2. By Presentment or Indictment. 3. By Information. The first was a charge by a private accuser, which, in that form, has long been obsolete. The second is a statement made by a body of men specially constituted, called the grand jury, that they believe the person accused to be guilty of the crime charged, definitely describing it. The third is a charge of a crime presented by a public officer, authorized to proceed in that way. 1 Stephen, Hist. Cr. L. 244-254, 294-296; 1 Bish. Cr. Pr. (3d Ed.) §§ 130-154, 4 Bl. Com. 301-311.

The indictment was, at common law, and still is, the most common method of accusation, and unless expressly restricted, is applicable to all crimes. The information was allowable only in cases of misdemeanor. The statutes of the several states sometimes provide for a trial of minor offences upon what is called an information or complaint of a private prosecutor, before an inferior court; but such informations or complaints are not the same as informations at common law and are allowable only in summary proceedings.

CONSTITUTIONAL REQUIREMENTS. —By the fifth amendment to the federal constitution, a person cannot be "held to answer for a capital or otherwise infamous crime, unless on a presentment or indictment of a grand jury" with certain exceptions not here important; and in most of the state constitutions are found provisions preserving to the accused the right to be tried only upon indictment as to higher crimes, while as to minor crimes some other form of accusation may be provided. What is an "infamous crime" has been the subject of much discussion. It is considered as referring to the punishment provided for the crime, rather than the crime itself, and a crime punishable by imprisonment in the penitentiary is considered infamous, within the meaning of the constitutional provisions. Cooley, Const. Law, 290; *Jones v. Robbins*, 8 Gray, 329; *U. S. v. Yates*, 6 Fed. Rep. 861; *U. S. v. Baugh*, 1 Fed. Rep. 784; *U. S. v. Maxwell*, 3 Dill. 275; *U. S. v. Brady*, 3 Cr. L. Mag. 69.

DUE PROCESS OF LAW. — It being the rule at common law that accusation of a felony must be by indictment and could not be by information, it is perhaps a question as yet unsettled whether a statutory provision for trial of such crimes upon information instead of indictment would be in violation of the guaranty of due process of law in the state constitution and the fourteenth amendment to the federal constitution. *Rowan v.*

State, 30 Wis. 145, 11 Am. Rep. 559; *State v. Ledford*, 3 Mo. 102; *Jones v. Robbins*, 8 Gray 329, 342, 355; 2 Story, Const. §§ 1782–1786.

PRESENTMENT OR INDICTMENT. — The federal constitution, in using the terms "presentment or indictment," recognizes a distinction existing at common law between a charge made by a grand jury on their own motion, and by them presented to the court, and an approval by them of a bill of indictment laid before them by the proper officer. Every indictment is a presentment, but a presentment need not, by the common law, be in the form of an indictment. *Com. v. Keefe*, 9 Gray, 290. But the distinction is of no practical value, and when an accusation of a crime is made by a grand jury in such legal manner that the accused may be brought to trial thereon, it is now called an indictment. "An indictment is a written accusation of an officer, preferred to, and presented on oath as true, by a grand jury at the suit of the government." 2 Story, Const. § 1786.

In discussing accusation by indictment it is necessary to consider the organization of the grand jury, its method of procedure in investigating charges, the form and requisites of an indictment, and the method of its presentation.

THE GRAND JURY. HOW CONSTITUTED. — A legal grand jury, at common law, consisted of not less than twelve, nor more than twenty-three freeholders of the county, selected by the sheriff. The concurrence of twelve members was essential to any valid accusation by them, and the higher limit was so fixed that there might be the largest attainable possibility of finding an indictment without the possibility of its being the expression of less than a majority. These limits are not varied by statute. Indeed wherever the right to be tried only on indictment found by grand jury is guaranteed, it is understood that a grand jury of twelve is intended and a less number would not be considered a grand jury. Statutes, however, often provide that the actual number summoned shall be less than twenty-three; they also usually provide definitely as to the method of selection. 1 Bish. Cr. Pr. (3d Ed.) §§ 849–860,

4 Bl. Com. 301, 302; Whart. Cr. Pl. & Pr. §§ 341–353; *Rex v. Marsh* (6 A. & E. 236), 33 E. C. L. 143, 1 Lead. Cr. Cas. 260 and note; *Clyncard's case*, Cro. Eliz 654; 2 Burr. 1088; *Hudson v. State*, 1 Blackf. 317; *People v. Thurston*, 5 Cal. 69; *State v. Symonds*, 36 Maine, 128.

HISTORY. — It is not proposed to go into the interesting but rather obscure history of the grand jury system, further than to suggest that the institution is thought to be an outgrowth of the usage of very early times, by which the representatives of the various townships summoned to the county court seem to have been sworn to make presentment of criminals to the justices. This presentment was doubtless upon their own knowledge, and was so far conclusive of guilt that the accused could only escape legal punishment by successfully undergoing trial by ordeal of water, or later, by appealing to twelve recognitors to find the facts; and even if he was thus justified he suffered some legal disadvantage from having been presented for crime. The appeal to recognitors who at first simply testified on oath from their own knowledge, as to the facts concerning the crime charged, finally became trial by a pettit jury, and the presentment of the grand jury came to be merely an accusation, and not in any sense a finding upon, or decision of, the direct question of guilt. 1 Stephen, Hist. Cr. L. 251–260; 1 Stubbs, Const. Hist. 617–621; note in 2 Hale, P. C., 1st Am. ed. 164.

QUALIFICATIONS OF MEMBERS; OBJECTIONS.— The statutes of particular states will be found to contain provisions as to the qualifications of persons to serve on grand juries. Various causes of disqualification are usually mentioned, among them that the juror has formed or expressed an opinion as to the guilt of a party whose case is to come before them, or that he is a prosecutor, or interested in the prosecution of such party, or is an alien, or not a resident of the county, etc., etc. There may be objections, also, to the array or panel, that is to the entire body of the grand jury, on the ground of some irregularity in the method of selecting or summoning them. There are two methods for raising objections of either kind; one by challenge

to the array or the individual juror, as the case may be, which must be made before the grand jury has acted upon the particular case in which the objection is to be raised; the other, by objecting in some way to the indictment after it is found; which objection might be by motion to quash, or plea in abatement, or in some other way provided; but it seems that in the absence of any statutory provision, no objection will lie to an indictment after it is found, on account of the prejudice or other disqualification which may be made ground of challenge, even though the accused had no opportunity of challenge. *People v. Jewett,* 3 Wend. 314, 321; *State v. Easter,* 30 Ohio St. 542; 4 Cr. L. Mag. 171.

Objections of this kind, as they are preliminary matters and do not touch the question of guilt or innocence, ought to be raised as early as practicable, and if not made until after defendant has joined issue as to the truth of the matters in the indictment, cannot be made at all. 1 Bish. Cr. Pr. (3d Ed.) §§ 871–879.

CHALLENGES.— A challenge to the array, or to an individual grand juror, must be taken at the organization of the grand jury, and by a person whose case is to come before it for action, that is, by any one who has been arrested and bound over on a preliminary examination to await further proceedings. But as will hereafter appear, the grand jury is not limited in its action to such cases, and may indict persons who have not been arrested and bound over; and of course such persons would not have the opportunity of challenge. Some way is usually provided, therefore, as suggested in the last paragraph, in which such persons may object to the indictment after it is found for such grounds, among others, as would have been grounds of challenge to the array or a juror, and it is often also provided that it is only persons who had not the opportunity of challenge that can raise such objections to the indictment when found. *State v. Gibbs,* 39 Iowa, 318.

ORGANIZATION; OATH; CHARGE.—The grand jurors being in the presence of the court, those who have a valid excuse for not serving, or who are exempt from liability to such service (if they choose to interpose such privilege, which is personal and cannot be made ground of objection; *State v. Adams*, 20 Iowa, 486; *State v. Wright*, 53 Maine, 328, 344; *State v. Forshner*, 43 N. H. 89), being discharged; also all legal challenges having been allowed, and any vacancies caused in any of these methods, or by failure to attend, being filled so far as necessary, the court administers to them an oath for the faithful discharge of their duties, and also charges them specially as to what such duties are. A foreman to act as the presiding officer of the grand jury is usually appointed by the court before the oath is administered, and he is usually first sworn.

SECRECY. — One of the obligations usually imposed in the oath is to keep secret the proceedings of the grand jury; and a violation of this duty is a crime. However, where it becomes essential to the ends of justice to inquire into anything said or done in the course of such proceedings, a grand juror may be required as a witness to testify with respect thereto, for instance, in a prosecution for perjury in testifying before the grand jury. But their action cannot be inquired into before the court for the purpose of impeaching the regularity or validity of their proceedings; for instance, to show that the requisite number did not concur in the action. 2 Hale, P. C. 161 and note in 1st Am. Ed.; *Rex v. Marsh*, 1 Lead. Cr. Cas. 260, and note; *State v. Hayden*, 45 Iowa, 11; *State v. Gibbs*, 39 Iowa, 318.

PROCEEDINGS. — Being duly organized, sworn, and charged, the grand jury acts largely at its own discretion in the discharge of its duties, subject, however, to some extent, to the direction of the court. There are three ways in which criminal charges may be brought to its attention: 1. By its members on their personal knowledge; 2. By action of the prosecuting officer in laying matters before them for action; and 3. Through charges brought to its attention by private accusers. The first method is the most ancient, and the charge agreed upon in this way is laid before the court as a presentment, which need not have the formality of an indictment. It will be sufficient to authorize the arrest of the person charged, but must be embodied in a regular indictment and thus presented to the court

before accused can be tried. The prosecuting officer, who has general charge of the business before the grand jury, and is their legal adviser, lays before them the charges against persons who have, on preliminary examination, been bound over or committed to prison by a committing magistrate to await further proceedings; he may also lay before them any cases brought to his attention by private prosecutors, so far as he sees proper to do so. It is quite common for grand juries to allow private prosecutors to come before them directly, without having their cases pass through the hands of the prosecuting officer, and present charges and evidence to support them, but such practice has sometimes been characterized as improper. *McCullough v. Com.*, 67 Penn. St. 30; 4 Cr. L. Mag. 182; Whart. Cr. Pl. & Pr. §§ 332-339; 1 Stepen, Hist. Cr. L. 293.

The grand jury is usually required by express statutory provision to examine into the charges against all persons found in prison, whether such charges be laid before them or not.

INDICTMENT. — At common law, there being no public prosecutor, the indictment was usually prepared by or under direction of a solicitor employed by the private prosecutor, but in this country the prosecuting officer usually drafts and signs the formal charge on which the accused is to be put upon trial, and he may do it beforehand and present it to the grand jury, or he may do it after the case has been examined and the jury has determined as to its action. At early common law the indictment was an exceedingly technical and formal instrument, drafted on parchment, and in the Latin language. At present it is in English, and much simpler in form; but it must be in writing, and must be drawn with legal accuracy and skill. 1 Stephen, Hist. Cr. L. 273; 1 Bish. Cr. Pr. (3d Ed.) §§ 319, 340-359, 702-4.

WITNESSES. — The prosecuting officer summons such witnesses to support charges presented by him, as he sees fit, and the grand jury may, also, on their own motion, call witnesses before them. The witnesses are sworn, and examined by the prosecuting officer, or the foreman, or any other member, and minutes of their evidence are usually required to be preserved. As the whole proceedings are presumed to be without the knowledge of accused, he is not present nor represented, and has no right to testify, nor make a statement nor call witnesses in his own behalf (*State v. Wolcott*, 21 Conn. 272), but if the jury think that the charge may be disproved or explained away, they may call witnesses for that purpose, at their option. It is often required by statute that the grand jury endorse on the indictment the names of the witnesses upon whose testimony it is found, and also return to the court with the indictment the minutes of the evidence of such witnesses. These provisions are intended to furnish the accused a clue as to the evidence which he may have to meet on the trial. But the prosecution is, under such statutory regulations, allowed to introduce on the trial witnesses whose names are not so endorsed, upon giving some specified notice to accused of their names and the nature of their evidence. Whart. Cr. Pl. & Pr. § 358.

ACTION. — During the investigation of a charge the prosecuting officer may be present, and the presence of other persons, though improper (except when being examined as witnesses), will not necessarily render the proceeding invalid. But final action must be taken only by, and in the presence of, the grand jurors authorized to act upon the particular case, and the presence of any other person will render their proceedings void. *State v. Clough*, 49 Maine, 573.

Their final action is in approving or disapproving a bill of indictment already prepared, and they are said to either " find " or " ignore " the bill, according as their action is favorable or unfavorable to it. It is not requisite that all the jurors be present and acting, twelve are sufficient; but twelve must concur in the finding of a bill to make it valid. The grand jury ought to find an indictment when all the evidence before them, taken together, if unexplained or uncontradicted, would, in their judgment, warrant a conviction by a trial jury; and it would seem, therefore, that it ought to be stronger than is necessary to warrant a committing magistrate in binding a

prisoner over. 4 Cr. L. Mag. 185; 1 Bish. Cr. Pr. (3d Ed.) §§ 866, 867; Whart. Cr. Pl. & Pr. § 361.

PRESENTATION. — The fact that a bill is "found" by twelve jurors is usually evidenced by the indorsement on the back of the indictment, of the words, "a true bill," with the foreman's signature. (As to whether this indorsement and signature are indispensable, see *State v. Freeman*, 13 N. H. 488; 2 Lead. Cr. Cas. 250 and note; *State v. Magrath*, (N. J.) 3 Cr. L. Mag. 831.) The fact that the action of the grand jury is adverse to an indictment is indicated by a similar indorsement of "not a true bill," or "ignoramus," but such action does not preclude another investigation of the same charge by the same or a subsequent grand jury. The indictment properly indorsed is presented to the court by the foreman in the presence of the grand jury and the connection of the grand jury with the case is ended. 1 Bish. Cr. Pr. (3d Ed.) §§ 695–701; Whart. Cr. Pl. & Pr. §§ 368–376. If the jury have found it a true bill, the person charged may be arrested, if not already in custody. If they have ignored it, the person charged therein, if in custody or on bail, is released unless the court order his case re-submitted to the same or another grand jury.

It seems that although the grand jury may be, and by some statutes must be, directed to inquire into certain matters, such as the conduct of public officers, etc., they have no right to report to the court the result of their investigations, except by way of indictment if they find an indictable offence to have been committed. *Rector v. Smith*, 11 Iowa, 302.

NAME OF PROSECUTOR INDORSED. —It is frequently provided by statute that if the indictment is found at the instance of a private prosecutor, his name shall be indorsed on the bill, and that the costs may be taxed to him if the prosecution fails and appears to have been malicious or without probable cause. 1 Bish. Cr. Pr. (3d Ed.) §§ 690–694.

BENCH WARRANT. — Arrest in pursuance of a charge made by the grand jury through a presentment or indictment is authorized by a bench warrant, issued under authority and seal of the court; that term being used to distinguish it from a warrant issued by a magistrate. Upon the arrest of accused the court has before it the subject matter and the person, and is ready to proceed with the case according to the rules of pleading and procedure in criminal cases.

BAIL AFTER INDICTMENT. — An indictment is presumptive proof of the truth of the crime charged, except for purposes of trial; therefore, if the charge is of a capital crime, the rule is, under the usual constitutional provision, that accused is not, of right, entitled to bail; and the court will not, on an application for bail, inquire into the testimony before the grand jury, nor hear evidence *aliunde*. *People v. Tinder*, 19 Cal. 539.

INFORMATIONS.—The question as to what cases can properly be tried upon information, has already been discussed. All that remains to be said is, that in cases where information was a proper method of procedure at common law, and is not in violation of some constitutional or statutory restriction, the accusation may be made in that method, although it is considered that leave of court is essential to the commencement of the proceeding. When properly filed, a bench warrant may issue and the subsequent proceedings are the same as upon indictment. The requisites of an information as to the form of allegation, etc., are substantially the same as those of an indictment, which are now to be considered. *U. S. v. Maxwell*, 3 Dill. 275; *State v. Cowan*, 29 Mo. 330; 1 Stephen, Hist. Cr. L. 294; *Merwin v. People*, 26 Mich. 298.

PLEADING.

WHAT TO BE CONSIDERED. — The method of making an accusation has been described, but the form remains yet to be considered. The indictment (or information, as the case may be) is the first formal step toward bringing to the attention of the court the facts which, it is claimed, constitute a crime in the person charged therewith. It corresponds to the petition in a civil action, for, although the presentation of an indictment is attended with many more preliminary formalities than the presentation of a petition or declaration, yet its object is the same. It constitutes the first pleading, and the question as to what

must be averred, and the proper method of making the averments, is to be considered in connection with like questions relating to other pleadings in the case, under the general head of pleading.

The rules of criminal pleading apply equally to every form of accusation on which a defendant is brought to trial in a criminal cause. *State v. Allen*, 32 Iowa, 471.

The Accusation.

WHAT IT MUST CONTAIN. — Due process of law undoubtedly requires that the accusation, whatever its form, shall contain some statement of the crime with which the accused is charged. But in view of the forms of accusation in use at the time that our national and state governments were organized, it must mean also that this statement shall be in accordance with the general notions of pleading then existing, which required that the facts — that is, the acts or omissions on the part of accused which are relied on as constituting his guilt — shall be stated, and not merely the conclusion from such facts, drawn by the law for itself when the facts are known, that accused is guilty of some crime in the abstract. 1 Bish. Cr. Pr. (3d Ed.) § 329; 1 Stephen, Hist. Cr. L. 293; *Arnold v. State*, 52 Ind. 281, 21 Am. Rep. 174.

As the object of the accusation is, however, not only to bring to the knowledge of the court the facts, and all the facts, relied on as showing the guilt of accused, but to do so in such manner that their truth may be denied by accused and thus an issue raised for determination, if guilt is not admitted, it is evident that not only must the facts alleged be such as, if true, lead necessarily to the conclusion of guilt, but they must be averred with such directness and certainty that their truth may be readily put in issue. Whart. Cr. Pl. & Pr. §§ 115-166; *U. S. v. Cruikshank*, 92 U. S. 542, 562; *U. S. v. Simmons*, 96 U. S. 360; *State v. Rochforde*, 52 Mo. 199, 1 Green, Cr. L. R. 756.

The federal constitution gives accused the right " to be informed of the nature and cause of the accusation" (Am. Art. VI), and a similar clause is found in most state constitutions. Such provisions make necessary an adherence to the general requirements above stated. *Fink v. Milwaukee*, 17 Wis. 26. It also renders it imperative that accused shall only be convicted and punished, if at all, for the identical offence described in the indictment, and not for some other offence. *Com. v. Blood*, 4 Gray, 31.

In short, "the first principles of law require that the charge should be so preferred as to enable the court to see that the facts amount to a violation of law, and the prisoner to understand what facts he is to answer or disprove." Opinion of Lord Denman and Sir William Horn, quoted in Heard's Cr. Pl. 30.

HOW BROAD. — The accusation must therefore contain an allegation of every fact legally essential to the punishment to be inflicted. 1 Bish. Cr. Pr. (3d Ed.) §§ 79–88, 95–112; *Koster v. People*, 8 Mich. 431; *Lacy v. State*, 15 Wis. 13; *State v. Stiles*, 40 Iowa, 148.

If there are different degrees of the same crime, punishable differently, the facts constituting the degree charged, as distinct from any lower degree, ought to be stated. Thus, in case of a charge of murder, it is the better rule that the facts which constitute murder in the first degree as distinct from the second, must be alleged if it is sought to put accused upon trial for the higher degree. *Fouts v. State*, 8 Ohio St. 98, 110; *State v. McCormick*, 27 Iowa, 402, 407; though on this precise point see *contra*, *Green v. Com.*, 12 Allen, 155, 170; *State v. Verrill*, 54 Maine, 408; *Davis v. State*, 39 Md. 355, 2 Green, Cr. L. Rep. 381.

However, facts which do not affect the nature or degree of the crime, but may be taken into consideration by the court in guiding its discretion within limits allowed in affixing the punishment to be inflicted, need not be alleged, nor need matters of defence be anticipated and negatived. If the facts stated in the indictment show a completed crime, it is sufficient. *State v. Fuller*, 33 N. H. 259.

CERTAINTY. — Lord Coke makes a threefold division of certainties, as he calls them, in pleadings: F rst, to a common intent; second, a certain intent in general; third, a certain

intent in every particular. The second degree is sufficient in indictments, the first or lowest degree in pleas in bar, while the third or highest degree is required in dilatory pleas. The reason of the rule in the last two cases will appear when those pleas come to be considered. What is required in the indictment is that the facts be stated with reasonable precision and directness. 1 Bish. Cr. Pr. (3d Ed.) §§ 323–327; 1 Stephen, Hist. Cr. L. 280; *Com. v. Phillips*, 16 Pick. 211. The facts must be stated also, directly, and not argumentatively, or by way of conclusion or belief. *Com. v. Dean*, 110 Mass. 64; *Fouts v. State*, 8 Ohio St. 98, 121.

But where it is not any particular act, but a succession of acts, giving the person a certain character (such as that of a common scold, or a common barrator, or a common seller of spirituous liquor), which is made criminal, it not necessary that the acts be specifically described, it being the practice, or habit, which constitutes the offence. 2 Hawk. P. C. ch. 25, § 59; *Com. v. Pray*, 13 Pick. 359; *Com. v. Wood*, 4 Gray, 11; *Com. v. Davis*, 11 Pick. 432.

If essential facts are stated in the alternative, or the allegation is susceptible of two meanings, one of which would charge a crime and the other would not, the indictment is insufficient. *State v. Drake*, 30 N. J. Law 422, 427; *Vannatta v. State*, 31 Ind. 210; *State v. Dooly*, 64 Mo. 146; *People v. Williams*, 35 Cal. 671; *State v. Parker*, 43 N. H. 83; *Com. v. Grey*, 2 Gray, 501, 2 Lead. Cr. Cas. 150; *Com. v. Green*, 3 Heisk. 131, 1 Green, Cr. L. Rep. 459; *Cunningham v. State*, 5 W. Va. 508, 2 Green, Cr. L. Rep. 669 and note.

The common law required a minuteness of description, in some respects, which seems to us abused. For the causes which led to this technicality in the common law, see *McKinney v. People*, 7 Ill. 540, 548; *Lasure v. State*, 19 Ohio St. 43, 52. However, the same strictness is generally adhered to, unless expressly made unnecessary by statute. (See variance and amendment, *post.*) The following cases illustrate the minuteness required in particular cases: *Merwin v. People*, 26 Mich. 298, 12 Am. Rep. 314; *State v. Blake*, 39 Maine, 322; *State v.*

Williams, 32 La. Ann. 335, 36 Am. Rep. 272; *Arbintrode v. State*, 67 Ind. 267, 33 Am. Rep. 86; *State v. Patrick*, 79 N. C. 655, 28 Am. Rep. 340.

COMMON LAW PRECEDENTS; STATUTORY MODIFICATIONS.— An accusation according to the common law precedents is held sufficient to comply with constitutional requirements. *Com. v. Davis*, 11 Pick. 432, 438. But so far as the common law precedents were unreasonably technical, diffuse, or minute, they may be changed in accordance with statutory provision, and only the essential matters preserved. *Rowan v. State*, 30 Wis. 129, 149, 11 Am. Rep. 559; *Wolf v. State*, 19 Ohio St. 248; *State v. Corson*, 59 Maine, 137. The necessity of reform in the rules regulating the forms of indictment was forcibly urged over two hundred years ago by Lord Hale. After pointing out that owing to the great strictness required and the easy ear given to exceptions to indictments by which many offenders escape, to the reproach of the law, he says: " And it were very fit that by some law this overgrown curiosity and nicety were reformed, which is now become the disease of the law, and will, I fear, in time grow mortal, without some timely remedy." 2 Hale, P. C. 193.

But it is not within the power of the legislature to dispense with such requirements of common law forms as are essential to full, formal and precise description of the offence. *State v. Learned*, 47 Maine, 426; *Fink v. Milwaukee*, 17 Wis. 26; *Landringham v. State*, 49 Ind. 186; *McLaughlin v. State*, 45 Ind. 338; *State v. Calendine*, 8 Iowa, 288, 297.

FOLLOWING PRECEDENTS.— Although the tendency is to do away with the extreme subtlety and nicety formerly characterizing pleadings, (*McKinney v. People*, 7 Ill. 540, 548; *Com. v. Woodward*, 102 Mass. 155) yet, except so far as statutory provisions, either general or special, may require or authorize a change, it is still the practice, commended by the courts, to adhere to old forms, for the sake of uniformity and certainty. *Rex v. Marsden*, 4 M. & S. 164, 168; *Rex v. Stevens*, (5 B. & C. 246) 11 E. C. L. 448; *Com. v. Keefe*, 9 Gray, 290.

Formal Parts.

VENUE. —At the beginning of the indictment or information, in the left margin, it was usual to insert the venue, consisting of the name of the county, followed by the words
" to-wit," thus :

HAMPSHIRE }
   to-wit: }

the object being to indicate the local jurisdiction of the court
to which the indictment is returned. It is necessary afterward
to so allege the facts stated in the indictment as that it shall
appear the offence charged was committed within such territorial jurisdiction. After the name of the county has thus
been mentioned in the margin it may afterward be referred to
in the caption as " the county aforesaid." But if the name of
the county is properly set out in the caption of the indictment
the failure to insert it in the margin is not a defect. 1 Stephen,
Hist. Cr. L. 276; *Com. v. Quin*, 5 Gray, 478; *Com. v. Desmond*,
103 Mass. 445; *Reg. v. O'Connor* (5 Q. B.) 48 E. C. L. 16;
Reg. v. Albert, id. 37; *Reg. v. Stowell*, id. 44.

In the United States it is common in the venue to mention
the name of the state and county, thus:

STATE OF IOWA,   } ss.
COUNTY OF JOHNSON. }

Some such form is often provided by statute, and it is sometimes provided, also, that when the venue is laid in the margin,
all the other allegations of the indictment shall be taken to be
made with reference to such venue, unless otherwise stated.
But these statutes do not, generally, dispense with the necessity of proving the offence to have been committed within
the jurisdiction of the court. *Com. v. Quin*, 5 Gray, 478;
Nichols v. People, 40 Ill. 395; *State v. Grable*, 46 Mo. 350;
State v. Simon, 50 Mo. 370; *State v. Keel*, 54 Mo. 182; 1 Bish.
Cr. Pr. (3d Ed.) § 385.

Unless required by statutory form it is doubtful if the name
of the state is any essential part of the venue, as the court will
take judicial notice that the county named is within the state,
just as the courts of England take notice that the county named

is within the realm. *Foster v. State*, 19 Ohio St. 415; 1 Bish. Cr. Pr. (3d Ed.) § 383.

CAPTION AND COMMENCEMENT.—An explanation of the meaning and use of these terms in the English courts would not be profitable. The caption was no part of the indictment proper, but a part of the record showing the organization of the grand jury. The commencement was simply the formal opening of the indictment in some such form as "The jurors for our Lady the Queen, upon their oaths, present," &c. In the United States the caption no longer serves the purpose that it did in England, and is sometimes blended with the commencement, the whole being often regulated by statute. The following commencements will serve as examples of the usual form, with minor variations. If a formal venue is used the commencement, after the venue, may be:

"The jurors of the state of ——— in and for said county, on their oath present, that," &c.

If no venue is set out in the margin the commencement may be:

"The jurors of the county of ——— (*sometimes*, in the name and by the authority of the State of ———) on their oath present, that," &c.

It is essential that it expressly appear that the presentation is on the oath of the grand jury, and that fact should appear in each count. 1 Bish. Cr. Pr. (3d. Ed.) §§ 653-698; Whart. Cr. Pl. & Pr. §§ 91-95; *State v. McAllister*, 26 Maine, 374.

COUNTS.—As will be hereafter explained, more than one offence may be charged, in form at least, in the same indictment, and when it is desired so to do each is set out in a separate count, just as separate causes of action are set out in separate counts of a declaration. Each count of the indictment must be complete in itself, so that, without the others, it would charge a complete offence, and must have a commencement and conclusion of its own; yet statements made in one count may be incorporated into another by proper reference without being again set out in full; and the commencement of any count subsequent to the first is usually abbreviated by reference

to the first, as for instance, " The jurors aforesaid, on their oath aforesaid, do further present." Averments of qualities or adjuncts of a subject, but separate from it, made as to such subject in one count, are not, however, imported into another count merely by reference to the same subject as " aforementioned." 1 Bish. Cr. Pr. (3d. Ed.) §§ 421–431; *Reg. v. Waverton*, (17 Q. B.) 79 E. C. L. 562, 2 Lead. Cr. Cas. 157; *Reg. v. Stevens*, (5 B. & C. 246) 11 E. C. L. 448.

CONCLUSION. — At common law the indictment concluded, when for an offence not statutory, "against the peace of our Lady the Queen," to which was usually added, though not essential, "her crown and her dignity," and when for a statutory offence, "against the form of the statute (or statutes) in that case made or provided." Such a conclusion was essential to the validity of the indictment. 1 Stephen, Hist. Cr. L. 282; 1 Bish. Cr. Pr. (3d Ed.) §§ 647–649; Whart. Cr. Pl. & Pr. §§ 280–284.

When the constitutions of the various states were formed, it was seen to be necessary to substitute some other expressions for those which were common in law, and especially in criminal law, recognizing the queen (or king, as the case might be) as the representative and embodiment of sovereign power and the fountain of justice. Process, which had issued at common law in the name of the queen, was directed to run in the name of the state, the commonwealth, or the people; and so in regard to indictments it was sometimes provided that in place of the conclusion then necessary, in case of common law offences, an expression should be substituted embodying the same change in sovereignty. Thus it come about that many constitutions expressly provide that an indictment in such cases shall conclude "against the peace and dignity of the state" or with other similar forms. In this way a formal conclusion is made imperative beyond statutory regulation, although in England formal conclusions are no longer essential. In many states, however, the formal conclusion is unimportant. 1 Bish. Cr. Pr. (3d Ed.) §§ 650–652; Whart. Cr. Pl. & Pr. § 279; *Rice v. State*, 3 Heisk. 215, 1 Green, Cr. L. R. 366; *Lemons v. State*, 4 W. Va. 755, 1 Green, Cr. L. R. 666; *Cox v. State*, 8 Tex. Ct. App. 254, 34 Am. Rep. 746.

Matters of Description.

VARIANCE.—Before the rules as to' minuteness and accuracy of description required are more fully gone into, it will be proper to point out the effect of a misdescription. The pleader in preparing a criminal accusation, is between two dangers. If his allegations are not sufficiently complete and certain, his accusation may be attacked by defendant, as will hereafter appear in discussing defendant's pleadings, either before trial or after conviction. If, on the other hand, the pleader goes too minutely into details, there is likely to be a failure on the trial to prove such details at all, or there may be a discrepancy between the allegations made and the facts proved. Failure of proof is of course fatal if the allegation is one necessary to be proved; that is, if it is not surplusage within the meaning of that term soon to be discussed, or does not relate to one of those few things which must be alleged, but need not be proved. As a rule, however, where an allegation must be made, it must be proved; and it must be proved as charged and not otherwise. A discrepancy between a description in the allegation and the proof is a variance, and is equally fatal with a failure of proof, if the allegation is material, that is, not surplusage; for to warrant conviction defendant must be proven not only guilty of some crime, but of the identical crime charged, otherwise he is entitled to acquittal. 1 Bish. Cr. Pr. (3d Ed.) §§ 485-488.

WHEN FATAL. — The strictness of the common law as to the minuteness of description has already been referred to (*ante* p. 167). It was equally strict in requiring the proof to correspond to the allegations. *Burcus v. State*, 49 Miss. 17, 19 Am. Rep. 1; *Com. v. Gavin*, 121 Mass. 54, 23 Am. Rep. 255; *Brisco v. State*, 4 Tex. Ct. App. 219, 30 Am. Rep. 162.

STATUTORY PROVISIONS.— While constitutional guarantees entitle accused to a statement of the essential elements of the offence charged, and a proof of these facts as distinct from any other facts, it is universally recognized that the unreasonable minuteness of allegation and proof required by common law

is not made obligatory by the constitutional provisions, and that these strict requirements of the common law may be modified by statute. If the legislative power may say that certain allegations, previously regarded as essential, shall no longer be deemed so, it may also provide that a failure to prove them at all, or to prove them as alleged, shall not be fatal to the prosecution. *Rowan v. State*, 30 Wis, 129, 149, 11 Am. Rep. 559; *Lasure v. State*, 19 Ohio St. 43, 52; *Mulrooney v. State*, 26 Ohio St. 326; *State v. Cuningham*, 21 Iowa, 433.

AMENDMENTS. — As an indictment must come from a grand jury and cannot be found by the court, it cannot be amended by the court in any material respect; but so far as the legislature may properly declare any of the common law requisites immaterial and dispense with them, so far it may provide that the indictment may be amended by the court. *State v. Startup*, 39 N. J. Law, 423; *State v. Kelly*, 6 Cal. 210; 1 Bish. Cr. Pr. (3d Ed.) §§ 97, 98; Whart. Cr. Pl. & Pr. § 90.

As informations are filed by a prosecuting officer by leave of court, there is no reason why they may not be amended in the same manner. *State v. Merchant*, 38 Iowa, 375; *State v. Doe*, 50 Iowa, 541.

In England, where the legislative power is not trammeled by constitutional limitations, the power of amendment is so far put into the hands of the court that scarcely any variance which it does not think material is to be regarded as fatal. 1 Stephen, Hist. Cr. L. 285.

SURPLUSAGE. — Any averment without which the indictment would be sufficient is called surplusage. It does not vitiate the indictment, and a failure to prove it, or a variance in the proof with respect thereto, is immaterial. Thus, if, by striking out defective allegations, enough is left to charge a complete crime, the defective allegations may be treated as surplusage; but this cannot be properly done as to allegation not defective. Thus, also, unnecessary words and phrases may be disregarded, and also words and phrases which obstruct the sense, but which, when stricken out, leave the indictment sensible. *Com. v. Randall,* 4 Gray, 36; *Com. v. Hunt,* 4 Pick. 252; *State v. Bailey,* 31 N. H. 521; *State v. Corrigan,* 24 Conn. 286; *Com. v. Jeffries,* 7 Allen, 548, 571; *Com. v. Pray,* 13 Pick. 359; 1 Bish. Cr. Pr. (3d Ed.) §§ 477–484; Whart. Cr. Pl. & Pr. § 158.

However, if the needless averment shows that no crime has been committed, or that the prosecution cannot, for some other reason, be maintained, it cannot be disregarded, and the indictment must fail. *Dukes v. State,* 11 Ind. 557; *Rex. v. Murray,* (5 Car. & P. 146) 24 E. C. L. 496, in note.

NEEDLESS PARTICULARITY.—The doctrine of surplusage does not apply to needless particularity of description. Even though a description is more minute than necessary, or some of the terms might have been omitted, yet the proof must correspond with the description as given, and no part of it can be treated as surplusage. *Com. v. King,* 9 Cush. 284; *State v. Crogan,* 8 Iowa, 523; *State v. Verden,* 24 Iowa, 126; *Shearm v. Burnard,* (10 A. E. 593, 596) 37 E. C. L. 318; *Com. v. Wade,* 17 Pick. 395; *State v. Noble,* 15 Maine 476; *Aklenbrack v. People,* 1 Denio, 80.

VIDELICET.— The word *videlicet* or *scilicet* (contracted as "viz." or rendered in English, "to-wit," "that is to say") is used to introduce a clause stating a fact generally, by way of information, without making it a part of the description so as to render strict proof thereof necessary. If the clause thus introduced is repugnant, or for any other cause improper, it may be rejected as surplusage; if in fact immaterial, want of exact proof thereof will not create a variance; but if in fact material, so that without it the pleading would be defective, the averment must be proved as fully and exactly as if the videlicet had not been used. The advantage in laying a clause under a videlicet was to prevent its being considered a material averment unless it was necessary, and to escape the rule that a description though more minute than necessary must still be proved as laid. Whart. Cr. Pl. & Pr. §§ 122–158 a; 1 Bish. Cr. Pr. (3d Ed.) § 406.

NAME AND ADDITION OF DEFENDANT.—The name of defendant is of importance in two ways, first as securing the arrest and trial of the right person; second as enabling him afterward to show that he has already been tried for the same offence. If the wrong person is arrested, he can show that fact on a writ of *habeas corpus* or on the trial, and secure his release. If one John Smith should commit a crime and an indictment should be found properly charging the offence as committed by John Smith, but under that charge another person of that name should be arrested, the latter would escape punishment, not by showing a defect in the indictment, but by proving that he was not guilty. In short, the name under which a person is arrested and tried is not, as to the proceedings themselves, of any importance, provided the right person is brought to trial; for mere proof of identity of name between the criminal and accused will not convict the latter, nor is proof of the name of defendant required of the prosecution; the question being, whether the person on trial is the one who committed the offence. Therefore, if the wrong name is used in the indictment, but the person intended is arrested, he must take preliminary steps to attack the defect. He cannot wait until the trial and then rely for acquittal upon proof that he is incorrectly named, when the proof shows him guilty. At common law the defect must be made available under plea in abatement, to be hereafter referred to, a peculiarity of which pleading rendered a disclosure of the real name necessary, whereupon the party could again be indicted in his right name. In various states, statutes will be found simplifying the procedure by providing that when the accused is brought in to answer the indictment he shall be asked if he is indicted in his right name, and if he answers affirmatively, or refuses to give his true name, he shall be proceeded against under that name, while if he does give another name as his true one, the latter shall be substituted; but in either case the proceedings shall not be abated. The record is thus made to show the correct name if the defendant chooses that it shall. *Lasure v. State,* 19 Ohio St. 43; *State v. Schricker,* 29 Mo. 265.

NAME UNKNOWN; FICTITIOUS NAME.— If the name of the person accused is not known to, nor ascertainable by, the grand jurors, they may allege that fact in the indictment and describe him in some other way, as accurately as possible, or they may indict him under a fictitious name, the result being that of using the wrong name, as suggested in the last paragraph, which, as there shown, is not fatal to the prosecution of the right person. 1 Bish. Cr. Pr. (3d Ed.) §§ 676–680; Whart. Cr. Pl. & Pr. §§ 96–104; 2 Hale, P. C. 238; *Geiger v. State,* 5 Iowa, 484; *Jones v. State,* 11 Ind. 357; *State v. White,* 32 Iowa, 17; *State v. Brunell,* 29 Wis. 435.

ADDITIONS.— By a statute of Henry V. it was required that in prosecutions in which outlawry was awarded the addition should be made to the name of defendant, of his estate, or degree, or mystery, and of the name of his town, or hamlet, or place, and county. The addition of defendant, as it was called, became therefore very important in those cases where outlawry might be had, but as with us there is no outlawry the whole learning on the subject is useless. By legislation, if not otherwise, the addition is no longer important. 1 Bish. Cr. Pr. (3d Ed.) §§ 671–675; 2 Hawk. P. C. ch. 23 §§ 104–125.

ALIAS DICTUS.— As the name is a matter of description, and a person may be known by more than one name, it may be proper to give both, connecting them with the words "otherwise called," or similar expression corresponding to the Latin phrase *alias dictus.* 1 Bish. C. Pr. (3d Ed.) § 681.

NAMES OF OTHER PERSONS.— Whenever it becomes essential to refer in the indictment to another person than accused, the name of such person is his proper description, and should be used if known; if unknown, that fact may be stated and some other description used, but it must actually appear that the name was in fact unknown. 1 Bish. Cr. Pr. (3d Ed.) §§ 683–689; *Com. v. Sherman,* 13 Allen, 248; *Com. v. Glover,* 111 Mass. 305.

The effect of a mistake in the name of a third person is more serious than a similar mistake as to the name of accused. The

purpose of inserting the name of a third person is in some way to aid in the description of the offence charged, so that accused may be fully informed of its nature and may know what he has to meet. On a charge against a defendant of stealing the horse of A , it might be a very great surprise to him, and very unjust, if he were required to defend himself against evidence that he stole the horse of B., while no such inconvenience or injustice would follow from disregarding an error in his own name. Therefore, failure to prove the name of a third person as it is stated in the indictment, if the allegation containing it is not surplusage, is a material variance, within the rules as to variance heretofore stated, and is therefore fatal to the prosecution; and such an error in description in an indictment cannot be cured by amendment on the trial (except in so far as statutes may have changed the common law rule). 1 Bish. Cr. Pr. (3d Ed.) §§ 488, 689 b; *Com. v. Pope*, 12 Cush. 272.

NAME BY WHICH KNOWN; MIDDLE NAME. — A person may be known by some other name than his true one, and proof that the name used is one by which he is generally known will be sufficient. *State v. Lincoln*, 17 Wis. 579.

A person is presumed to have a christian name, and the initials of such name do not generally constitute a good description, but if it could be shown that he was known by those initials alone, they would perhaps be sufficient.

It is sometimes said that a middle name is not a part of the name at all, that is, that the law only recognizes one christian name, but the better rule seems to be that a middle name is part of the christian name, and if used in the indictment must be proved as charged. *Com. v. Perkins*, 1 Pick. 388; *Com. v. Hall*, 3 Pick. 262; *Com. v. McAvoy*, 16 Gray, 235; *Com. v. Shearman*, 11 Cush. 546.

The foregoing cases even hold that a middle initial is a part of the name and must be proved as laid, but most authorities hold that, however it may be with a middle name, a middle letter is no part of the name and may be disregarded. *King v. Hutchins*, 28 N. H. 561, 578; *Hart v. Lindsey*, 17 N. H. 235; *Erskine v. Davis*, 25 Ill. 251.

The additions senior and junior are no part of the name, and need not be used; and if used are probably to be regarded as surplusage. *Rex v. Peace* (3 B. & Ald. 579), 5 E. C. L. 334; *People v. Collins*, 7 Johns. 549.

IDEM SONANS. — The law pays no attention to arbitrary orthography. If a name is spelled in different ways in the indictment, or if not correctly spelled therein, the defect is not material, provided the name as there spelled may be sounded like the true name without doing violence to the power of the letters used; but if the spelling is correct, it makes no difference how far it varies from its pronunciation. The whole question depends less upon spelling than upon usage, and is for the jury. *Com. v. Jennings*, 121 Mass. 47, 53; *Com. v. Gill*, 14 Gray, 400; *Com. v. Desmarteau*, 16 Gray, 1, 15; *Com. v. Donovan*, 13 Allen, 571; *State v. Havely*, 21 Mo. 498; *Gahan v. People*, 58 Ill. 160, 1 Green, Cr. L. Rep. 704; *Parchman v. State*, 2 Tex. Ct. App. 228, 28 Am. Rep. 435.

NAME OF PERSON INJURED.— One of the requisites of the common law indictment was a statement of the name of the person injured, or that it was to the jurors unknown, but statutory provision is often made dispensing with proof of the name of such person, and making a variance therein immaterial, especially in case of acts done with intent to defraud. *State v. McIntyre* (Iowa), 13 N. W. Rep. 286; *State v. Cuningham*, 21 Iowa, 433; *State v. Maxwell*, 47 Iowa, 454.

NAME OF OWNER OF PROPERTY.— In describing property in connection with which the offence charged was committed, it is usually considered essential to proper certainty of description that the name of the owner be alleged, and proved as alleged: *State v. Morrissey*, 22 Iowa, 158; *People v. Hall*, 19 Cal. 425; *Jackson v. State*, (Wis.) 13 N. W. Rep. 448; Bish. Stat. Cr. § 453.

ALLEGATIONS OF TIME.— It is a rule of common law pleading that a year and a day for each material fact must be alleged, and that the time thus alleged for any fact must be consistent with the other allegations. It must be prior to the

finding of the indictment and must be on a possible date. But in general the time need not be proved as alleged, a discrepancy in that respect not being considered a variance. Proof of the doing of the offence charged at any time prior to the finding of the indictment (within the limit of time made necessary by the statute of limitations hereafter to· be explained) will be allowed, and will warrant a conviction. *Rex. v. Hollond,* 5 Term R. 607, 624; *Reg. v. Brownlow,* (11 Ad. & El. 119) 39 E. C. L. 87; *Rex. v. Francis,* 2 Stra. 1015; *Com. v. Doyle,* 110 Mass. 103; *Com. v. Adams,* 1 Gray, 481; *State v. Baker,* 34 Maine, 52; *State v. Hanson,* 39 Maine, 337, 340; *Com. v. Sego,* 125 Mass. 210; *State v. Offutt,* 4 Blackf. 355; *Markley v. State,* 10 Mo. 291; 2 Hawk. P. C. ch. 25,·§ 77; 1 Bish. Cr. Pr. (3d Ed.) §§ 386–404; Whart. Cr. Pl. & Pr. §§ 120–138.

In case of continuing offences, it is proper to allege their commission on a certain day and each day thereafter until a certain other day, as for instance that of the finding of the indictment; or for a definite length of time after the day mentioned. If the continuous act is one which might consistently have been committed upon a single day, it is proper to so allege it, and it may thereupon be proved on several days without creating a variance. *Com. v. Wood,* 4 Gray, 11; *Com v. Mitchell,* 115 Mass. 141; *State v. Ransell,* 41 Conn. 433; *Reg. Firth,* L. R. 1 C. C. 172.

By statute the formal allegation of time, when not material, is frequently dispensed with, and the charge that the crime was committed prior to the finding of the indictment is made sufficient.

TIME MATERIAL.— The allegation of time is not always merely formal. Some acts are made criminal only when committed within a certain period of time, or part of the year, or on a particular day of the week, or during a particular part of a day, and some acts will constitute one crime or another according to the portion of the day when committed. In all such cases the time must be so alleged and proved as to bring the case within the definition of the crime, though it is still not essential that the proof correspond with the allegations as to particulars.   2 Hale, P. C. 179; *Lehritter v. State,* 42 Ind. 383; *Com. v. Crowther,* 117 Mass. 116; *Wells v. Com.* 12 Gray, 326.

Further, where the allegation of time is not merely as to the happening of an event, but is a matter of description, it must be proved as laid; for example, where it constitutes the date of an instrument set out, or of a newspaper in which a libel is charged to have been published. *Com. v. Varney,* 10 Cush. 402; 1 Bish. Cr. Pr. (3d Ed.) § 488 a.

STATUTES OF LIMITATION.— By common law there was no limit to the time within which prosecutions might be commenced, but statutes of limitation as to criminal actions have been passed in England and in this country, requiring the prosecution of various classes of crimes to be brought within a specified time after the commission of the offence, the time being different for different crimes. Any period of absence from the state is usually excepted from computation. The various statutes must be consulted on all questions of detail. Whart. Cr. Pl. & Pr. §§ 316-329; 2 Stephen Hist. Cr. L. 1; 1 Bish. Cr. Pr. (3d Ed.) § 405.

How RAISED. — If the statute contains no exception, it is said an accusation charging an offence as committed at a time so long previous, as that it would be barred, will be defective, and may be attacked on that ground before or after verdict, but that where there are exceptions, the fact that the offence appears to be barred is no ground of objection, for the case may be brought, by the evidence, within one of the exceptions. Another line of reasoning is, that as a statute of limitation is, in itself, a general exception to all laws declaring certain acts to be punishable, therefore, within the rule as to exceptions and provisos (see *post,* p. 185), this is something to be relied upon by accused as a defence, and need not be negatived in the indictment. Of course, also, the fact that the case comes within an exception to this general exception, need not be alleged until the general exception is urged by accused. Whatever the reasoning, it is generally held that the fact that the prosecution for the offence appears to be barred, is not a ground of objection to the indictment, nor to the conviction

thereon, and that it must be raised by the accused as a defence on the trial, by special plea or under the general issue, although the contrary is also maintained. *U. S. v. Cook*, 17 Wall. 168, 2 Green, Cr. L. Rep. 88 and note 96; *State v. Hussey*, 7 Iowa, 409; *State v. Deitrick*, 51 Iowa, 467; *State v. Hobbs*, 39 Maine, 212; *People v. Santvoord*, 9 Cowen, 655; *State v. Rust*, 8 Blackf. 195; *People v. Miller*, 12 Cal. 291; 1 Cr. L. Mag. 451.

The same difficulty as to whether the statute of limitations may be taken advantage of by demurrer, or whether it must be specially pleaded, has arisen under code procedure in civil actions. Pomeroy, Remedies, §§ 713, 714; Bliss, Code Pl. §§ 205, 355, 414. It seems but natural that in criminal procedure the rule of the common law procedure in civil cases should be followed, which did not permit the statute to be raised by demurrer, rather than that of the courts of equity, which has generally been adopted under reformed procedure, and which was to the contrary effect.

If the statutory period to bar a prosecution has not yet expired, a statute may extend the time for prosecution without being unconstitutional as *ex post facto*. *Com v. Duffy*, 96 Penn. St. 506, 39 Am. Rep. 577. But if the prosecution has become fully barred, the legislature cannot revive it. *Moore v. State*, 43 N. J. Law, 203; 39 Am. Rep. 558.

PLACE. — At common law it was essential that the place of each material event be averred, and such averment must designate the vicinage, that is, the vill or neighborhood, one of the purposes of such allegation being to indicate from what vicinity the jurors were to be summoned. The allegation of the county alone was not deemed sufficient. But since the jurors are now summoned from the body of the county, and not with reference to any particular vicinage therein, it is, in general, sufficient to allege the offence as committed within the territorial limits over which the court has jurisdiction; for it remains essential that the allegations and proof shall bring the case within the jurisdiction of the court. 2 Hawk. P. C. ch. 23, § 92; 1 Bish. Cr. Pr. (3d Ed.) §§ 360–385; Whart. Cr. Pl. & Pr. §§ 139–150; *State v. Cotton*,

24 N. H. 143; *U. S. v. Reyburn*, 6 Pet. 352; *Reg. v. O'Connor*, (5 Q. B.) 48 E. C. L. 16, 31; *Rex v. Mathews*, 5 Term R. 162.

In many states are found statutes dispensing with allegation or proof of place except to bring the case within the jurisdiction of the court, unless the place be material.

WHEN PLACE MATERIAL. — When an act is a crime, or criminal to a greater degree, when done in one locality rather than another, the locality becomes material to the criminality or degree of criminality of the act, and must be alleged and proved; and the same is true where subsequent proceedings as to the place, such as its abatement as a nuisance, are asked. *Hagan v. State*, 4 Kan. 89.

. Also, the place may be made part of a description, and if the description is material, as it usually is, must be proved as laid. It is thus held as to the particular locality of the house in burglary, etc. *State v. Crogan*, 8 Iowa, 523; *State v. Verden*, 24 Iowa, 126; *Moore v. State*, 12 Ohio St. 387; *People v. Slater*, 5 Hill, 401; *Com. v. Heffron*, 102 Mass. 148; *Reg. v. Cranage*, 1 Salk. 385.

WRITTEN INSTRUMENTS; TENOR; PURPORT. — Where the offence charged consists in the writing, printing, or issuing of a written instrument, or of words of a certain character, that is, where the written (or printed) words are of the gist of the offence, the instrument must be set out in its exact language in the indictment, and must be proved as laid, the slightest variance being fatal. This rule is applicable in case of libel, forgery and the like. This is called setting out the instrument by its tenor, while in referring to it by its purport, only its general character or effect need be stated. *Com. v. Wright.* 1 Cush. 46; *Com. v. Houghton*, 8 Mass. 107; 1 Bish Cr. Pr. (3d Ed.) §§ 559-565; Whart. Cr. Pl. & Pr. §§ 169-202.

Where the instrument is not in the possession of the party pleading, or is lost, or is of such scandalous or obscene nature that it is not proper to spread it upon the records of the court, its nature alone may be alleged, with the reason for its omission. *Com. v. Holmes*, 17 Mass. 336.

DUPLICITY; JOINDER OF OFFENCES; COMPOUND OFFENCES.
— The rule at common law as to charging more than one
offence in the same indictment was, that but one offence could
be charged in the same count; but that distinct offences might
be charged in different counts of the same indictment, subject,
however, to this restriction, that felonies and misdemeanors
could not be charged in the same indictment, and further, that
where felonies were charged the defendant might require the
prosecution to elect which one of distinct offences it would
proceed upon, and the charge as to others would be dis-
missed; but where different counts are used to charge the
same transaction in different ways as constituting the same or
different offences, to cover uncertainties as to what the evidence
may be on the trial, the court will not require an election to be
made, but will confine the evidence to the one transaction.
Where an offence is compound, that is, the same acts constitute different crimes, one included within the other, they
may be charged in the same count and a conviction had upon
any one of the included offences.   1 Stephen, Hist. Cr. L. 289-
292; 1 Bish. Cr. Pr. (3d Ed.) §§ 432-462; Whart. Cr. Pl. & Pr,
§§ 243-255, 285-300; *State v. McPherson*, 9 Iowa, 53; *State v.
Shaffer*, (Ia.) 13 N. W. Rep. 306; *State v. Brannon*, 50 Iowa,
372; *Jennings v. Com.*, 105 Mass. 586; note in 2 Lead. Cr.
Cas 38.

If two offences are included in one count, but the averments
as to one are so defective as not to charge the offence referred
to, such averments may be considered surplusage and the count
will be good for the other offence. *State v. Smouse*, 50 Iowa,
43.

Where a statute provides that any one of several acts shall
constitute an offence, the indictment may charge in the same
count any number of such acts, conjunctively, without being
objectionable for duplicity. *State v. Dean*, 44 Iowa, 648; *State
v. Barrett*, 8 Iowa, 536; *Reg. v. Bowen* (1 Car. & K.), 47 E.
C. L. 501; *State v. Gray*, 29 Minn. 142.

It is not duplicity to charge, as committed against two or
more persons, an offence which is capable of being so com-

mitted, and proof of the complete offence as against one of them
will sustain a conviction. *Com. v. O'Brien*, 107 Mass. 208;
State v. Nash, 86 N. C. 650, 41 Am. Rep. 472 and note; *Teat
v. State*, 53 Miss. 439, 24 Am. Rep. 708; *Woodford v. People*,
62 N. Y. 117, 20 Am. Rep. 464; Whart. Cr. Pl. & Pr. § 286.

JOINDER OF DEFENDANTS.—All or any member of the guilty
participants in the same crime may be jointly indicted, or each
may be indicted separately. Thus, principals and accessories,
before or after the fact, may be jointly charged in the same
count. But it does not follow that they must be jointly tried,
as will appear in considering the subject of trial. 1 Bish. Cr.
Pr. (3d Ed.) §§ 463–467; Whart. Cr. Pl. & Pr. §§ 301–315.

INDICTMENTS UNDER STATUTES. — Where the offence is
statutory, as in some states all offences are, the indictment must
follow the statute and state every element which is made a part
of the statutory description. While it is not indispensable that the
exact language of the statute be used, that is the better course
when the act is therein described. *State v. Gove*, 34 N. H.
510; *State v. Beasom*, 40 N. H. 367; *State v. McKenzie*, 42
Maine, 392; *U. S. v. Cahill*, 9 Fed. Rep. 80; *Com. v. Turner*, 8
Bush. (Ky.) 1, 1 Green, Cr. L. Rep. 293; *State v. Lockbaum*, 38
Conn. 400; *State v. Hussey*, 60 Maine, 410, 11 Am. Rep. 209;
1 Bish. Cr. Pr. (3d Ed.) §§ 610–622; Whart. Cr. Pl. & Pr. §§
220–242; 2 Hawk. P. C. ch. 25, § 110.

But if the statute simply names the offence without describing it, leaving the description to be determined by the common
law (as is the method as to most common law offences in states
having complete criminal codes), it will not be sufficient to
follow the language of the statute in the indictment, but the
facts constituting such offence at common law must be charged.
On the other hand, if the facts constituting the offence are thus
charged, an error in the name of the offence will be immaterial.
State v. Shaw, 35 Iowa, 575; *State v. Davis*, 41 Iowa, 311;
State v. McIntyre, (Ia.) 13 N. W. Rep. 287.

If the statute uses general terms, the indictment must specifically describe the offence, and if any element essential to
constitute the offence which the statute contemplates, is not

mentioned therein directly, it will not be sufficient to follow the words of the act, but such essential element must be particularly set out. *U. S. v. Carll,* 105 U. S. 611, 13 Rep. 673; *State v. Brandt,* 41 Iowa, 593, 607; *Com. v. Bean,* 11 Cush. 414, 2 Lead. Cr. Cas. 172 and note; *State v. Jackson,* 39 Conn. 229; *U. S. v. Cruikshank,* 92 U. S. 542, 558.

EXCEPTIONS AND PROVISOS IN STATUTES. — An exception contained in the enacting clause of a penal statute, that is, embodied in the very definition of the thing forbidden or made punishable, must be negatived in an indictment thereon, but a proviso or exception not thus embodied need not be negatived. The fact that in the enacting clause there is a general reference to the provisions found in other portions of the statute will not render subsequent provisos or exceptions a part of the enacting clause within this rule. Where the proviso or exception is such that it need not be negatived in the indictment, the defendant relying thereon must, by proof, as a part of his defence, bring himself within its terms. See *ante,* p. 18; also, *Com. v. Jennings,* 121 Mass. 47, 23 Am. Rep. 249; *U. S. v. Cook,* 17 Wall 168, 2 Green, Cr. L. Rep. 88; *Com. v. Hart,* 11 Cush. 130, 2 Green, Cr. L. Rep. 247 and note, 2 Lead. Cr. Cas. 1 and note; *Rex v. Turner,* 5 M. & S. 206.

ALLEGATIONS OF INTENT. — Although it is a general principle that to render an act criminal it must have been done with a criminal intent (*ante,* p. 19), yet it by no means follows that any criminal intent need be alleged in the indictment. If the facts charged are such as give rise to a presumption of criminal intent (*ante,* p. 22), it is not, in general, necessary to allege any intent; and want of intent, by reason of mistake, want of capacity, or compulsion, is matter of defence. 1 Bish. Cr. Pr. (3d Ed.) §§ 521–525; Whart. Cr. Pl. & Pr. § 163 a; *Com. v. Hersey,* 2 Allen, 173; *Com. v. York,* 9 Met. 93, 114.

But where a specific intent is essential to constitute the crime, it must be alleged, and proved as alleged. *Ante,* p. 22; *Drake v. State,* 19 Ohio St. 211; 1 Hale P. C. 561; 2 East. P. C. 510.

Thus in many statutory offences, the intent is specified as an ingredient of the crime, and the indictment must charge such intent; and it may even be necessary to charge the intent more specifically than it is described in the statute. *Com. v. Slack,* 19 Pick. 304; *U. S. v. Carll,* 105 U. S. 611.

Defendant's Pleadings

MOTION TO QUASH.— At common law the court might, at any time, on motion of defendant or on its own motion, quash the indictment, that is, discontinue the proceedings thereunder, when it became evident to it that it was not sufficient to sustain a conviction. As the whole subject is a matter of statutory regulation in most states, a further discussion of it is not necessary. Sometimes the statutes supply other means for reaching such defects, and this motion is not contemplated. 1 Bish. Cr. Pr. (3d Ed.) §§ 758-774; Whart. Cr. Pl. & Pr. §§ 385-397.

PLEAS TO THE INDICTMENT.— At common law the defendant might raise an issue of law or fact upon the indictment in the following ways: 1. By plea to the jurisdiction; 2. By declinatory plea; 3. By plea in abatement; 4. By demurrer; 5. By plea in bar; 6. By plea of not guilty, or the general issue. 1 Bish. Cr. Pr. (3d Ed.) §§ 734-757; 4 Bl. Com. 332, 341; 2 Hale, P. C. 236.

PLEA TO JURISDICTION. — This plea called in question the jurisdiction of the court over the crime charged, not on account of its having been committed beyond the territorial jurisdiction of the court, which is a question of fact to be raised under the general issue, but on account of the jurisdiction not extending to the class of crimes to which the one charged belonged. This plea is not common, as the objection can always be raised subsequently in another manner. 1 Bish. Cr. Pr. (3d Ed.) § 794; Whart. Cr. Pl. & Pr. § 422.

DECLINATORY PLEAS.— If a defendant was at common law entitled to benefit of clergy he might decline to be tried at all by the secular courts; but it was not usual to insist upon this privilege until after conviction, and declinatory pleas had gone out of use before Lord Hale's time.

PLEAS IN ABATEMENT.— These corresponded in their object with pleas of same name in civil actions. They might be for

matter appearing upon the record, as some defect in the proceeding, but such an objection could usually be raised after conviction, and therefore was not generally raised before. By plea in abatement the defendant might also raise the question of fact as to whether he was indicted under his right name and addition.

DEMURRER.—If the fact stated in the indictment, if true, would not be sufficient to show defendant to be guilty of the crime charged, he might raise that question by demurrer. But the same objections can be raised after conviction, and they are usually left to be relied upon at that stage. 1 Bish. Cr. Pr. (3rd Ed.) §§ 775–786; Whart. Cr. Pl. & Pr. §§ 400–407.

PLEAS IN BAR.—That defendant had been previously acquitted, convicted, attainted, or pardoned, for the same offence was a matter to be pleaded in bar to the indictment.

PLEA OF GUILTY OR NOT GUILTY.—By pleading "guilty" defendant could confess the crime charged, whereupon the court would proceed as upon a conviction. By pleading "not guilty" the defendant denied every fact necessary to constitute the crime as charged, and under this plea he might not only disprove the facts directly alleged, but also introduce evidence of any matter of justification or excuse.

MODERN PRACTICE.—The whole subject being regulated by statute in most states, it is practicable to give but a brief outline of the lines of defence open to accused. Something corresponding to the demurrer is generally provided. If his demurrer is sustained the indictment fails, but he may be held to answer a new indictment by the same or a new grand jury. If it is overruled he may plead over. The advantage in leaving any defect which might be raised by demurrer, and urging it, instead, after conviction, is that if the conviction is found to be erroneous and set aside, defendant cannot be again tried and goes free. Pleas in abatement are usually resorted to only in cases of misnomer; and as they are dilatory in nature, the highest degree of certainty is required of the pleader, which makes it necessary that he shall point out not only the defect in his name, but also state what his name really is; whereupon, if the plea is sustained he may be indicted again under the true name thus disclosed. The plea in bar is used now to raise the question of previous conviction or acquittal, pardons before conviction being no longer granted· There were at common law many fine distinctions and much confusion, as to whether two or more pleas could be interposed at the same time, and whether after a plea raising a question of fact was adjudged against the defendant he could plead the general issue. The present rule is to allow defendant all the defences which he has, by allowing either a pleading over or simultaneous pleas. Thus he is permitted in some method to avail himself of both a plea in bar and the plea of not guilty. 1 Bish. Cr. Pr. (3rd Ed.) §§ 744–757, 775–804; Whart. Cr. Pl. & Pr. §§ 408–433; 1 Stephen, Hist. Cr. L. 297.

DEFENCES; CERTAINTY.—The practical result is, that defendant's defences are, either that he has been previously convicted or acquitted of the same offense, or that he is not guilty. In setting up these defences the lowest degree of certainty is required of the pleader, so that he does no more than state the conclusion of law in a general form, without stating the facts upon which he relies to establish his defence. What may be proved under these defences will be considered in discussing the subject of defences under the head of The Trial.

THE TRIAL.

PRELIMINARIES.—Having traced the orderly course of proceedings down to the filing of the indictment or information, and the arrest of the accused thereunder, supposing him not previously under arrest or·bail, it is now proper, after having turned aside to consider various general principles ·of pleading in criminal cases, to take up the proceedings again in their regular order. In so doing, various steps intervening between the indictment and the actual trial remain to be considered.

PRESENCE OF DEFENDANT.—In civil cases the court gets jurisdiction to proceed after defendant has had proper notice and opportunity to appear, but in criminal cases it is essential that he be brought personally within the jurisdiction of the court. It is sometimes provided that in proceedings before· magistrates or

inferior courts the defendant may be summoned, without arrest, to appear; but if he does not appear and submit to the jurisdiction, actual arrest is necessary; the proceedings cannot be conducted as upon default. The necessity for his actual personal presence at subsequent stages of the proceeding will be found in many states determined by statute, but in the absence of statute the common law rule is that at every stage of the trial down to verdict his presence is essential if the offense charged be a felony, while if it is a misdemeanor, the rule is uncertain, the matter resting, perhaps, largely in the discretion of the court. When actual presence is required, it cannot be waived nor the presence of an attorney substituted. On the other hand, even when his presence is not essential to the validity of the proceeding, he has the right to be present and no step can properly be taken in his absence if such absence is not voluntary. In any case, if the prisoner escapes from custody the trial must be suspended until he is again in custody. The presence of defendant at proceedings had upon appeal does not seem to be regarded as essential. In view of the conflict in statutory provisions and in the exposition of the common law in different states it does not seem possible to state any more definite rules on the subject; *Prine v. Com.* 18 Penn. St. 103; *Bigelow v. Stearns*, 19 Johns., 39; *People Genet*, 59 N. Y. 80; *Dunn v. Com.* 6 Penn. St. 384; *State v. Reckards*, 21 Minn. 47; *Jones v. State*, 26 Ohio St. 208; *Maurer v. People*, 43 N. Y. 1; *State v Wilson*, 50 Ind. 487; *State v. Costello*, 121 Mass. 371; *State v. Decklotts*, 19 Iowa, 447; *State v. Shepard*. 10 Iowa, 126; *State v. Westfall*, 49 Iowa, 328. 1 Bish. Cr. Pr. (3rd Ed.) §§ 265–277; Whart. Cr. Pl. & Pr. §§ 540–550.

CORPORATIONS.—As a corporation cannot be brought corporally before the court, it is necessarry, in prosecuting it for a crime, that there be some other way of acquiring jurisdiction. It is said there was a proper proceeding at common law, but statutory provisions may be made allowing service of some kind of notice, as for instance, a copy of the indictment, upon the corporation and thereupon considering it in court for all purposes of the case

See cases, *ante*, p. 48, and in addition to cases there cited, see as to criminal prosecutions against corporations, *State v. B. & O. R. R. Co.*, 15 W. Va. 362, 36 Am. Rep. 803; *State v. Atchison*, 3 Lea, 729, 31 Am. Rep. 663.

ARRAIGNMENT.—The next step after the arrest of the prisoner and his appearance before the court, is to secure his plea to the indictment, in order that the issue may be made up for trial. For this purpose he is arraigned, which consists in reading the indictment to him and asking him whether he is guilty or not guilty. The object of arraignment being to secure a plea, it may be waived by pleading without arraignment. 1 Bish. Cr. Pr. (3d Ed.) §§ 728–733 b; Whart. Cr. Pl. & Pr. §§ 699–701; 4 Bl. Com. 322–324; 1 Stephen, Hist. Cr. L. 297.

The trial can only properly proceed upon a plea. Without this there is no issue to try, and the proceeding is a nullity. *Hoskins v. People*, 84 Ill. 87, 25 Am. Rep. 433; *People v. Corbett*, 24 Cal. 328; *Douglas v. State*, 3 Wis. 820; *contra*, (under statutory provisions) *State v. Cassady*, 12 Kan. 550, 561.

RIGHT TO COUNSEL.—At common law a defendant upon trial for misdemeanor was entitled to the assistance of counsel, but upon trial for treason or felony he had no such privilege, the theory being that in such cases the court would see that his rights were protected. In the constitution of the United States and those of the various states are found provisions securing to the accused in every case the right to be assisted by counsel. It is often provided, also, that if defendant is unable to procure counsel the court shall appoint members of its bar to act in his defence; and it is the duty of attorney so appointed to act, even though no compensation is provided; however, it is usual to provide compensation by the state in such cases. In connection with the arraignment it is usual to inform defendant of his right to counsel and allow him opportunity to secure such assistance. 1 Bish. Cr. Pr. (3d Ed.) §§ 14–19, 296–313; Whart. Cr. Pl. & Pr. §§ 557–560; Cooley, Const. Lim. *330–338; *Valle v. State*, 9 Tex. Ct. App. 57, 35 Am. Rep. 719.

STANDING MUTE.—If the prisoner refused to plead, the common law provided that proceedings be had to determine whether such refusal was willful, or by visitation of God. If the former was found, he was in contempt and was subjected to severe penalties; if the latter, the trial was proceeded with as though he had pleaded not guilty. It is a usual provision of statute that in all cases of standing mute the plea of not guilty shall be entered and the trial proceed. *In re Smith*, 3 Cr. L. Mag. 835, 13 Fed. Rep. 25 ; 4 Bl. Com. 324–329 ; 1 Stephen, Hist. Cr. L. 298–301 ; 2 Hawk. P. C. ch. 30.

PLEAS.—Upon arraignment defendant may, instead of pleading to the merits, interpose any objection to the sufficiency of the indictment, or to the regularity of prior proceedings. Objections to the indictment need not be taken at this stage, as they will be good after verdict, but objections to prior irregularities, as to the constitution of the grand jury and the like, and in general matters pleadable in abatement, should be raised before pleading to the merits or they will be deemed waived, although the court may, in its discretion, allow the withdrawal of a plea to the merits and the interposition of a motion or demurrer or plea in abatement or bar. That it may be provided by statute that formal objections can only be raised at a certain stage in the proceedings, see *Green v. Com.* 111 Mass. 417.

PLEAS ORAL OR WRITTEN.—Pleas of guilty or not guilty are usually oral ; other pleas were usually written, at common law, though perhaps they might be oral at the discretion of the court, being entered of record by the clerk.

PLEAS BY SEVERAL DEFENDANTS.—If two or more defendants are indicted together, each may plead as he sees fit, and it is not necessary that they join in a plea.

TRIAL OF SEPARATE PLEAS.—The motion to quash and the demurrer raise questions for the court only. Also, the plea in abatement or in bar may raise a question of law, or a question to be determined on the record alone, in which case it is to be tried by the court. But each of these pleas, as well as the plea to the merits, may raise an issue of fact, upon which defendant is entitled to a jury trial. Issues on different pleas could not at common law be tried simultaneously, and thus it might happen that at successive steps the defendant might have successive trials; but it is sometimes provided by statutes that different issues (as for instance, former accquittal and not guilty) may be tried at the same time to one jury, thus avoiding successive trials. 2 Hawk. P. C. ch. 23, § 128; 2 Hale, P. C. 239.

SEVERANCE.—Where two or more defendants are jointly indicted, it is the common law rule that they shall be tried together unless the court in the exercise of its discretion shall, on the application of a defendant or the state, grant separate trials. Sometimes statutes give to such defendants the right to separate trials in certain classes of cases. *State v. Collins,* 70 N. C. 241, 16 Am. Rep. 771; 1 Bish. Cr. Pr. (3d Ed.) §§ 1017–1041; Whart. Cr. Pl. & Pr. § 309.

PLEA OF GUILTY.—If the defendant, being properly arraigned, pleads guilty, he thereby admits the truth of all material facts well pleaded in the indictment, and the court should proceed to sentence as upon a verdict of guilty. But the court should exercise caution in receiving such plea, and a liberal discretion in allowing it to be withdrawn if the defendant desires to interpose a defence. Of course the plea cures no defect which might be taken advantage of after verdict, and defendant may therefore object to the sufficiency of the indictment or to any fatal irregularity in the proceedings by arrest of judgment. It is sometimes provided by statute that upon plea of guilty to a crime consisting of degrees the court must examine witnesses to determine the degree. 1 Bish. Cr. Pr. (3rd Ed.) § 795; Whart Cr. Pl. & Pr. §§ 413–416.

METHOD OF TRIAL.—As has already been suggested, the earliest form of trial upon public accusation was by ordeal of fire or water, although if the accused was of good character he might have trial by oath, that is, might escape the punishment for the crime of which he was accused by producing compurgators, the number varying with the crime, who should swear that he was innocent. Trial by jury being afterward introduced, it became the custom to ask the defendant upon issue being joined upon his plea, how he would be tried, and it is probable he had the

election of trial by ordeal, that is, as was then understood, by God, or by jury, that is, by the country. As the trial by ordeal went out of use it seems the two formulas were united in one response, so that, although there was but one method of trial, the formality was still preserved of asking defendant how he would be tried, to which his response uniformly was, " By God and my country." This formality, however, as well as that of joinder of issue by the prosecution upon defendant's plea, is frequently rendered obsolete by statutes. 1 Stephen, Hist. Cr. L. 70-73, 297, 301 ; 4 Bl. Com. 342.

RIGHT TO TRIAL BY JURY.—It was provided by Magna Charta that no free man should be taken, or imprisoned, or destroyed, except upon judgment of his peers or by the law of the land. It has been supposed by some that trial by jury was implied in the term " by judgment of his peers," but is probable that such phrase was intended only to secure to the peers trial by their fellows, which right is still preserved to them in England, and that " trial by the law of the land " was all that was guaranteed to those of lower rank. However this may be, the law of the land did require trial of issues of fact in criminal prosecutions to be by jury. Consequently our federal and state constitutions all guarantee the right of jury trial in criminal cases. 1 Stephen, Hist. Cr. L. 162 ; Cooley, Const. Lim. 319 ; 4 Bl. Com. 349 ; 1 Bish. Cr. Pr. (3d Ed.) §§ 890-894.

DUE PROCESS OF LAW.—As the term " due process of law " used in the fourteenth amendement to the federal constitution is equivalent to "the law of the land," as used in Magna Charta, and as the law of the land required jury trial in criminal cases, it is doubtful whether a state could, even by constitutional provision, dispense with that form of trial in such cases without interfering with the guaranties contained in that amendment, which is a limitation upon the powers of the states. *Saco v. Wentworth*, 37 Maine, 165.

ESSENTIALS OF JURY TRIAL.—In using the term "trial by jury" it was intended in the constitutional provisions to preserve the incidents of such trial, as for instance, that the jury must consist of twelve jurors, and that they must unanimously concur

in a verdict. Cooley, Const. Lim. 319, and Const. Law, 293; 1
Bish. Cr. Pr. (3d Ed.) §§ 897–899; *Work v. State,* 2 Ohio St. 297,
1 Lead Cr. Cas. 482 and note; 4 Bl. Com. 349; Opinion of Judges,
41 N. H. 550.

A jury of more than twelve is illegal and its verdict will be set
aside, or judgment thereon reversed on appeal. *Bullard v. State,*
38 Tex. 504, 19 Am. Rep. 30.

SUMMARY PROSECUTIONS WITHOUT JURY.—Statutory provisions for trial of minor offences without a jury are upheld in two
ways:

1. The right of trial by jury as it existed at common law, did
not exclude summary proceedings for petty offenses, such proceedings being well recognized in England when the common
law was brought to this country, and our constitutional guaranties of jury trial only contemplate the preservation of the right so
far as it was recognized at common law. *Byers v. Com.* 42 Penn.
St. 89; *Bryan v. State,* 4 Iowa, 349.

2. The state constitutions in guaranteeing jury trial in criminal
cases usually provide for trial of minor offenses, in a summary
proceeding without a jury, or with a jury of less than twelve,
preserving to defendant, however, the right of appeal to the court
of general criminal jurisdiction, and a full jury trial there. This
provision is supposed to prevent the summary proceeding from
being in violation of right of jury trial, even if it would otherwise
be. See *ante,* p. 116; Cooley, Const. Lim. *410, note; *State v.
Beneke,* 9 Iowa, 203; *State v. Everett,* 14 Minn. 439.

WAIVER OF JURY TRIAL.—There is a direct conflict among
the authorities as to whether the right of jury trial is one
which can be raised. It has been said that a trial of a question
of fact in a criminal case by a court without a jury of twelve
men (except in case of summary prosecution), was a proceeding not known to the law, and before a tribunal created only
by consent, and therefore not valid. *State v. Maine,* 27 Conn.
281; *State v. Lockwood,* 43 Wis. 403; *U. S. v. Taylor,* 3
McCrary, 500, 11 Fed. Rep. 470; Cooley, Const. Lim. *319.
But it is held that where a statute expressly authorizes a trial

by the court without a jury, by consent of defendant, 'the proceedings are valid. *State v. Worden*, 46 Conn. 349, 33 Am. Rep. 27, 1 Cr. L. Mag. 178 and note; *Connelly v. State*, 60 Ala. 89, 31 Am. Rep. 34.

The weight of authority seems to support the doctrine that in the absence of any statutory authority the defendant cannot (at least in prosecution for felony) waive a defect in the number of jurors and consent to a trial by less than twelve. *Cancemi v. People*, 18 N. Y. 128; *Brown v. State*, 8 Blackf. 561; *State v. Mansfield*, 41 Mo. 470; *Hill v. People*, 16 Mich. 351. *Contra, State v. Kaufman*, 51 Iowa, 578, 33 Am. Rep. 148, 1 Cr. L. Mag. 57 and note.

SPEEDY TRIAL. — A speedy trial is guaranteed in the various constitutions. There can be no absolute rule as to what this provision requires, but it is generally considered that if, at the next term of court after the finding of the indictment, the defendant is not put upon trial, and no reason appears why the prosecution should not have been ready and the case tried, the prisoner is entitled to be discharged, which right he may secure by *habeas corpus*. *In re Fox*, (Montana) 2 Cr. L. Mag. 329; *Exparte Stanley*, 4 Nev. 116.

CONTINUANCES. — The time of trial, with the limitation as to speedy trial just specified, is within the control of the court. Statutes usually provide for the granting of continuances to either party upon a proper showing. I Bish. Cr. Pr. (3d Ed.) § 951; Whart. Cr. Pl. & Pr. §§ 583–601.

THE JURY. — The method of securing a jury for the trial of causes is pointed out by statute. It is usual to provide for the selecting and summoning from the persons qualified to act as jurors of a certain number, more than twelve, from whom the twelve jurors for the trial of any particular cause are to be taken. The persons thus summoned serve as jurors for the trial of all causes, civil and criminal, to be tried at the same term of court. But if the names on the list are for any cause exhausted without the requisite number being obtained for any particular jury, bystanders may be called in to fill up the requisite number, unless the statute makes special provision for

selecting and summoning additional jurors. There are sometimes statutory directions intended to prevent bystanders who
frequent court rooms for the purpose of being selected to fill
up juries, from being called. Jurors whose names are
not on the regular jury list, and who are selected to act only in
a particular case, are called talesmen.

QUALIFICATIONS.— In general, persons to be qualified to act
as jurors must be male citizens of the state, resident in the
county, over twenty-one years of age, of good character, sound
mind, in full possession of the senses of seeing and hearing,
and able to understand the English language. Certain classes
of persons are exempted from jury services, but this exemption is a personal privilege and does not constitute a disqualification. See on this last point cases cited to same effect as to
grand jurors, *ante*, p. 160; also 1 Bish. Cr. Pr. (3d Ed.) §§
853, 926.

DISABILITY.— Besides possessing the general qualifications
above specified, the jurors must be free from certain disqualifi-
cations as to the particular case, which the law considers such
as to render it improper that the juror act in such case. These
are usually expressly specified by statute, but in conformity
with common law principles. Among the more important of
them are, relationship within a specified degree of affinity or
consanguinity to the person injured or accused; relationship
by employment, dependence, or otherwise, to one or the other
of such parties; previous incidental connections with one party
or the other likely to prejudice the juror in favor of, or against
such party; interest in the result of the action, as by reason of
being a party in a similar action or otherwise; having formed
or expressed an opinion as to the guilt or innocence of the
prisoner; having passed upon some question involving the
facts in the case, while acting in another capacity. 1 Bish. Cr.
Pr. (3d Ed.) §§ 900–930; Whart. Cr. Pl. & Pr. §§ 622–669;
State v. Collins, 70 N. C. 241, 16 Am. Rep. 771; *Guetig v.
State*, 66 Ind. 94, 32 Am. Rep. 99 and note; *State v. Arnold*,
12 Iowa, 479; *State v. Bruce*, 48 Iowa, 530; *Boyle v. People*,
4 Col. 176, 34 Am. Rep. 76; *State v. Medlicott*, 9 Kan. 257;

Com. v. Thrasher, 11 Gray, 57; *People v. Weil*, 40 Cal. 268; *Fleming v. State*, 11 Ind. 234; *Leach v. People*, 53 Ill. 311.

CHALLENGES. — The objection to the list of jurors from whom the trial jury is to be taken, that they have not been properly selected or summoned, is to be raised by a challenge to the panel or array. The objection that any particular juror does not possess the qualifications required, in general, or is disqualified to act in that particular case, is raised by challenge to the individual juror, and is called a challenge for cause. In addition, each party is usually allowed a limited number of challenges for which no cause need be assigned, called peremptory challenges. Where the challenge is to the panel or for cause, the court determines the question as to whether the objection is well taken, ascertaining the facts from the jurors themselves by examination upon an oath previously administered, requiring them to make true answers to questions touching their competency (which is often called an examination of the juror upon his *voir dire*, although the term applies primarily to a similar examination of witnesses touching their competency), and from such other evidence as may be presented. 1 Bish. Cr. Pr. (3d Ed.) §§ 931–935.

At common law a proceeding was recognized, known as a challenge to the favor, which was a challenge on the ground of general bias, not resulting from any of those things considered as necessarily indicating bias and therefore a ground of principal challenge such as is above described, but arising, or to be inferred, from other facts. The question upon a challenge to the favor is one of fact, whether the juror is indifferent between the parties, and at common law was determined by triers specially provided for that purpose, and not by the judge. *People v. Reyes*, 5 Cal. 347; 1 Bish. Cr. Pr. (3d Ed.) §§ 903–906; Whart. Cr. Pl. & Pr. § 670. The practice is quite frequently supplanted to a greater or less extent by statutory provisions making objections that were formerly raised in this manner, ground for a principal challenge, and determinable by the court.

WHO MAY CHALLENGE. — The challenge to the panel, or
to an individual juror for cause, may be taken by either the
prosecution or the defendant, though it must be by the party
against whom the bias is presumed to exist. If he chooses to
waive his objection, it is no ground of challenge by the other
party. At common law the defendant was allowed peremptory
challenges in case of trial for felony, not in case of misdemeanors, but now the statutes usually give the right in all cases, the
distinction between felonies and misdemeanors being preserved,
however, by allowing a greater number of such challenges in
the one case than the other. 1 Bish. Cr. Pr. (3d Ed.) §§ 941-
945; 2 Hawk. P. C. ch. 43, § 4.

STANDING JURORS ASIDE.— By early common law, it seems,
those who prosecuted in the name of the king were
allowed to challenge peremptorily any number of jurors. By
Stat. 4 of 33 Edw. I., it appears that the prosecutors sometimes took advantage of this privilege by challenging peremptorily so many jurors that there were not enough left on the
list to constitute a full jury, thereby preventing a trial of the
accused; the result being that if accused was in prison await-
ing trial he was kept in confinement without the truth of the
charges against him being investigated. To remedy this evil
the statute referred to provided that the prosecutors "shall
assign of their challenge a cause certain, and the truth of the
same challenge shall be inquired of, according to the custom
of the court." In construing this statute the courts did not
regard it as taking away entirely the right of peremptory
challenge by the prosecution, but considered that it only
required that the right should not be exercised so as to defeat
a trial by exhausting the list without securing a jury. Therefore they allowed the prosecutor to stand aside such jurors as
he saw fit, as they were called, without assigning any cause,
and only required such jurors to be accepted, or cause shown
for their rejection, in case the whole list was exhausted without
a full jury being obtained. If a jury was obtained without
such jurors the result was, as to them, the same as that of
peremptory challenge. In most of the states a certain number

of peremptory challenges is allowed to the prosecution, and the practice of standing jurors aside is not recognized. In others, it is still in force, and in Pennsylvania it has been held that a statutory provision giving the prosecution peremptory challenges does not take away the right to stand jurors aside as before. *Haines v. Com.* (Penn. 1882) 14 Rep. 603; *Mansell v. Reg.* (S E. & B.) 92 E. C. L. 54, 70; 1 Bish. Cr. Pr. (3d Ed.) §§ 936-940; 2 Hawk. P. C. ch. 43, §§ 2, 3.

IMPANELLING THE JURY; OATH. — The jury list having been provided in the proper manner, twelve names are selected by the clerk by lot from those on the list and the jurors thus chosen are called into the jury box. Applications by jurors to be excused on the ground of exemption from service, or other reason recognized by law, are then heard and the vacancies made by the granting of any such applications being filled in the same manner, challenges to the array may be interposed, and afterward, if the panel is found not to be objectionable, challenges for cause. Any vacancies occasioned by challenges of this kind being allowed by the court must be filled by jurors not subject to objection for cause before either party is required to exercise the right of peremptory challenge.

All objections must be interposed at this stage, that is, after the jurors are called into the box, and before they are finally sworn as the jury in the case, or they will be deemed waived, except that, as to defendant, the right of objection on grounds not known to, or reasonably discoverable by, him at the time of impanelling may, to some extent, be ground for new trial. *Yanez v. State*, 6 Tex. Ct. App. 429, 32 Am. Rep. 591; *State v. Groome*, 10 Iowa, 308; *State v. Tuller*, 34 Conn. 280; *State v. Ross*, 29 Mo. 32, 52.

Twelve jurors being obtained as to whom no valid cause of objection is raised, and the parties having exhausted, or waiving their peremptory challenges, the jury is sworn. Sometimes the form of oath is prescribed by statute. Otherwise some such formula as this is probably sufficient: " You, and each of you, do solemnly swear that you will well and truly try the issues joined between (the prosecution) and (the defendant) and a true verdict render according to the evidence; so help you God." Whart. Cr. Pl. & Pr. § 716, note; *State v. Ostrander*, 18 Iowa, 435, 452.

The swearing of the jury is the first step in the actual trial.

PUBLIC TRIAL. — The various constitutions guarantee a public trial. It is said that this does not necessarily involve the admission of the entire public, but that those having an interest in the proceeding, including defendant and his friends, shall be allowed to be present. 1 Bish. Cr. Pr. (3d Ed.) §§ 957-959; Cooley, Const. Lim. *312; and see *Hobart v. Hobart*, 45 Iowa, 501, 504.

INCIDENTS OF TRIAL; OPENING. — The order of procedure upon the trial is largely regulated by statute, or within the discretion of the court. The prosecution has, in general, the burden of sustaining its accusation, and must first introduce evidence to support it before the defendant is called upon to introduce evidence in defence; but if he has put in a plea in abatement or bar, it is for him to support the issue on his part, raised by such plea.

WITNESSES. — Our constitutions generally guarantee to defendant the right to have compulsory process to secure the attendance of witnesses in his favor; and this right is secured by statutes directing the officers of the court to subpoena such witnesses for defendant as he may direct, whose attendance may thereupon be compelled in the same way as in case of witnesses for prosecution. But the state is under no obligation to provide for the fees of such witnesses. *State v. Waters*, 39 Maine, 54.

They also provide that he shall have the right to be confronted with the witnesses against him. This makes it necessary that all evidence of witnesses for the prosecution be oral, and not by means of depositions, unless defendant waives his privilege; Cooley, Const. Lim. 318; *State v. Reidel*, 26 Iowa, 430; *State v. Collins*, 32 Iowa, 36; *State v. Polson*, 29 Iowa, 133; *People v. Lambert*, 5 Mich. 349; *People v. Jones*, 24 Mich. 215; *State v. Frederic*, 69 Maine, 400; *U. S. v. Sacramento*, 2 Mont. 239, 25 Am. Rep. 742; *Bell v. State*, 2 Tex. Ct. App. 216, 28 Am. Rep. 429.

This right to be confronted by the witnesses is not violated by allowing in prosecution for homicide, evidence of dying declarations of the person killed, under such restrictions as the law imposes. *State v. Dickinson,* 41 Wis. 299; *Robbins v. State,* 8 Ohio St. 131, 163.

The defendant is, by provision of the federal constitution (Am. Art. V.), not compellable in criminal prosecutions in the federal courts, to be a witness against himself; a similar provision may be found in some state constitutions. The common law not only did not compel him to be a witness in his own case, but considered him wholly incompetent to testify under such circumstances. Statutes of the United States and of some states make him a competent witness, and allow him to waive the privilege of not testifying if he sees fit to do so, but they do not compel him to be a witness, and often make special provision that his election not to testify shall not be commented upon by the court or counsel to his disadvantage. If he does elect to become a witness in his own behalf, he thereby waives his exemption and may be subjected to the same cross-examination to test his credibility, memory and intelligence, as other witnesses; but the cross-examination must be strictly confined to the matter called out in the examination in chief. The waiver of the right not to be a witness does not constitute a waiver of the privilege possessed by all witnesses to refuse to answer criminating questions. *State v. Flanders,* 38 N. H. 324; *State v. Red,* 53 Iowa, 69; *State v. Beal,* 68 Ind. 345, 34 Am. Rep. 263; *Brandon v. People,* 42 N. Y. 265; *Angelo v. People,* 96 Ill. 209, 36 Am. Rep. 132; *Com. v. Scott,* 123 Mass. 239, 25 Am. Rep. 87; *State v. Ober,* 52 N. H. 459, 13 Am. Rep. 88, 1 Green, Cr. L. Rep. 211; Cooley Const. Lim. *316 and note; 1 Greenl. Ev. § 451; 1 Bish Cr. Pr. (3d Ed.) §§ 1181–1187; Statutes of U. S. 1877–8, p. 30.

The general rules as to the competency of witnesses, methods of impeachment, weight of testimony, etc., are the same in criminal cases as civil and need not be here specially referred to.

THE ISSUES; DEFENCES. — The defences which may be interposed to an indictment are either in the nature of denial, or of confession and avoidance. Denial of guilt is made by the plea of not guilty, and simply negatives the charge of crime by the prosecution. Special pleas in abatement or in bar confess, for the time being, the truth of the matters well pleaded, but set up some reason why defendant should not be tried in that proceeding or at all. They are outside the allegations of the accusation, and may be properly styled affirmative defences, which must be specially pleaded, and cannot be proved under a general denial. *Com. v. Chesley*, 107 Mass. 223.

THE GENERAL ISSUE; NOT GUILTY. — Under the plea of not guilty, which is said to raise the general issue, defendant may introduce evidence of any matter of defence which he may have, such as infancy, insanity, compulsion, mistake, or any matter of justification or excuse. Under such plea he may show that the prosecution is barred by statute of limitation (see *ante*, p. 180). Also, if intent is of the gist of the offence, he may prove lack of intent. 4 Bl. Com. 338; 1 Bish. Cr. Pr. (3d Ed.) § 799.

The elements of a crime, and the evidence to prove or disprove the existence of each element, as well as the burden of proof in regard to the same, will be considered hereafter.

SPECIAL PLEAS; FORMER JEOPARDY. — Pleas in abatement being of little practical importance, need not be further considered. Pleas in bar are now reduced to plea of former conviction, and of former acquittal. The nature of these pleas and the evidence sufficient to support them will hereafter be considered.

BURDEN OF PROOF. — The term burden of proof is used to indicate the obligation resting upon the party having the affirmative of an issue to support his side of such issue by evidence sufficient to entitle him to a verdict in his favor. In other words, the burden of proof rests upon the party against whom the issue would be determined if no evidence was produced by either party. It is evident from the statement already made as to the nature of the issues that upon a

plea of not guilty the affirmative of the issue is with the prosecution, while on a plea of previous conviction or acquittal the burden is with defendant. 1 Greenl. Ev. § 74; 1 Bish. Cr. Pr. (3d Ed.) §§ 816, 1048–1051; Bouv. Law Dic. s. v. Burden of Proof; *Leete v. Gresham &c. Soc'y*, 7 Eng. L. & E. 578; 1 Lead. Cr. Cas. 300; note, 37 Am. Rep. 148; Whart. Cr. Ev. §332; *Com. v Sutherland*, 109 Mass. 342; *Cooper v. State*, 47 Ind. 61. As an illustration of the rule that as to affirmative defences the burden is upon defendant, see *Ake v. State*, 6 Tex. Ct. App. 398, 32 Am. Rep. 586.

AFFIRMATIVE PROOF OF FACTS IN DENIAL. — Although by the plea of not guilty defendant simply denies the truth of the charge of crime, yet he is by no means limited to merely negativing the proof produced by the prosecution. He may rely upon that, or he may by affirmative proof of other facts inconsistent with the truth of the evidence for prosecution, or showing the absence of some essential element of the crime charged, overthrow the case made out against him. If he desires to rely upon such affirmative proof of facts not necessarily involved in the case for prosecution, such as matter of justification, excuse, or the like, he must first introduce affirmative evidence thereof, and until he does so the prosecution is under no obligation to negative such possible defence; but though defendant has the affirmative as to such facts he does not have the affirmative of the issue, which is as before, is defendant guilty, upon which the prosecution still has the burden of proof and must overcome the negative evidence, including the affirmative facts relied upon by defendant, as will appear below, by proof of guilt beyond a reasonable doubt.

It is at this point that the main disagreement among the authorities as to the burden of proof arises. Some writers and judges speak of the defendant as having the affirmative of the issue as to such facts, as though a new issue was raised thereby, whereas, in truth, the issue remains the same, and these new matters shown by defendant simply tend to support the negative of it. If the evidence for prosecution tends to show the doing of the criminal acts by defendant at a particular time and place, and instead of attempting to disprove the acts thus charged he introduces evidence that at that exact time he was elsewhere, it is plain that, although he introduces evidence of a new fact, his being at the other place, a fact as to which he must, of course, take the initiative, yet he does so merely to overcome the evidence against him, that is, to maintain the negative of the issue of not guilty.   It is clearly erroneous to call the fact which he attempts to prove, namely, that he was elsewhere, an affirmative defence.   *Toler v. State*, 16 Ohio St. 583.

PRESUMPTIONS.— It does not follow that because the burden of proof is upon the prosecution in case defendant pleads not guilty, it must therefore, as to every imaginable ingredient necessary to constitute the crime, introduce evidence in the first instance.   There are many facts which are so universally in accordance with human experience that they may be presumed true until something appears to indicate an exception.   Thus capacity of defendant to commit crime is as necessary an element of guilt, as the doing of the wrongful act, yet such capacity is ordinarily possessed by human beings, and need not be proved until something is shown indicating its absence.   In other cases one fact will be presumed upon proof of another fact with which it is usually, but not necessarily, associated. Proof of the doing of an act gives rise to the presumption of the intent to do the act, and such intent need not be proved in the first instance; but the existence of such intent might be overcome by proof of a mistake of fact such as to disprove it.   In other words presumption is a method of proof supplied by the law and rendering actual proof unnecessary, so long as nothing appears to destroy such presumption.   1 Bish. Cr. Pr. (3d Ed.) §§ 1096-1101; 1 Greenl. Ev. §§ 33-42; Whart. Cr. Ev. §§ 734-740.

DOES THE BURDEN OF PROOF SHIFT.—It is not uncommon to speak of the shifting of the burden of proof from one party to the other, the idea being that when the one party has proved those things which give rise to a presumption in its behalf, the burden of overcoming such presumption shifts to the other

party. Such a use of the term burden of proof is, however, erroneous. The party having the affirmative of the issue does not change his relations to that issue when he has introduced sufficient proof to entitle him to recover in the absence of any evidence to the contrary. If the opposite party introduces evidence overcoming the case made, the party having the affirmative must still maintain the issue on his part or he will fail. *State v. Flye*, 26 Maine, 312; *Powers v. Russell*, 13 Pick. 69; *Small v. Clewley*, 62 Maine, 155, 16 Am. Rep. 410; *Central Bridge Co. v. Butler*, 2 Gray, 130; 1 Greenl. Ev. §§ 74, n. 1, 81 b; *Com. v. McKie*, 1 Gray, 61, 1 Lead. Cr. Cas. 295, note; *Turner v. Com.* 86 Penn. St. 54, 27 Am. Rep. 683; *State v. Wingo*, 66 Mo. 181.

PRIMA FACIE CASE.—The effect of a presumption as taking the place of direct evidence is simply to enable the party in whose favor it exists to make out a prima facie case, that is, a showing which will entitle him to succeed if nothing further appears. If evidence is introduced by the opposite party negativing the presumption, the prima facie case is gone, and the party having the affirmative must make out the issues in his favor on the actual evidence; that is, must introduce enough evidence in support of his position to establish it as against any evidence introduced to the contrary. *Com. v. Kimball*, 24 Pick. 366, 373; *Chaffee v. U. S.* 18 Wall. 516, 544; Whart. Cr. Ev. § 330.

PRESUMPTION OF INNOCENCE. — In civil cases the court stands indifferent between the parties. If the party having the affirmative of the issue supports his side of the issue by evidence which preponderates ever so little over that on the negative, he is entitled to succeed. But in criminal prosecutions the presumption is that defendant is innocent until his guilt is established. The court does not stand indifferent, but leans to the side of defendant and requires more than a mere preponderance of evidence against him to establish his guilt. 1 Bish. Cr. Pr. (3d Ed.) §§ 1103–1106; Whart. Cr. Ev. § 1.

AMOUNT OF EVIDENCE; REASONABLE DOUBT.—The amount of evidence which is required to establish defendant's guilt is such as establishes the crime charged beyond a reasonable doubt. Mere preponderance of evidence is not enough. The words themselves express the idea better than any others that could be used, and further definition is scarcely possible. The result of the doctrine is, simply, that each juror, in weighing the evidence in his own mind, should be convinced beyond a reasonable doubt of the guilt of the prisoner, before concurring in a verdict of guilty. Whart. Cr. Ev. § 718; 1 Bish. Cr. Pr. (3d Ed.) §§ 1091–1095; 14 Cent. L. Jour. 446; 1 Stephen, Hist. Cr. L. 438.

The reason of the rule ceases when the burden as to any issue is upon defendant, and therefore as to such issues he is only required to sustain the burden of proof upon him by preponderance of evidence.

Proof beyond a reasonable doubt is not required in civil cases, even where the fact to be proved constitutes a crime. *Welch v. Jugenheimer*, 56 Iowa, 11; *Ellis v. Buzzell*, 60 Maine, 209, 11 Am. Rep. 204; Cooley on Torts, 208.

EVIDENCE. -- The general principles of the law of evidence are the same in criminal as in civil cases, and need not here be discussed. 1 Bish. Cr. Pr. (3d Ed.) § 1046. It is only the application of those principles to particular cases, in view of the peculiar presumptions which obtain in criminal law, that need be considered. The elements of a crime will first be considered, and some rules as to the proving or disproving of each element; after that, the nature of the affirmative defence of previous jeopardy and the evidence necessary to support it.

ELEMENTS OF A CRIME. — For the purposes of this discussion it will be convenient in considering whether a person charged with a crime is punishable therefor, to divide the crime into three elements: 1. the act; 2. the connection of defendant with the act; 3. the intent. And it may be added in a general way, that as to all the elements of the crime, the burden of proof on a plea of not guilty is on the prosecution.

THE ACT; CORPUS DELICTI. — When an act appears to have been done through human agency and is of such nature as to give rise to the presumption that the person doing it was

guilty of a crime, the act itself may be called criminal. It may be that the facts when developed will show that it was not a crime in the person actually doing it, but if so it will be for some reason inhering in the person and not the act. It will often be necessary to prove the act itself by evidence entirely distinct from the evidence that defendant committed it, and in such cases the evidence that the act was committed is called proof of the *corpus delicti*. As there can be no crime, in the eye of the law, without the doing of a criminal act, it is plain that where the defendant denies the crime by plea of not guilty, the prosecution has the burden of proving the *corpus delicti*, and must prove it beyond a reasonable doubt. 1 Bish. Cr. Pr. (3d Ed.) §§ 1056–1060; Whart. Cr. Ev. §§ 324–328, 633, 787; 3 Greenl. Ev. § 30.

CONFESSIONS.—As showing that the law distinguishes between the *corpus delicti* and the connection of defendant with the crime, the rule as to extra-judicial confessions may be stated. Such confessions are those not made in open court (*i. e.* by plea of guilty), but which must be proved by witnesses; and the rule seems to have been settled on common law principles, though it is in many states specially enacted by statute, that they are not sufficient to establish the *corpus delicti*; but that the act being proven, they may be sufficient to connect the defendant with its commission. 1 Greenl. Ev. § 217; *State v. Grear*, 29 Minn. 221; *State v. German*, 54 Mo. 526; *Gray v. Com.* (Penn.) 4 Cr. L. Mag. 253; Whart. Cr. Ev. § 632; 1 Bish. Cr. Pr. (3d Ed.) § 1058.

CORPUS DELICTI IN MURDER.—It is in cases of felonious homicide that the necessity of conclusive proof of the *corpus delicti*, that is, of the death of a human being under circumstances indicating criminality in some one, is most strenuously insisted upon. It is said that without clear proof of the death of the supposed deceased, a conviction for the crime should not be allowed to stand.

ALIBI OF ALLEGED DECEASED.—An affirmative fact showing that there is no *corpus delicti* in case of felonious homicide, and therefore that defendant is not guilty, would be that the supposed deceased is still alive, or as it is called, an alibi of the alleged deceased. (The meaning of the term alibi will appear from its use a little further on.) According to the rule heretofore laid down as to burden of proof, this fact would negative guilt and the burden of proof would be on prosecution to prove guilt, including the *corpus delicti* as charged, beyond a reasonable doubt. In violation, however, of this rule, it is decided in one case that under such circumstances the burden of proof is upon defendant to establish such alibi, which he must do by preponderance of evidence. *State v. Vincent*, 24 Iowa, 570. The principle will be further discussed under alibi hereafter.

CHASTITY OF PROSECUTRIX IN SEDUCTION. — The statutes defining seduction make it an essential element of the crime that the person seduced shall have been of previously chaste character. That fact is, therefore, an essential element of the *corpus delicti*. Some cases hold that the presumption of chastity is sufficiently strong to make out a prima facie case for prosecution, without direct proof in the first instance of the fact of chastity (*Andre v. State*, 5 Iowa, 389, 397; *State v. Higdon*, 32 Iowa, 262; *Slocum v. People*, 90 Ill. 274, 281. *Contra, West v. State*, 1 Wis. 209), but however this may be there is a concurrence of the best authorities in holding that the burden of proof as to chastity is upon the prosecution. *Com. v. Whittaker*, 131 Mass. 224, 12 Rep. 16; *Zabriskie v. State*, 43 N. J. Law, 640, 39 Am. Rep. 610; *People v. Roderigas*, 49 Cal. 9.

IDENTITY OF DEFENDANT. — Just as important an element as the *corpus delicti* in the proof of defendant's guilt, is the fact that it was he, and not some one else, who committed the crime implied in the criminal act, or, as it is sometimes called, the identity of defendant, that is, as the perpetrator of the crime. If there is any doubt on this point, no matter how clear may be the proof of the *corpus delicti*, and even of the criminal intent on the part of defendant, he cannot be convicted. *People v. Woody*, 45 Cal. 289; *Campbell v. People*, 16 Ill. 17.

ALIBI. — The affirmative fact most frequently attempted to be proved to negative the connection of defendant with the *corpus delicti* is that defendant was elsewhere than where he must

have been to have committed the crime in the manner indicated by the evidence for the prosecution. Such fact is called an alibi, and most of the best authorities hold that when the defendant has, by evidence tending to prove an alibi, thrown doubt upon his guilt, the prosecution still has the burden of proof on the issue of guilt, and must overcome such evidence and establish the commission of the crime by defendant beyond reasonable doubt. *Toler v. State*, 16 Ohio St. 583; *French v. State*, 12 Ind. 670; *Creed v. People*, 81 Ill. 565; *Stuart v. People*, 42 Mich. 255; *Turner v. Com.* 86 Penn. St. 54, 73; *Com. v. Choate*, 105 Mass. 451; 1 Bish. Cr. Pr. (3d Ed.) §§ 1061–1068; Whart. Cr. Ev. § 333. *Contra, State v. Hamilton*, 57 Iowa, 596; *Fife v. Com.* 29 Penn. St. 429, 439.

RECENT POSSESSION OF STOLEN PROPERTY.—Where the *corpus delicti* in larceny is established, the fact that defendant soon after the commission of the larceny was found to be in possession of a portion of the property stolen, will, in the absence of any explanatory circumstances, raise the presumption of his guilt. But in overcoming this presumption by showing that he came into the possession of the property in some manner consistent with innocence, defendant has not the burden of proof, but need only introduce enough evidence as to the innocence of his possession to raise a reasonable doubt of his guilt, the burden being still upon the prosecution to overcome it. *State v. Richart*, 57 Iowa, 245; *State v. Merrick*, 19 Maine, 398; *Comfort v. People*, 54 Ill. 404; *People v. Brown*, 48 Cal. 253.

CRIMINAL INTENT.—That criminal intent is a necessary element of a crime has already been stated (*ante*, p. 19). It has also been stated that when it is necessarily inferred from the nature of the act itself, it need not be alleged in the indictment; while if the act may be either criminal or innocent, according to the specific intent with which it is done, the specific wrongful intent must be stated (*ante*, p. 185). It is clear on principle that in the former case the intent will be presumed and need not be proved by the prosecution until it is in some way negatived by the defendant, while in the latter case no such presumption arises and the specific wrongful intent must be proved in the first instance by the prosecution. *U. S. v. Taintor*, 11 Blatch. 374, 2 Green, Cr. L. Rep. 241 and note; *Com. v. York*, 9 Met. 93; *Com. v. Hersey*, 2 Allen, 173, 180; *State v. Bell*, 29 Iowa, 316; *Roberts v. People*, 19 Mich. 401, 414; 2 Stephen, Hist. Cr. L. 118; 1 Greenl. Ev. 18.

EVIDENCE OF DISTINCT CRIMES.—Nevertheless, the specific criminal intent may be shown as an inference from other acts; it need not be proved directly. For instance, the doing of previous acts of the same character may be shown to throw light upon the intent. Also, other acts, previous or subsequent, forming with the one charged a system, may indicate an intent in the one charged which would not otherwise be apparent, and may be shown for that purpose. Both these cases are exceptions to the general rule that upon trial for one crime proof of a distinct crime is not admissible. *State v. Neagle*, 65 Maine, 468; *Com. v. Edgerly*, 10 Allen, 184; *Com. v. McCarthy*, 119 Mass. 354; *Thayer v. Thayer*, 101 Mass. 111; *State v. Bridgman*, 49 Vt. 202, 24 Am. Rep. 124; *Kramer v. Com.* 87 Penn. St. 299; *Com. v. Goersen*, 2 Cr. L. Mag. 233; *People v. Corbin*, 56 N. Y. 363.

How CRIMINAL INTENT REBUTTED.—If the crime charged involves a specific criminal intent it may be rebutted like any other fact. It is said that defendant, in states where he is made a competent witness in his own behalf, may testify directly, in such cases, as to what his intent was. *Kerrains v. State*, 60 N. Y. 221, 228.

But in cases where the intent involved is simply the intent to do the act done, that being in itself wrongful, the defendant must disprove the criminal intent inferred from the doing of the act by proof of some independent fact, such as mistake, compulsion, infancy, insanity, or the like, which the law regards as sufficient to overcome the presumption. If the previous reasoning as to burden of proof and the effect of presumptions is correct, then the presumption of guilty intent from the act itself will only sustain the case for the prosecution until defendant has introduced evidence of some such independent fact sufficient

to throw a doubt upon the actual existence of the intent thus presumed, and the burden of proof will still be on prosecution to overcome such evidence by disproving the mistake, compulsion, infancy, or insanity, as the case may be, beyond a reasonable doubt.

COMPULSION; JUSTIFICATION; EXCUSE; PROVOCATION.—The authorities are in conflict as to the application of the rule above suggested as the correct one, to cases where a defendant attempts to justify or excuse an act otherwise criminal, on the ground of compulsion; or to mitigate its criminality (as in case of homicide in heat of blood) by showing provocation. Some support the rule just laid down; others hold that the defendant has the burden of proof as to facts justifying, excusing, or mitigating his act, and must prove them by a preponderance of evidence. On the one hand see *Com. v. McKie*, 1 Gray, 61, 1 Lead. Cr. Cas. 295, and note; *State v. Patterson*, 45 Vt. 308, 12 Am. Rep. 200; *State v. Porter*, 34 Iowa, 131; *Maher v. People*, 10 Mich. 212; *State v. Wingo*, 66 Mo. 181; *Stokes v. People*, 53 N.Y. 164, 182; Whart. Cr. Ev. § 334. On the other hand, see *People v. Stonecifer*, 6 Cal. 405; *Weaver v. State*, 24 Ohio St. 584; *Com. v. Drum*, 58 Penn. St. 9.

INSANITY.—The conflicting authorities as to which party has the burden of proof when defendant attempts to negative a criminal intent by proof of insanity, have already been quite fully collected (see *ante*, pp. 44–46). The following may be added in support of the doctrine that when the presumption of sanity is overthrown by evidence to the contrary, the burden of proving it, beyond a reasonable doubt, is upon the prosecution: *Com v. Heath*, 11 Gray, 303; *O'Connell v. People*, 87 N. Y. 377; *State v. Jones*, 50 N. H. 369, 9 Am. Rep. 242; *McDougal v. State* (Ind.), 4 Cr. L. Mag. 509; *Wright v. People*, 4 Neb. 407. As supporting the contrary doctrine, that the burden of proving insanity by a preponderance of evidence is upon defendant, see the following cases aside from those heretofore cited: *Com. v. Eddy*, 7 Gray, 583; *State v. Hoyt*, 46 Conn. 330; *State v. Grear*, 29 Minn. 221; *Bond v. State*, 23 Ohio St. 349.

EXCEPTIONS AND PROVISOS; LICENSE.—The rule determining whether, as to an exception or proviso in a statute defining a crime, the burden is upon prosecution to prove beyond a reasonable doubt that defendant, or the act charged to him, does not come within the exception or proviso, or is upon defendant to bring his case, by a preponderance of evidence, within such exception or proviso, is the same as that already stated as to when such exception or proviso must be negatived in the accusation and when it is matter of defence (*ante*, p. 185). In the former case it is essential to the prima facie case for prosecution that the exception be negatived; in the latter it is a matter of affirmative defence. *Fleming v. People*, 27 N. Y. 329; *State v. Stapp*, 29 Iowa, 551; *State v. Ourley*, 33 Iowa, 359; *Colson v. State*, 7 Blackf. 590; *State v. Williams*, 20 Iowa, 98; *Stanglein v. State*, 17 Ohio St. 453; *State v. Edwards*, 60 Mo. 490; *Mehan v. State*, 7 Wis. 670; *Com. v. Thurlow*, 24 Pick. 374, 1 Lead. Cr. Cas. 308; *Conyers v. State*, 50 Ga. 103, 15 Am. Rep. 686.

AFFIRMATIVE DEFENCES.—It has been already shown that the only affirmative defence generally available to the defendant is that of a previous conviction or acquittal, or former jeopardy, as it is called, and that, as to this, defendant has the burden of proof, and must establish it by a preponderance of evidence. In addition to authorities, *ante* p. 203, see on this point *Com. v. Daley*, 4 Gray, 209. It remains to consider more fully what constitutes a former jeopardy, and what evidence is sufficient to prove it.

FORMER JEOPARD.—It is a provision of the federal constitution (Am. Art. V.) that "no person shall be subject, for the same offence, to be twice put in jeopardy of life or limb," and similar provisions are found in the state constitutions. There was such a maxim at common law, but it was merely a deduction from adjudications, a matter of practice, while under the constitutional provisions it is a principle which must be strictly observed, guaranteeing to a defendant immunity from a second prosecution. The provision in the federal constitution does not strictly apply to misdemeanors, for it is only treason and felo-

nies which were ever punishable by taking life or limb; but the provisions in state constitutions are usually applicable equally to misdemeanors, and the rule generally recognized makes no practical distinction between different classes of crimes. 4 Bl. Com. 335; Broom's Leg. Max. (6th Am. Ed.) [*340]; *Winsor v. Reg.* L. R. 1 Q. B. 289, 303; 1 Bish. Cr. L. (6th Ed.) §§ 978–1070; Whart. Cr. Pl. & Pr. §§ 490–520; Cooley, Const. Lim. *325–328; 4 Cr. L. Mag. 487.

As between different Sovereignties.—It is a general rule of comity between different sovereignties that the result of a trial in the courts of one, as to a matter fully within its jurisdiction, shall be regarded as conclusive in the courts of another. Wheat. Int. Law, § 182. As to crimes, however, it is very seldom that, under common law doctrines, jurisdiction over the same act could be exercised by different sovereignties. Moreover the same act might constitute a crime against different sovereignties, and if so, there is no reason why each might not properly punish the offender for the crime against itself, irrespective of the offence against the other. Thus it is held that, as between the United States and a state, an act may constitute a crime against each (*ante*, p. 123) and may be punished by each. *Moore v. Illinois*, 14 How. 17, 20. Thus, too, it is held that if a crime is within the jurisdiction of two different states to punish, the fact of a conviction in one will not bar a prosecution in the other. *Phillips v. People*, 55 Ill. 429.

Acquittal in a court of the United States which has no jurisdiction will not prevent subsequent trial in a state court. *Com. v. Peters*, 12 Met. 387.

It is said that while the punishment of an offence by one sovereignty will not bar its prosecution by another, yet the fact that the offender has been punished may, by comity, be taken into consideration when he is a second time put on trial, and the court may decline to punish him further; but it must appear that the punishment has actually been inflicted. *Marshall v. State*, 6 Neb. 120, 29 Am. Rep. 363; Whart. Conflict of Laws, § 934.

As between the State and a City. — An act may be

at the same time an offence against the state laws and the municipal regulations of a city; and punishment under one will not preclude punishment under the other. Cooley, Const. Lim. *199; 1 Dillon, Mun. Corp. 366, 367; *Robbins v. People*, 95 Ill. 175, 10 Rep. 42; *Greenwood v. State*, 6 Baxt. 567, 32 Am. Rep. 539; *McRea v. Mayor*, 59 Ga. 168, 27 Am. Rep. 390; *Bloomfield v. Trimble*, 54 Iowa, 399, 37 Am. Rep. 212. *Contra, State v. Cowan*, 29 Mo. 330; *State v. Welch*, 36 Conn. 215.

WHAT CONSTITUTES PREVIOUS JEOPARDY. — If defendant has once been, within the same jurisdiction, legally acquitted or convicted, of course he is not to be again tried, but the constitutional provision, in its usual form, implies more than merely the conclusiveness of the prior proceeding. The defendant has been once in jeopardy if he has before been put on trial for the same offence in a proceeding so far regular that a conviction therein would have been valid. The jeopardy commences when a jury is impanelled and sworn for the trial of the charge. 1 Bish. Cr. L. (6th Ed.) §§ 1012–1047; *State v. Redman*, 17 Iowa, 329; *Com. v. Cook*, 6 S. & R. 577; *McFadden v. Com.* 23 Penn. St. 12; *O'Brian v. Com.* 9 Bush. 333, 15 Am. Rep. 715; *Weaver v. State*, (Ind.) 4 Cr. L. Mag. 27; 1 Lead. Cr. Cas. 528.

But the pendency of another indictment for the same offence, on which defendant has not been tried, cannot be pleaded in bar, or even in abatement. *Com. v. Drew*, 3 Cush. 279; *Com. v. Murphy*, 11 Cush. 472; *Dutton v. State*, 5 Ind. 533.

JURISDICTION OF THE COURT. — Jeopardy does not result from being put on trial, if the court in which the prosecution is brought has not jurisdiction, for its judgment would be void. *State v. Odell*, 4 Blackf. 156; *Com. v. Peters*, 12 Met. 387; *State v. Hodgkins* 42 N. H. 474.

SUFFICIENCY OF INDICTMENT. — As will hereafter appear, a verdict of guilty upon an indictment so defective as not to conform to the essential requirements of law, can be set aside on motion in arrest of judgment, or on writ of error, or appeal. Therefore, if the indictment is not sufficient to support a conviction if secured, it does not constitute jeopardy that defendant

is put upon trial thereon. *People v. Cook*, 10 Mich. 164; *People v. March*, 6 Cal. 543; *Com. v. Bakeman*, 105 Mass. 53.

However, even if the conviction is erroneous and might have been set aside, yet if defendant has actually suffered the punishment adjudged thereon he cannot again be tried. *Com. v. Loud*, 3 Met. 328.

DISMISSAL; NOLLE PROSEQUI. — When defendant has been once put on trial on a sufficient indictment in a court having jurisdiction, he is entitled to have that trial proceed to its proper conclusion. Therefore, while at common law the prosecutor might discontinue his prosecution at any time (which was called the entry of a *nolle prosequi*, or as it was usually abbreviated, a *nol. pros.*) and the prosecuting officer may, in general, still do the same, under statutory regulations, such a dismissal after the trial has commenced will amount to acquittal and the defendant cannot be again tried. *Lee v. State*, 26 Ark. 260, 7 Am. Rep. 611; *State v. Calendine*, 8 Iowa, 288; *O'Brian v. Com.* 9 Bush. 333, 15 Am. Rep. 715; *Baker v. State*, 12 Ohio St. 214; *Contra, State v. Champeau*, 52 Vt. 313, 36 Am. Rep. 754; *Hines v. State*, 24 Ohio St. 134.

TERMINATION OF TRIAL WITHOUT VERDICT. — The trial may, however, be brought to a termination by mischance, before a verdict is reached, and without fault on the part of the prosecution; for instance, by the sickness of a juror or the judge, by expiration of the term of court, by inability of the jury to agree upon a verdict, and in various other ways. The principle applied in such cases is, that if the prosecution and the court have done all that they could legally do to secure a verdict, and the trial has, by mischance or by fault of defendant, come to an end without one, the proceeding does not constitute jeopardy. *Ex parte McLaughlin*, 41 Cal. 211, 10 Am. Rep. 272; *Mixon v. State*, 55 Ala. 129, 28 Am. Rep. 695; *State v. Vaughan*, 29 Iowa, 286; *People v. Cage*, 48 Cal. 323, 17 Am. Rep. 436; *State v. McGimsey*, 80 N. C. 377, 30 Am. Rep. 90; *People v. Goodwin*, 18 Johns. 187; *Com. v. McCormick*, 130 Mass. 61, 39 Am. Rep. 423.

WAIVER OF RIGHT. — The right of defendant to have a

trial proceed to verdict, or to insist that the result of such trial shall be final and that the same offence shall not again be made the basis of prosecution, is one which defendant may waive. As suggested in the last paragraph, if by his fault (*e. g.* if he should escape from custody) the trial is terminated without verdict, he cannot afterward take advantage of it. So, if he takes proceedings by motion in the same court, or by writ of error, or appeal to a higher court, to secure a new trial, and succeeds, he waives the former jeopardy and can be again tried. Further, the former jeopardy, although complete, might be waived by failure to plead it on a subsequent trial. 1 Bish. Cr. L. (6th Ed.) §§ 995–1011; *People v. Higgins,* 59 Cal. 357, 13 Rep. 105.

NEW TRIAL. — The effect of waiver of former jeopardy by asking a new trial is strictly limited to so much of the result as is unfavorable to defendant. As will appear in connection with verdict, the jury may, if there are different degrees of the offence with which defendant is charged, find him guilty of a less degree of the offence than that for which he is put on trial; or they may convict him of any other offence necessarily included in that with which he is charged. The effect of such a verdict is twofold; it is not only a conviction of the lower degree or the included offence, but an acquittal of the higher degree or greater offence charged. Therefore, if defendant applies for a new trial in such case he waives the result only so far as it is against him but not that part which is in his favor. Therefore, upon re-trial he can only be tried for that degree or offence of which he was convicted, not for the higher degree or greater offence for which he was first put on trial. *State v. Tweedy,* 11 Iowa, 350; *State v. Clemons,* 51 Iowa, 274; *State v. Ross,* 29 Mo. 32, 41; *State v. Belden,* 33 Wis. 121, 14 Am. Rep. 748; *State v. Martin,* 30 Wis. 216, 11 Am. Rep. 567; *People v. Gilmore,* 4 Cal. 376; *Simco v. State,* (Tex. Ct. App.) 2 Cr. L. Mag. 26. *Contra, State v. Behimer,* 20 Ohio St. 572; *State v. McCord,* 8 Kan. 232, 12 Am. Rep. 469, 1 Green, Cr. L. Rep. 406 and note.

It has already been suggested that a plea of guilty has the

same effect as a verdict of guilty, but no greater, and that if there is a fatal defect in the indictment or proceedings, it may be taken advantage of to set aside the conviction on such plea. Therefore, if a defendant pleads guilty to a less degree of an offence than that of which he is indicted, or to an included offence, and such plea is accepted, he cannot afterwards, upon the conviction being set aside, be put on trial for a higher degree or offence than that to which he pleaded guilty. *Kring v. Missouri*, 15 Rep. 769.

On the same principle as above, if defendant is convicted on only one or a part of several counts in an indictment, and acquitted as to others, he cannot again be put on trial as to the latter, although the conviction is set aside. *U. S. v. Davenport*, Deady 264, 1 Green, Cr. L. Rep. 429; *Guenther v. People,* 24 N. Y. 100.

VERDICT DETERMINES THE JEOPARDY.—It is the verdict, and not the judgment, which determines whether defendant has previously been in jeopardy. Therefore, if an erroneous judgment is rendered, on a verdict or plea of guilty, and the judgment is reversed on appeal, or if no judgment is entered a new trial cannot be had. Perhaps upon reversal of the erroneous judgment the defendant is entitled to discharge, although in reason it would seem that all he could insist upon would be that the case be sent back for proper judgment. *People v. Goldstein*, 32 Cal. 432; *State v. Elden*, 41 Maine, 165; *Shepherd, v. People*, 25 N. Y. 406, 418.

NO NEW TRIAL AFTER ACQUITTAL.—The various rules as to new trials apply, as will be seen, only in case of convictions. An acquittal is final, provided the court has jurisdiction and the indictment sufficiently charges the offence. Therefore, no matter what errors have been committed upon the trial, and no matter how erroneous may be the conclusion of the court or the jury, the acquittal cannot be set aside on the motion of the prosecution, or on an appeal or writ of error brought by it, and a new trial secured; such new trial would be a second jeopardy. *State v. Van Horton*, 26 Iowa, 402; *People v. Corning*, 2 N. Y. 1; *Com. v. Cummings,* 3 Cush. 212; 1 Lead Cr. Cas. 599, 604, 610; *State v. Shields*, (Ind.) 1 Cr. L. Mag. 611.

It is sometimes provided by statute that the prosecution may appeal for the purpose of reversing error committed in the trial court, but a reversal can have no effect in that case; it will simply settle the law for other cases not yet tried.

IDENTITY OF CRIME.—It is only as to the *same offence* that defendant is not to be a second time put in jeopardy. The former accusation is the test as to whether the former prosecution was for the same or a different offence. If it appears that the offense for which defendant is put on trial is the one for which he was before tried, and one for which there might have been a valid conviction under the indictment or information on which the former trial was had, such former trial constitutes jeopardy as to the same offence, though the evidence to support the crime embodied in the second charge was not introduced on the former trial. *Com. v. Roby*, 12 Pick. 496; *Com. v. Robinson*, 126 Mass. 259, 30 Am. Rep. 674. *Com. v. Sutherland*, 109 Mass. 342, 1 Green. Cr. L. Rep. 189; 1 Lead Cr. Cas. 516; 1 Bish. Cr. L. (6th Ed.) §§ 1048–1069.

DEGREES OF THE CRIME; INCLUDED CRIME.—Of course a former trial for a higher degree of the same crime, or for a crime necessarily including the one charged on the second trial, is a bar, for defendant might, on the former trial, have been convicted of the lower degree or the included crime. On the other hand, a previous jeopardy as to the lower degree or the included crime will also, it seems, bar a second prosecution as to the higher degree or crime, for, as the lesser is included in the greater, the defendant is twice put in jeopardy as to the lower degree or crime. 1 Lead. Cr. Cas. 537-541; *Moore v. State*, (Ala.) 4 Cr. L. Mag. 429; *State v. Cooper* 13 N. J. Law, 361; *Wilcox v. State*, 6 Lea, 571, 40 Am. Rep. 53; *Com. v. Squire*, 1 Met. 258. Contra. *State v. Foster* 33 Iowa, 525.

This reasoning does not apply to previous convictions of an assault with an intent to commit murder, or great bodily injury, if the person assaulted dies therefrom after the first prosecution, but within a year and a day so as to make the offence murder. *Reg. v. Morris*, L. R. 1 C. C. 90; *Com. v. Evans*, 101 Mass. 25.

COMPOUND INJURIES FROM ONE ACT.—One act may result in

injuries to two or more persons, or may involve different articles of property, belonging to one or more persons. In such case it seems a prosecution for the act as constituting a crime affecting one or more of the persons, or a part of the property, will bar a subsequent trial as to the whole, or any other part of the transaction. *Clem v. State,* 42 Ind. 420, 13 Am. Rep. 369; *State v. Egglesht,* 41 Iowa, 574, 20 Am. Rep. 612; *Quitzow v. State,* 1 Tex. Ct. App. 47, 28 Am. Rep. 396; *Hudson v. State,* 9 Tex. Ct. App. 151, 35 Am. Rep 732; *State v. Benham,* 7 Conn. 414. But see, *State v. Nash,* 86 N. C. 650, 41 Am. Rep. 472, and note; *State v. Teat,* 53 Miss. 439, 24 Am. Rep. 708; 1 Lead. Cr. Cas. 533.

MERGER; LOWER DEGREES. — At common law a person put on trial for a felony could not be convicted of a misdemeanor; therefore an acquital for a felony would not bar a subsequent prosecution for an included misdemeanor. Also, it was said that the misdemeanor was merged in the felony, in case the same transaction included both, and that the misdemeanor could not, therefore, be prosecuted. Both rules were based on reasons which do not now exist, but the question as to how far they are still to be recognized is not very definitely settled, except as the matter is regulated by statutory provisions. 1 Bish. Cr. L. (6th Ed.) §§ 786-790, 804-815.

VARIANCE. — Where the first prosecution failed on account of a fatal variance between the charge and the proof, it will not bar a second prosecution for the offence which the evidence on the former trial tended to prove.

PROOF ALIUNDE OF IDENTITY OF CRIME. — As allegations of time and place are not, in general, material, and need not be proved as alleged, it would be easy in the second charge to so vary the allegations that the offence would not appear to be necessarily identical; but evidence of witnesses who heard the first trial would be received on the trial of the issue on the plea of former jeopardy to show that the transaction charged in the second prosecution was the same as that which was sought to be proved under the first. *Maher v. State,* 53 Ga. 448, 21 Am. Rep. 269; *Com. v. Bosworth,* 113 Mass. 200, 18 Am. Rep. 467.

IDENTITY OF PERSON. — That defendant's name is the same as that of defendant in a previous prosecution does not establish identity of person, nor does the fact that a former prosecution was against a person under a different name necessarily show that the person was not the same. Therefore, in the one case as in the other oral, proof is admissible to show whether the defendant in the one is actually the same as in the other or not.

FRAUD. — If the former prosecution was not in good faith, but was fraudulent or collusive, in the interest of defendant, it will not be permitted to bar a new prosecution. *State v. Green*, 16 Iowa, 239; *Watkins v. State*, 68 Ind. 427, 34 Am. Rep. 273; *Com. v. Dascom*, 111 Mass. 404; *State v. Simpson*, 28 Minn. 66, 41 Am. Rep. 269; 1 Lead. Cr. Cas. 529.

PREVIOUS ATTAINDER. — It was a rule at common law that after a defendant had once suffered attainder for a felony he could not be prosecuted for another. No such rule is now recognized.

ORDER OF THE EVIDENCE. — The question as to the order of evidence, and many points of practice in relation to its introduction, depend upon principles not peculiar to criminal actions and need not be specially discussed. Moreover, in these matters the court is given a large discretion and fixed rules cannot well be laid down. As a general rule, however, the party having the burden of proof, which would be the prosecution if the plea be not guilty, must first introduce evidence making out a prima facie case. The defendant then introduces evidence, either directly rebutting that of prosecution as to the facts already testified to by its witnesses, or negativing guilt by proof of independent facts. Thereupon the prosecution may introduce rebutting evidence on its part, but cannot, except as a favor, for good cause shown, introduce evidence as to new matters, nor merely cumulative evidence.

ARGUMENTS OF COUNSEL. — When the evidence is all in, the counsel on the respective sides sum up the case to the jury, the party having the affirmative opening and closing, being confined in closing to a reply to the arguments for the other

party. Improprieties committed by the counsel for the prosecution in his address may sometimes be a ground for setting aside the verdict if the jury should convict; as, for instance, gross and uncalled for abuse of defendant, statement of matters as facts which have not been proved, or reference (in violation. of statute forbidding it) to the fact that defendant has not testified when he might have done so, (see *ante* p. 201). *Coble v. Coble,* 79 N. C. 589, 28 Am. Rep. 338; *State v. Reilly,* 4 Mo. App. 392; *Cross v. State,* (Ala. 1881) quoted from in 3 Crim. L. Mag. 627; 1 Bish. Cr. Pr. (3d Ed.) §§ 974, 975.

It has been questioned whether, as defendant has the right to have his case argued by counsel, the court can limit the time of such arguments. It is considered, however, that the time may be limited, provided the limitation is reasonable and allows full and fair opportunity to present the case. 1 Bish. Cr. Pr. (3d Ed.) § 313; Whart. Cr. Pl. & Pr. § 560; Cooley, Const. Lim. *336; *Hunt v. State,* 49 Ga. 255, 15 Am. Rep. 677; *Williams v. State,* 60 Ga. 367, 27 Am. Rep. 412; *People v. Keenan,* 13 Cal. 581; *White v. People,* 90 Ill. 117, 32 Am. Rep. 12; *State v. Hoyt,* 47 Conn. 518, 36 Am. Rep. 89; *Dille v. State,* 34 Ohio St. 617; *State v. Collins,* 70 N. C. 241, 16 Am. Rep. 771, and note; 3 Crim. L. Mag. 622.

JUDGE AND JURY; LAW AND FACT. — The respective provinces of court and jury, the one determining questions of law, the other those of fact, is the same as in case of jury trials in civil cases. As a result of the doctrine, it is proper for an attorney to argue questions of law and cite authorities to the court instead of to the jury, although the practice in this respect is not uniform. Cooley, Const. Lim. *336; 1 Bish. Cr. Pr. (3d Ed.) § 986.

INSTRUCTIONS. — The court has the right, and it is in general its duty, to state to the jury the law applicable to the case. This it does after the closing of arguments of counsel, by a charge to the jury, consisting of instructions, oral or written (though sometimes required by statute to be written) stating the different propositions of law which it deems applicable to the evidence before them. Cooley, Const. Lim. *321; 1 Bish.

Cr. Pr. (3d Ed.) §§ 976–982; Whart. Cr. Pl. & Pr. §§ 708–714; *State v. Brainard*, 25 Iowa, 572; 8 Southern Law Rev. 402.

If the evidence is clearly insufficient to support a conviction, so that, if the jury should return a verdict of guilty the court would be bound to set it aside, it may direct the jury to acquit the defendant, and such direction will constitute an acquittal; but under no circumstances has the court the right to direct a verdict of guilty, not even where the evidence of guilt is uncontradicted. The defendant has the right to the verdict of a jury. *State v. Smith*, 28 Iowa, 565; *U. S. v. Taylor*, 3 McCrary, 500, 11 Fed. Rep. 470, 3 Cr. L. Mag. 552. *Contra*, *U. S. v. Anthony*, 11 Blatchf. 200, 2 Green, Cr. L. Rep. 208 and note, 226.

JURY AS JUDGES OF THE LAW.— Although it is the duty of the jury to accept the law as stated to them by the court, they cannot be compelled to do so, nor punished for not doing so. It will appear hereafter more fully that an erroneous conviction may, under provisions in many states, be set aside, but as we have already seen, the verdict, if for acquittal, is final and it would constitute a second jeopardy to put the prisoner again on trial, no matter how erroneous the verdict might be. Nor can the jury be required to return a special verdict, leaving to the court the question as to the legal effect of the facts thus found; but they have a right to return a general verdict of guilty or not guilty, and if they choose to do the latter, it cannot be questioned by the court. Therefore, in acquitting, their judgment not only as to the facts, but as to the application of the law to the facts, is final. It is in some such sense that the jurors are sometimes said to be judges of the law in criminal cases. 1 Bish. Cr. Pr. (3d Ed.) §§ 983–988; Cooley, Const. Lim. *321; 2 Curtis' Works, 176–190; Conkling's Treatise, U. S. Courts, 612; 1 Stephen, Hist. Cr. L. 306; *Kane v. Com.* 89 Penn. St. 522, 33 Am. Rep. 787 and note, 1 Cr. L. Mag. 47 and note; *State v. Buckley*, 40 Conn. 246, Am. L. Reg. June, 1874, and note; *State v. Wright*, 53 Maine, 328; *Bell v. State*, (Md.) 2 Cr. L. Mag. 664; *Washington v. State*, 63 Ala. 135, 35 Am. Rep. 8; *U. S. v. Taylor*, 3 McCrary, 500, 11

Fed. Rep. 470, 3 Cr. L. Mag. 552; *State v. Croteau*, 23 Vt. 14, 1 Lead. Cr. Cas. 363, and note, 428; Hallam, Const. Hist. ch. 13; 8 Southern L. Rev. 409; 3 Cr. L. Mag. 484.

In cases of libel it is quite frequently provided by constitution or statute, that the jury shall be judges of the law, as well as the fact. See cases above, also, 2 Stephen, Hist. Cr. L. 313, 343-345, 350.

CONDUCT OF JURY DURING TRIAL. — The jury, from the time it is sworn, is under the control of the court. During the trial it is in the presence of the court. During intermissions it may be kept in charge of a sworn officer, or the members may be allowed to separate, being cautioned not to converse with one another, or allow others to converse with them on the case.

DELIBERATIONS OF JURY.— After the charge of the court, the jury is sent out to deliberate upon a verdict. The members are to be kept together in charge of a sworn officer, and not to be allowed to communicate with anyone, except with the court and, for necessary purposes, with the officer in charge. The old rule was that they were to be kept without food or drink or fire until they reached an agreement. The modern practice is to allow them all necessaries, so far as consistent with their being kept together in the charge of the officer.

VERDICT; RENDITION.— Concurrence of all the jurors is, as has already been stated, necessary to a verdict. When it is reached, that fact is announced to the court through the officer in charge, and the jury comes into court, which is considered always in session for that purpose, so that the judge, with the usual officers of the court, in the usual place for holding court, may receive a verdict at any hour, although the presence of defendant is necessary (except in case of misdemeanors, when he may waive the right). The verdict may be oral or in writing, and announced or delivered by the foreman, whom the jury has chosen. It is sometimes directed by statute that the jury upon agreeing to a verdict during adjournment of court, may reduce it to writing, seal it up, and separate, returning into court at its next opening and rendering it as their verdict as before. This is usually allowed, however, only upon order of court, by consent of the parties. 1 Bish. Cr. Pr. (3d Ed.) §§ 1001–1016; *State v. Callahan,* 55 Iowa, 364; *Rowan v. State,* 30 Wis. 129, 11 Am. Rep. 559; *Stewart v. People,* 23 Mich. 63, 9 Am. Rep. 78; *Com. v. Durfee,* 100 Mass. 146; *Com. v. Tobin,* 125 Mass. 203, 28 Am. Rep. 220.

FORM OF VERDICT. — The verdict may be simply guilty or not guilty, specifying the offence, which is a general verdict; or the jurors may, at their option, return a special verdict as to the facts found, and allow the court to render such judgment thereon as the law may warrant. The verdict must be perfectly clear and explicit, although the court may, if not in proper form, refuse to receive it and require it to be properly rendered. But very slight defects in the verdict as actually received have been held fatal. *Woolridge v. State,* (Tex. Ct. App.) 4 Cr. L. Mag. 515, 16 Cent. L. Jour. 314, and note 321.

It was the common law rule that a defendant might be convicted of any crime necessarily included in that charged in the indictment, or of any lower degree of the crime than that charged unless the crime charged and the included crime or lower degree were of different classes, that is, the one a felony, the other a misdemeanor; and statutes quite frequently abrogate this exception, so that on trial for felony there may be conviction of lower degree or included crime, though it be a misdemeanor. *State v. Jarvis,* 21 Iowa, 44; *State v. Clemons,* 51 Iowa, 274; *Benham v. State,* 1 Iowa, 542; *State v. White,* 45 Iowa, 325.

POLLING THE JURY. — To ascertain positively whether the verdict is concurred in by all the jurors they may be asked individually if it is their verdict, which is called polling the jury. This may be done on the request of one of the parties, or by direction of the court, but is not otherwise necessary; in some states it is not recognized as a right of defendant to have the jury polled. 1 Cr. L. Mag. 170; *James v. State,* 55 Miss. 57, 30 Am. Rep. 496 and note; *State v. Hoyt,* 47 Conn. 518, 36 Am. Rep. 89.

NEW TRIAL.—At common law in England a new trial might be granted by the court on the motion of defendant upon proper ground in case of a misdemeanor, but not in case of a felony. Statutes of the various states usually authorize new trials on specified grounds in all cases, and the power to grant them is also maintained without statute. The motion is addressed to the discretion of the court, and may be for any irregularity which has deprived defendant of a fair trial. The court may consider, among other things, whether the evidence was sufficient to warrant the conviction. For reasons already stated it cannot be granted on motion of the prosecution. 1 Bish. Cr. Pr. (3d Ed.) §§ 1272–1281; Whart. Cr. Pl. & Pr. §§ 784–902; 1 Stephen, Hist. Cr. L. 310; *State v. Groome,* 10 Iowa, 308; *Com. v. Green,* 17 Mass, 515, 533.

MOTION IN ARREST OF JUDGMENT.— After the rendition of the verdict of guilty and at any time before sentence, the defendant may still urge, by way of motion in arrest of judgment, any defect in the proceedings, which is apparent on the record, showing that sentence should not be passed upon him, for instance, that the indictment is defective, that the verdict is not sufficient, or does not correspond to the indictment, &c., &c. Thus matters which might have been ground of demurrer may usually be raised. 1 Bish. Cr. Pr. (3d Ed.) §§ 1282–1288.

SENTENCE.— The judgment of the court as to the kind and amount of punishment to be inflicted is called the sentence. The punishment is usually fixed by statute in such way as to leave to the judge a discretion, within certain limits, as to the kind or amount, and in exercising this discretion the judge may take into consideration the evidence on the trial, and also matters of aggravation or mitigation not appearing in the evidence, but brought to his attention otherwise. It is the general practice, to ask the defendant, before sentence, whether he has anything to say as to why sentence should not be passed upon him, and he may then, by himself or counsel, make a statement or appeal to the court. 1 Bish. Cr. Pr. (3d Ed.) §§ 1289–1334; Whart. Cr. Pl. & Pr. §§ 906–945; *State v. Hoyt,* 47 Conn. 518, 36 Am. Rep. 89, and note; *Mullen v. State,* 45

Ala. 43, 6 Am. Rep. 691; *Jones v. State*, 51 Miss. 718, 24 Am. Rep. 658; *McCue v. Com.* 78 Penn. St. 185, 21 Am. Rep. 7, and note.

APPEAL; WRIT OF ERROR. — At common law a writ of error was allowable, as matter of favor only, from a judgment in a criminal case, but as such proceeding simply called in question errors appearing upon the record, it was of little practical value, for the record did not show the evidence, nor the instructions of the court. Later, a court was established for the determination of questions of law arising in criminal cases, and certified by the judge trying the case, but it was still discretionary with the judge whether he would reserve a question of law to be passed upon in this manner or not, so that the defendant had no method of compelling a rehearing of his case in this manner. 1 Stephen, Hist. Cr. L., 308–318; 1 Bish. Cr. Pr. (3d Ed.) §§ 1362–1374.

In this country, however, the various state statutes provide methods by which, in some form, not only errors of law, but also, to some extent, the sufficiency of the evidence may be inquired into; and this right of appeal is absolute in defendant, and not a favor.

For reasons already explained in connection with the doctrine of former jeopardy, a writ of error prosecuted by the state cannot affect a verdict of not guilty, and indeed, in the absence of special statutory authority, the prosecution cannot have the case reviewed on writ of error, even to settle a question of practice for other cases. *Ante*, p. 217; *State v. Kemp*, 17 Wis. 669; *People v. Corning*, 2 N. Y. 9; *Com. v. Cummings*, 3 Cush. 212; *State v. Tait*, 22 Iowa, 140.

EXECUTION.

FINES. — If the sentence be a fine, it amounts to a judgment, enforceable on execution as in a civil case. There is usually a statutory provision, also, authorizing imprisonment for a length of time corresponding in a fixed ratio to the amount of fine, unless the fine be sooner paid. *State v. Myers*, 44 Iowa, 580; *State v. Jordan*, 39 Iowa, 387.

IMPRISONMENT; CAPITAL PUNISHMENT.—The states provide penitentiaries and jails for the confinement of persons sentenced to imprisonment in the one or the other. The only other kind of corporal punishment now generally recognized is that of death, to be inflicted in the manner which the law points out. The officers having general charge of the enforcement of these punishments is the sheriff, who executes the sentence of death or takes the prisoner to the penitentiary, or confines him in the jail (which is generally under his charge), according to the directions of the judgment. The whole subject of the execution of sentence is outside the range of legal practice, and is of little general interest.

INDEX.

Abatement, pleas in, 186.

Accessories, 51–54; out of jurisdiction, 126.

Accessory before the fact in suicide, 69.

Accident, death from, excusable, 64.

Accomplice, 52.

Accusation, earliest form of, 108; method of, 155–157; essentials of, 165–168.

Acquittal, without jurisdiction, no bar, 213; of higher degree or offence by conviction of lower, 216; no new trial after, 217.

Act, intent inferred from, 22; intent must concur with, 23; producing unintended result, 23; of another carrying out wrongful intent, 24; malum in se, malum prohibitum, 8; what sufficient to constitute assault, 85, 86; burden of proving, 207.

Acts, of Legislature, see Statutes; what should be made crimes, 7.

Addition of defendant, 176.

Adultery, as provocation for killing by husband, 76.

Affirmative of issue, what is, 203.

Age of criminal accountability, 39.

Agent, liability of principal for acts of, 24; of corporation, not authorized to commit crime, 48; responsible for criminal act, 51.

Aider and abettor, 52.

Alias dictus, 176.

Alibi, burden of proof of, 208; of alleged deceased, 207.

Allegiance, 122; necessary in case of treason, 58.

Alternative allegations in indictment, 167.

Ambassadors, exemption of, from jurisdiction, 122; exempt from arrest, 142.

Amendment of indictments and informations, 173.

Animals, what subjects of larceny, 95.

Appeal of felony, 108; as form of accusation, 155.

Appeal, from conviction in summary proceeding, 116, 194; in criminal cases in federal courts, 119; from courts of original jurisdiction, 117; not allowed to prosecution, 217, 226.

Appearances justify self-defence, 36.

Arguments of counsel, 220.

Arraignment, 190.

Arrest, death caused in making, 63, 77, 78; death resulting from resisting, 71, 78; purpose of, 133; warrant of, 134–136; how made, 136–142; exemption from, 142; illegal, effect of, 142; upon bench warrant, 163.

Arrest of judgment, 225.

Arson, 90, 91.

Assault, upon sick person, malice presumed, 72; resistance to, in self-defence, 31–35; felonious, 88; prosecution for, does not bar prosecution for murder if death afterward results, 218.

Assault and battery, 84–87; liability of corporations for, 49.

Attainder as bar, 220.

Attempt, to kill, presumption from, 71; punishable by statute, 88; what criminal, 85.

Bail, 151–154; after indictment, 164.

Bailee, larceny from, 96; larceny, or embezzlement by, 98, 102.

Bar, pleas in, 187.

Battery, see assault and battery, 84–87.

Battle, trial by, 108.

Belief, justifying self-defence, 36; religious, not defence, 22.

Bench warrant, 163.

Benefit of clergy, how pleaded, 186.

Bigamy, territorial jurisdiction of, 126.

Binding over, to keep the peace and for good behavior, 131, 132; fugitive from justice, 148; upon examination, 150.

Bond to keep the peace, 131, 132.
Boundary of county, venue of crime committed near, 129.
Boundaries, territorial, between sovereignties, 121; between states, 122; between counties, 129.
Breach of the peace, 132.
Breaking, what sufficient to constitute burglary, 92.
Burden of proof, 202; of insanity, 44, 211; shifting of, 204; as to elements of crime, 206; of corpus delicti, 207; of chastity, 208; as to alibi, 209; to explain recent possession of stolen property, 209; of intent, 209, 210; as to compulsion, justification, excuse, provocation, 211; as to exceptions and provisos, 212; party having, to first offer evidence, 220.
Burglary, 91–94; intoxication as a defence in, 47.
Burning, what sufficient to constitute arson, 90, 91.

Caption of indictment, 170.
Certainty, in pleading, 166; in pleas in abatement, 187; in pleas in bar, 188.
Challenges, to grand jury, 158, 159; to trial jurors, 197–199.
Change of venue, 130.
Character of assailant as justifying self-defence, 36.
Charge to jury, 221.
Chastisement, death occurring in, 64, 72, 77, 78; lawful, not assault, 86.
Chastity in case of seduction, 208.
Child, unborn, not human being, 62, see Parent.
Choses in action, not subjects of larceny, 96.
Citizens, allegiance of, 122.
City, punishment by, not bar to prosecution by state, 213, 214.
Codes, criminal, 11.
Codification, 10; as to procedure, 109.
Coercion of wife by husband presumed, 38.
Combat, retreat required in cases of, 34, 35; passion arising from, as provocation, 76.
Combination, criminal liability of parties to, 25, 49, 50.
Commencement of indictment, 170.
Commitment on preliminary examination, 151; of witnesses, 151.
Common carrier, larceny or embezzlement by, 98, 102.

Common law as to crimes, 10, 11, 12, 56; effect of, on construction of statutes, 17; as to procedure in the states and U. S., 109.
Compensation for injuries, 5, 107.
Complaint, see preliminary information.
Compound offences, charged in same indictment, 183; when prosecution for one bars another, 218, 219; verdict in case of, 224.
Compulsion, burden of proving, 211.
Compurgators, 192.
Conclusion of indictment, 171.
Confessions, as evidence, 207.
Congress, powers of to declare and punish crimes, 13.
Consent, in case of rape, 83; to assault, 87; in case of larceny, 98.
Conservators of the peace, 111, 112.
Conspiracy, to levy war, 58; to accomplish unlawful object, 11; out of the jurisdiction, 127.
Constables, office and duties of, 115.
Constitution, powers conferred by as to crimes, 13; of U. S., limitations of, when applicable to states, 110.
Constitutional limitations as to procedure, 109, 110.
Construction of statutes, 14–19.
Consuls, not exempt from jurisdiction, 122; administer laws in foreign jurisdiction, 123.
Continuance, of preliminary examination, 149; of proceedings for trial, 195.
Continuando, 179.
Conviction of crime does not merge tort, 8.
Cooling time, what sufficient, in case of heat of blood, 77.
Coroner, office and duties of, 113.
Corporation, criminal responsibility of, 48; proceedings against, 189.
Corpus delicti, defined, proof of, 206–208.
Costs, taxation of, to prosecutor, 108, 163.
Counsel, on preliminary examination, 149; right to, 190; arguments of, 220.
Counterfeit, having with wrongful intent, criminal, 23.
Counterfeiting, 105; as treason, 60.
Counts, of indictment, 170; joinder of, 183; conviction of part set aside, no new trial as to others, 217.

County, jurisdiction of court limited to, 129, 130; venue of crime near boundary, 129; offense partly committed in, 129; name of, in indictment, 169; boundaries of, 129.

Court, judge of the law, instructions, 221.

Courts of United States, criminal jurisdiction of, 118, 119; venue in proceedings in, 128.

Courts of criminal jurisdiction, 115–117.

Coverture as relieving from criminal responsibility, 38.

Crime, defined, 6; distinguished from tort, 6; does not merge tort, 8; committed within jurisdiction by person beyond, 124; distinguished from tort as to procedure, 108; against U. S and state, 213; degrees of, jeopardy, 218.

Crimes, what shall constitute, 4; at common law, 10–12; declared by legislation, 12; classification of, 55; punishment of by federal government, 13; common law provisions as to, retained, 56; specific, how treated, 56; jurisdiction and venue of, 120, 130; punishable only within the jurisdiction where committed, 124–128; proof of identity of, to show previous jeopardy, 219.

Cumulative acts, 183.

Damages as a punishment, 3.

Danger necessary to justify self-defense, 36.

Dangerous appliances, acts, or business, death from, 74.

Death, how soon must occur to constitute homicide, 62; within jurisdiction from blow without, 125; in one county from blow in another, 130; see homicide.

Defense, of property, or person, or habitation, 31, 32; of person or property of another, 37; use of deadly weapons in, 77; insanity as, burden of proof, 44.

Defenses, what are, 188; under general issue, 202; affirmative, burden of proof upon, 203; what constitute, 203, 204, affirmative, 212.

Defendant, pleadings of, 186–188; as a witness, 201; testimony of, as to intent, 210.

Defendants, joinder of, 184.

Degrees of crime, jeopardy from trial of different, 216, 218, 219.

Deliberation, intoxication as showing absence of, 47.

Delirium tremens amounting to insanity, 46.

Delusions as a theory of insanity, 40, 43.

Demurrer, not proper to raise bar of statute of limitations, 180, 181; to indictment, 187.

Denial, affirmative proof in, 203.

Depositions, 200.

Description, in indictments, 167, 172–182; must be proved as laid, 174.

Detective, joining in an act, not criminally liable, 19.

Dilatory pleas, certainty in, 187.

Dismissal after jeopardy attaches, 215.

Distinct crimes, evidence of, 210.

Dogs, not subjects of larceny, 96.

Drunkenness, see intoxication.

Due process of law, 110, 111; requires accusation, 155; does it require indictment, 156; what sufficient accusation under, 165; as to jury trial, 193.

Duelling, death resulting from, murder, 72.

Duplicity in indictments, 183.

Duty, how enforced, 1, 2; failure to perform, negligence, 26; death caused in performance of, justifiable, 63; to resist felony, 32; death from omission of, manslaughter, 73.

Dwelling, meaning of term, 88; burning of, arson, 90; breaking and entering, burglary, 91.

Dying declarations, 201.

Elements of crime, 206.

Embezzlement, 102.

Enemy, alien, killing of, not justifiable, 64.

Entry, what sufficient to constitute burglary, 92, 93.

Escape from arrest, 140.

Evidence, what sufficient to warrant binding over, 150; to warrant indictment, 162; amount of, in criminal cases, 205, 206; of alibi, 209; as to intent, 209-211; of distinct crimes, 210; of indentity of crime and person to show previous jeopardy, 219; order of introduction, 220.

Ex post facto laws, 13 as to procedure, 110.

Examination, see preliminary examination.

Exceptions and provisos, in statutes, 18, 185; burden of proof in case of, 212.

Excuse, distinguished from justification, 34; burden of proving, 211.

Execution, 226.

Exemption from jury service, 160, 196.

Extradition of offenders, 143-148.

Fact, ignorance or mistake of, 28, 29.

False pretence, 102.

Federal courts, *see courts of U. S.*

Federal government, *see U. S.*

Felony, distinguished from misdemeanor, 32, 56; duty to prevent, 32; upon another, resistance of, 37; accessories recognized in, 54; derivation of term, 55; killing in resisting, justifiable, 32; malice aforethought presumed in attempting to commit, 70; death resulting from attempt to commit, 70, 79; assaults with intent to commit, 88; breaking and entry, with intent to commit, burglary, 93.

Fictions in presumption as to murder, 71.

Fine, how enforced, 226.

Firearms, death from careless use of, 74.

Fish, taking of, when larceny, 96.

Fixtures, taking of, when larceny, 95.

Foreman of grand jury, 160; indorsement and presentation of indictment by, 163.

Foreman of petit jury, delivery of verdict by, 223.

Forfeiture of bail, 154.

Forgery, 104.

Fraud, in burglary constitutes constructive breaking, 92; possession obtained by, in case of larceny, 98, 99, 101; what sufficient, in forgery, 104; in previous conviction or acquittal, 220.

Fugitive from justice, surrender of, 59, 143-148.

Games, death happening in, excusable, 64.

Government, represents the public in criminal proceedings, 4, 6; may declare what acts shall be crimes, 7; of U. S. offenses against, 59.

Governor, demand or surrender of fugitive from justice by, 144—148.

Grand jurors, qualifications of, challenges to, 158, 159; origin of indictment by, 108; accusation by, 157, 158; how constituted and organized, proceedings, 157-163; presentation on oath of, 170.

Great bodily harm, death in attempting, murder, 70.

Guilt, reasonable doubt of, 206.

Guilty, plea of, 187, 192.

Habeas corpus, by person surrendered as fugitive from justice, 147; to test commitment on examination, 151; to secure release on bail, 154.

Habitation, defense of, 32; retreat from, not required, 35; what constitutes, 88; offenses against, 88-94; no protection against arrest, 139, 140.

Heat of blood, does not imply absence of intent to kill, 69; reduces killing to manslaughter, 75.

Homicide, in protecting person or property, 31, 32; in resisting felony, 31, 34; justifiable, 63; excusable, 64; in self-defense, 64; by misadventure, 64; justifiable, and excusable, distinction, 65; felonious, 65; caused by blow beyond the jurisdiction, 125; when death is within the county from blow without, 130.

House, meaning of term, 88; burning of, arson, 90; breaking and entering, burglary, 91.

Hue and cry, 115.

Human being, how soon child considered to be, 62.

Husband, liability of for acts of wife, 24; protection of wife by, 37; wife not liable for crimes in presence of, 38; has no right to chastise wife, 86; burning of wife's house by, not arson, 90; wife's possession of property of, 99.

Idem Sonans, 178.

Identity, of defendant, 208; of crime and person to show previous jeopardy, 219, 220.

Idiocy, *see insanity.*

Ignorance or mistake of law or fact, as defense, 28, 29.

Imprisonment, 227.

Indictment, origin of, 108; accusation by, 155-157; form of, 161; finding and presentation of, 162, 163; as first pleading in criminal case, 164; amendment of, as to name, 177; joinder of defendants in, 184; under statutes, 184, 185; allegations of intent, 185.

Indictments, amendments of, 155, 173;
general requisites as to allegations,
165–168; formal parts, 169–171;
matters of description in, 172, 182;
duplicity in, 183; what sufficient to
constitute jeopardy, 214.
Infamous crimes, what are, 156.
Infancy as an excuse for crime, 39.
Infangthief, 107.
Information, accusation by, 155, 156;
form. 164; amendment of, 173; see
preliminary information.
Initials, use of, in stating name, 177.
Injury, to another, necessity excusing,
31; great bodily, resisting. 33.
Innocence, presumption of, 205.
Inquest of coronor, 113.
Insane person, rape upon, 83.
Insanity as a defense, 40–46; burden
of proving, 211.
Instructions to jury, 221.
Instrument, date of, as matter of description, 180.
Instruments, written, how pleaded,
182.
Intent, legislative, governs construction of statutes, 15; how ascertained, 16.
Intent, measures desert of punishment, 27; criminal, supplied by negligence, 25; necessary to constitute
criminal responsibility, 19–25; absence of, shown by ignorance or
mistake, 28, 29; necessity or compulsion, 30; infancy, 39; insanity,
40–46; intoxication, 46, 47; not
material in cases of negligence, 62;
to kill, as constituting malice aforethought, 69; to do great bodily
harm, death from, 70; to kill another, death from, 70; to kill, presumed from use of deadly weapon,
72; to kill, in case of manslaughter,
75; what sufficient to constitute
murder in first degree, 79; does not
constitute attempt, 85; what sufficient to constitute burglary, 93; in
case of larceny, 100; in case of forgery, 104; allegations of, 185; evidence
and burden of proof as to, 209–211;
how rebutted, 210; testimony of defendant as to, 210.
International law, as to jurisdiction
over crimes, 120–128.
Interpretation of statutes, 14–19.
Intoxication as showing want of criminal intent, 46, 47.
Issue, general, 202.

Issues, what, 202.

Jeopardy, former, burden of proof of,
212; what constitutes, 213–215;
waiver of, 215, 216; when new trial
is, 216, 217; is determined by verdict, 217; must be as to same offense, 218; in trial of another degree
of same crime, 218.
Joinder, of offenses, 183; of defendants, 184.
Judge and jury, respective, provinces
of, 221.
Judges as magistrates, 113, 117.
Judgment, for crime does not merge
tort, 8; arrest of, 225.
Jurisdiction, in summary proceedings,
116; of criminal proceedings, courts
having, 117; of federal courts, 119;
what gives, 120; as between different sovereignties, 121–128; pleas
to, 186; judgment by court having,
conclusive, 213; jeopardy does not
attach if court has not, 214.
Jurors, selected from vicinity of crime,
127, 181; qualifications, disabilities,
challenges, 195–199; standing aside,
198; see *grand jurors.*
Jury, right to trial by, 192; essentials
of, 193; summary prosecutions without, 194; waiver of, 194; how selected, qualification, disability, challenges, 195–199; impanelling, oath,
199; charge of court to, 221; as
judges of the law, 222; conduct and
deliberations, 223; verdict of, 223;
polling, 224; trial by, on appeal from
summary conviction, 116; see *grand
jury.*
Justice of the Peace, origin of the office and duties as magistrate, 113.
Justification, distinguished from excuse, 34; burden of proving, 211.

Knowledge of right and wrong as a
test of insanity, 40, 43; distinct
crimes as showing scienter, 210.

Lauguage, insulting, as provocation,
77.
Larceny, 94–102; territorial jurisdiction of, 125; recent possession of
stolen property as evidence of, 209.
Law, divisions of, 1; system of classification, of, 4; criminal, as a division
of municipal law, 1; genesis of, 5;
defined, 6; how prescribed, 9; both
written and unwritten, 9; codification of, 10; common and statutory
as to procedure, 109; argument upon

to jury, 221; instructions to jury upon, 221; jury as judges of, 222.

Law and fact, questions of, how determined, 221.

Law of the land, 110.

Laws, construction and interpretation of, 14–19.

Legislation, punishment of crimes by, 6, 12; as to surrender of fugitive from justice, 148; modification of forms of accusation, 168.

Legislature, power of, to regulate procedure, 109.

Libel, liability for, 24; as breach of bond for good behavior, 132; jury judges of law in, 223.

License, burden of proof as to, 212.

Life, taking of under necessity, 30.

Limitation of prosecutions, see statutes of limitation.

Liquors, intoxicating, sale of by agent or wife, 24, 25.

Machinery of criminal procedure, 111–119,

Magistrate, preliminary proceedings before, for arrest, 133–136; binding over fugitive from justice, 148; preliminary examination and binding over by, 149-151; bail by, on preliminary examination, 151–154.

Magistrates in the states, 112; in the U. S., 117; may require bond to keep the peace or for good behavior, 131, 132.

Maiming, see mayhem, 80, 81.

Mainprize, 152.

Malice, means wrongful intent, 22; what necessary in case of arson, 91.

Malice, aforethought, defined, 66 presumed, 67; express and implied, 67; murder distinguished by, 66, 68; premeditation not necessary to constitute, 69; presumed from intent to commit great bodily harm, 70.

Malicious mischief, 100, 103.

Manslaughter, death from negligence, constitutes, 27; history of the term, 66; definition of, 68; voluntary and involuntary, 68; may be intentional killing in heat of blood, 69; classification of cases of, 73; by statute, punishment, 80.

Master, liability for acts of servant, 24; liability for employing incompetent servant, 27; and servant, right of protection arising from relation of, 37; killing of, by servant, petty trea-

son, 57; may not chastise servant, 86; larceny from, by servant, 98.

Mayhem, 80.

Medicine, death from negligence in administering, 74.

Members of congress or legislature, exemption from arrest, 142.

Mental capacity, want of, as excusing from crime, 39–48.

Merger, of crime and tort, 8; of different crimes, 219.

Militia, may be called upon by civil authorities, 115.

Ministers, public, exemption of, from jurisdiction, 122; from arrest, 142.

Misadventure, homicide by, excusable, 64.

Misdemeanor, exciting to commit, is also misdemeanor, 10; no accessories recognized in, 54; meaning of team, 55.

Misnomer, pleadable in abatement, 187.

Misprison, of felony, recognized at common law, 49; of treason, 59.

Mistake, possession by, in case of larceny, 98, 100.

Motion to quash indictment, 186.

Motion for new trial, or in arrest waives jeopardy, 216.

Motive, distinct from intent, 21; as a defense, 22.

Municipal ordinance, punishment under, not bar to prosecution by state, 213, 214.

Murder, history of term, 65; what constitutes, 68; suicide constituting, 69; degrees of, 79, 80; punishment, 80; caused by blow beyond jurisdiction, 125; venue of when blow and death are in different counties, 130; degrees of, how charged, 166; corpus delicti in, 207; prosecution for assault before death does not bar prosecution for, 218.

Name and addition of defendant, 175, 176; abatement for mistake in, 187.

Name of person other than defendant, 176-178.

Necessaries, death from neglect to provide, 73.

Necessity, apparent as ground for killing in self-defense, 36; or compulsion as showing lack of intent, 30-38; in defense of person or property, 31; in preventing felony, 32.

Negligence, criminal, liability for, 25; what sufficient to constitute homicide, 61; death resulting from, manslaughter, 73.

New trial, 225; not after erroneous judgment on valid verdict, 217; not for higher crime or degree than conviction, 216; not after acquittal, 217; asked by defendant waives jeopardy, 216.

Night time, meaning of term, 91.

Nolle prosequi, 215.

Not guilty, plea of, 187; issue raised by, 202.

Oath, what sufficient to constitute perjury, 105.

Occupancy, what sufficient to constitute habitation, 89.

Occupant of dwelling, who deemed, 89, 90.

Offences against government, 57–60; against the person, 60–88; against the habitation, 88–94; against property, 94–105; see crimes.

Officer, see arrest.

Omission, criminal, what sufficient to constitute homicide, 61.

Opening and closing, 220.

Ordeal, trial by, 108, 192.

Outlawry, 108.

Parent, protection of child by, 37; chastisement of child by, 64, 86.

Participation, to constitute crime, 49.

Particulars governed by general provisions, 16, 17.

Passion, killing in heat of, manslaughter, 76.

Peace officers, who are, 112, 114, 118; see arrest.

Penalty attached, renders acts illegal, 8.

Perjury, 105.

Person, defence of, 31, 32; offences against, 60–88; jurisdiction of, necessary in criminal proceeding, 120; jurisdiction of sovereign over, 122; proof of identity of, to show previous jeopardy, 220.

Physicians and surgeons, criminal liability of, 27, 74.

Place of prosecution, see venue.

Place, how alleged, 169, 181, 182.

Plea, necessity of, 190.

Plea of guilty, 192; of lower degree, no new trial for higher, 217.

Pleas to indictment, 186–188; how and when interposed, 191; trial of, 191, 192; in abatement, in bar, 202; former jeopardy, 202.

Pleading in criminal prosecutions, 164–188.

Pleadings by defendant, 186–188.

Pleading over, 188.

Poison, furnishing to person committing suicide, 69; death from negligence as to, 74; killing by, murder in first degree, 79.

Posse comitatus, 115.

Possession, what sufficient in larceny, 97.

Polling the jury, 224.

Power of the county, 115.

Preamble, effect of in construction, 16.

Precedents for indictments, 168.

Preliminary information, 134, 135.

Preliminary examination, 149–152.

Presence, taking from, in case of robbery, 81.

Presence of defendant, when necessary at trial, 188, 189.

Presentation of indictment, 163.

Presentment by grand jury, 155, 157, 160.

Presumption, of intent from act, 22; as to infancy, as excusing crime, 39; of insanity, 44; of malice aforethought, 67, 71; defined, 204; as affecting burden of proof, 204, 205; of innocence, 205; of chastity, 208; from recent possession of stolen property, 209; of intent, 209, 210.

Prevention of offences, 131, 132.

Previous acquittal, conviction, or attainder pleaded in bar, 187; see jeopardy.

Prima facie case, 205.

Principal, liability of, for acts of agent, 24; and accessory, 49–54.

Principals, joint responsibility of, 49.

Prisoner, disposition of, upon arrest, 138.

Private person, arrest by, 137, 141.

Probable cause, what sufficient to warrant binding over, 150; what sufficient to warrant indictment, 162.

Proceedings, civil, for protecting right or enforcing duty, 2; distinguished from criminal, 3.

Procedure to be determined by statutes in force, 19; criminal, defined, history and present form, 107, 108.

Proof must correspond to allegation, 172; see burden of proof.

Property, defence of, 31, 32; what subject of larceny, 96; seizure of, upon arrest, or by search warrant, 139; description by name of owner, 178.

Prosecution, in behalf of public, 108.

Prosecution, no appeal by, 217.

Prosecuting officer, before grand jury, 160–162.

Prosecutor, before grand jury, 161; name indorsed on indictment, 163; private, in behalf of the public, 108.

Protection of person, property, or habitation, 31, 32, 34.

Provisos of statutes, 18; *see exceptions and provisos.*

Provocation, proof of intoxication in case of, 47; what sufficient to reduce killing to manslaughter, 76, 77; intentional killing, irrespective of, 78; unlawful arrest as constituting, 79; burden of proving, 211.

Public trial, 200.

Punishment, judgment in civil actions as, 2; criminal, 3; object of, 4; how fixed, 7, 10, 12; intent alone not subject to, 23; desert of, measured by intent, 27; in another jurisdiction, 213; under city ordinance, no bar to prosecution by state, 213, 214; under erroneous conviction constitutes bar, 215; discretion as to, 225; capital, 227.

Pupil, death in chastisement of, when excusable, 64.

Purport of written instrument, 182.

Pursuit, in case of self-defence, 35; of escaping prisoner 141, 142.

Quashing indictment, 186.

Rape, 83, 84.

Realty, taking, not larceny, 95.

Reasonable doubt, 205.

Rebutting evidence, 220.

Recent possession of stolen property, 209.

Recognizances of witnesses to appear, 151.

Removal of criminal cases to federal courts, 118.

Repeal of statutes, 18.

Representations, false, 103.

Requisition for surrender of fugitive from justice, 145–148.

Resistance, right or duty of, 31, 32, 34; of person about to be injured, 131; to arrest, 141.

Retreat in case of self-defence, 34.

Rights and duties, how protected and enforced, 1, 2.

Riot, killing in resisting, justifiable, 63.

Riots, suppression of, 132.

Robbery, 81, 82.

Sanity, presumption of, 44.

Sea, boundary of territory upon, 121, 122, 129; crimes upon, where cognizable, 121, 128.

Search warrant, 139.

Security, to keep the peace, 131; for good behavior, 131, 132.

Seduction, proof of chastity, 208.

Self-defence, homicide in, 31–35; 64, 77, 78; retreat and pursuit in case of, 34, 35.

Sentence, 225.

Servant, liability of master for acts of, 24; incompetent, liability of master for employing, 27; not excused by commands of master, 38; larceny from, 96, 97; larceny by, 97, 98; embezzlement by, 102; *see master and servants.*

Service of warrant of arrest, 135–142.

Severance, 192.

Sheriff, coroner as substitute for, 114; office and duties of, 114; may call upon militia or power of the county; 115.

Sovereign, foreign, exemption of, from jurisdiction, 122.

Sovereignties, former jeopardy as between, 213.

Sovereignty, jurisdiction of, over persons, 122–128.

Speedy trial, 195.

Standing jurors aside, 198.

Standing mute, 190, 191.

Sta e, treason against, 58; name of, in indictment, 169; boundaries of, 121, 122; territorial jurisdiction of 123; no jurisdiction over crimes against U. S., 123.

Statement of defendant before sentence, 225.

Statutes, construction of, 14–19; repeal of, 18; indictments under, 184; exceptions and provisos in, 185.

Statutes of limitation, 180.

Subornation of perjury, 106.

Suicide, 69.

Summary proceedings, 116, 118.

Summary prosecutions without jury, 194.

Summing up to jury, 220.

Supreme Court of U. S., appeals to, 119.
Sureties, to keep the peace, 131; for good behavior, 131, 132.
Surplusage, 173; second offence, defectively charged, 183.

Teacher, chastisement by, 64, 86.
Tenor of written instrument, 182.
Terms, common law, meaning of still retained, 56.
Territorial jurisdiction of sovereignties. 121–128.
Testimony of defendant, 201.
Thief, larceny from, 96.
Threats, as justifying self-defence, 36.
Time, allegations of, 178–181.
Title and preamble, effect of, in construction, 16.
Title, transfer of by fraud, not larceny, 98, 99.
Tort, distinguished from crime, 6; not merged in crime, 8; infancy, no excuse for, 39; appeal of felony developed into, 108.
Treason, no accessory recognized in, 54; high and petit, 57; in U. S., 57; what constitutes, 58, 59; misprison of, 59.
Trespass, necessary in larceny, 97; wrongful arrest constitutes, 138, 140.
Trial, 188; by battle and ordeal, 108; of extradited person, 143, 148; by ordeal, by compurgators, 192; method of, how chosen, 192; speedy, 195; public, 200; without verdict, may constitute jeopardy, 215; see new trial.
Trial by jury, see jury.

United States, power of, to define and punish crimes, 12; criminal procedure in courts of, 109; powers of officers and courts of, in criminal proceedings, 117–119; criminal jurisdiction of, exclusive, 123.

Vagrants, 132.
Variance, between allegation and proof, 172; in name, 176, 177; as to name of party injured, 178; as to time, 179, 180; as to place, 181, 182; as to written instrument, 182; trial failing from, not a bar, 219.
Vengeance, right of private, 107.
Venue, 127–130; change of, 130; of trials in federal courts, 128; of indictment, 169.
Verdict, direction of, by court, 222; special, cannot be required, 222; may be rendered, 224; rendition of, sealed, 223; form of, general and special, 224; determines the jeopardy, 217.
Videlicet, 174.

Waiver, of jury trial, 194; of privilege not to testify, 201; of former jeopardy, 216.
War, levying of, constitutes treason, 58.
Warrant, of arrest, 134–136; of commitment on preliminary examination, 151; upon indictment, 163; see search warrant.
Weapon, deadly, intent presumed from use of, 72; use of, implies intent to kill, 76; what sufficient provocation to. palliate use of, 76; use of, in self-defence, chastisement or arrest, 78.
Wife, liability of husband for acts of, 24; protection of, by husband, 37; criminal responsibility of, 38; not responsible as accessory after the fact to husband, 52; killing of husband by, petty treason, 57; burning husband's house by, not arson, 90; adultery of, as provocation for killing by husband, 76; no right in husband to chastise, 86; custody of husband's property by, 99.
Witness, defendant as, 201.
Witnesses, on preliminary examination bound over, 151; before a grand jury, 161; process for, 200; defendant confronted by, 200.
Words do not constitute assault, 86.
Wound, death from, amounting to homicide, 60; in one county causing death in another, 130.
Writ of error, see appeal.

Lightning Source UK Ltd.
Milton Keynes UK
UKHW020622220119
335962UK00012B/1290/P